Law and Capitalism

Law and Capitalism

What Corporate Crises Reveal about Legal
Systems and Economic Development
around the World

CURTIS J. MILHAUPT
KATHARINA PISTOR

The University of Chicago Press
Chicago and London

Curtis J. Milhaupt is the Fuyo Professor of Law and director of the Center for Japanese Legal Studies at Columbia Law School. A leading authority on the Japanese legal system and a frequent contributor to comparative corporate governance debates, Milhaupt's research and publications span a wide range of subjects at the intersection of legal institutions and economic organizations and development. Recent books (with coauthors) include *Economic Organizations and Corporate Governance in Japan* (Oxford University Press, 2004) and *Transforming Corporate Governance in East Asia* (forthcoming, Routledge, 2008).

Katharina Pistor is professor of law at Columbia Law School. She specializes in comparative legal systems and corporate governance in emerging markets. Pistor has published widely on privatization, corporate governance, and law in Russia and Eastern Europe and has contributed to the debate on the relation between and law and economic development and legal transplants in such journals as the *American Journal of Comparative Law, the American Review of Law and Economics, The Journal of Comparative Economics,* and the *European Economic Review.* She is coauthor of *The Role of Law and Legal Institutions in Asian Economic Development* (Oxford University Press, 1999).

The University of Chicago Press, Chicago 60637
The University of Chicago Press, Ltd., London
© 2008 by The University of Chicago
All rights reserved. Published 2008
Printed in the United States of America

17 16 15 14 13 12 11 10 09 08   1 2 3 4 5

ISBN-13: 978-0-226-52527-3 (cloth)
ISBN-10: 0-226-52527-9 (cloth)

Library of Congress Cataloging-in-Publication Data

Milhaupt, Curtis J., 1962–
    Law and capitalism : what corporate crises reveal about legal systems and economic development around the word / Curtis J. Milhaupt, Katharina Pistor.
        p.   cm.
    Includes bibliographical references and index.
    ISBN-13: 978-0-226-52527-3 (cloth : alk. paper)
    ISBN-10: 0-226-52527-9 (cloth : alk. paper)   1. Law and economics.   2. Corporate governance—Law and legislation.   3. Industrial laws and legislation.   4. Law—Political aspects.   5. Capitalism—Moral and ethical aspects.   6. Industrial organization (Economic theory)   I. Pistor, Katharina.   II. Title.
    K487.E3M55   2008
    340'.11—dc22   2007035753

For my dad
C. J. M.

For my parents
K. P.

CONTENTS

PREFACE

Several years ago, a series of conversations about our mutual interest in the role of law in economic development and our shared frustration with the current state of the literature about the topic led to a decision to teach a seminar in which we would explore the relation between legal institutions and market-oriented economic institutions. Early on, we decided that the best way to explore this relation was to combine the reading of theoretical and empirical studies about the topic with in-depth analyses of contemporary events in countries in different stages of economic development. We also decided that corporate governance, another of our shared research interests, provided an excellent focal point through which to examine this topic, for reasons that we explain in the introduction. We called the seminar "Law and Capitalism: A Comparative Approach," and we have taught it twice at Columbia Law School. This book is a direct outgrowth of those seminars.

Drafts of many chapters were presented at conferences and workshops around the world. The locations include Boalt Hall School of Law at the University of California at Berkeley, Columbia Law School, Hong Kong University Law School, the Latin American Law and Economics Association, the Research Institute of Economy, Trade, and Industry in Tokyo, Seoul National University, and the Tsinghua University Economics Department in Beijing. We are indebted to participants in those events for clarifying and challenging our arguments. Many people gave generously of their time to read all or portions of early versions of the manuscript. Others provided helpful feedback on our initial idea for this project, read all or parts of the manuscript, or discussed the major ideas of the book with us. Their criticisms and suggestions pushed us to make the book you are reading better than the one we would have produced if left to our own devices.

Thanks to John Armour, Harald Baum, Robert Cooter, Mel Eisenberg, Jesse Fried, Hwa-Jin Kim, Joongi Kim, Kon-Sik Kim, Bentley MacLeod, Mark Ramseyer, Charles Sabel, Ulrike Schaede, Mark West, Charles Whitehead and two anonymous referees for their comments.

Many other people helped us, directly and indirectly, to complete this book. Curtis Milhaupt received funding for research and travel from Columbia Law School. Katharina Pistor received financial support from the Milton Handler Faculty Research Fund. Young-Joon Kim, a partner at Milbank Tweed Hadley and McCloy in Hong Kong, and Kon-Sik Kim of the Faculty of Law at Seoul National University were instrumental in providing background information about the SK episode featured in chapter 6. Theodor Baums generously shared materials concerning the Mannesmann case, discussed in chapter 4. Jaewon Yoon provided excellent research assistance. Last but not least, we thank our seminar students at Columbia Law School, who explored much of the underlying material for this book with us.

INTRODUCTION

American law professors wrote the new corporate code for post-Soviet Russia at Boris Yeltsin's request. When the socialist bloc disintegrated, the World Bank's top priority was "drafting and quickly adopting new laws and regulations required to build a market economy."[1] And in Korea during the Asian financial crisis, the government, while urging housewives to donate their gold jewelry to avert budgetary meltdown, was negotiating a rescue package with the International Monetary Fund (IMF) conditioned on a massive overhaul of the country's corporate, bankruptcy, and securities laws.[2]

The applications are new, but the idea that law is essential to economic development—and the quest to understand the precise relation between legal systems and markets—is old. In late nineteenth-century Germany, Max Weber used law to explain the rise of capitalism in western Europe. Weber famously asserted that "rational"[3] law supports economic activity by lending predictability and legitimacy to the rules of market exchange. In the twentieth century Friedrich A. Hayek asserted that the common law, reflecting a tradition of constraint against governmental authority, is better suited to a market economy than is the civil law. As the twenty-first century approached, prominent economists produced a line of provocative empirical research whose critical explanatory variable was the origin of a country's legal system. The work linked differences in economic structures such as patterns of share ownership and the size of stock markets to the quality of shareholder protections provided by national legal systems. Common-law systems were found to provide higher quality protections than did civil-law systems—in particular, French civil law—resulting in more widely dispersed share ownership and larger stock markets. Extending the implications of this research early in the twenty-first century, scholars found evidence that in recent history, countries with common-law systems have experienced faster economic growth than those belonging to the civil-law family.[4]

Bringing this long line of important research into sharp focus in the past few years are two real-world developments that are at the center of this book. The first is a series of high-profile corporate crises around the world. Starting with the Enron debacle in the United States, major economies have witnessed extraordinary corporate governance controversies in the recent past that have shaken confidence—not only in the stock market but in the very institutional foundations of market activity in these countries. Each crisis has, in its own way, challenged the adequacy of the country's legal system and prompted institutional responses to repair the perceived shortcomings. The second development is globalization. Although the fact of economic globalization is well known, its implications for domestic legal systems have not been thoroughly examined (at least in scholarship concerned with corporate governance) outside the confines of the rather impoverished "convergence" debate.[5] Given these two developments, many countries facing serious institutional challenges as a result of corporate governance crises or broader macroeconomic problems[6] have over the course of the past fifteen years turned, either voluntarily or under pressure from international organizations such as the World Bank, to a fairly standard menu of legal reforms. The components of this menu, drawn predominantly from the U.S. legal system, were influenced by the recent economics scholarship linking favorable economic outcomes to "good" law. Not implausibly, because common-law regimes score well in this research, for many scholars and policy makers, good law is equated with Anglo-American (typically U.S.) law.

So we have arrived at a fascinating moment. Economists have provided us with important empirical results concerning the relation between legal institutions and economic outcomes that echo theories advanced by past generations of major thinkers. Simultaneously, the importance of creating effective legal systems for market activity has been underscored by a host of recent events such as the transformation of the former Eastern bloc regimes, the Asian financial crisis, and a series of corporate governance scandals around the world. The policy response, applied liberally from Seoul to Warsaw, is to re-create features of the U.S. legal system that are thought to account in some way for the comparative robustness of U.S. economic institutions.

But does the prevailing view of the relation between law and capitalism hold up under sustained scrutiny? Does law support market activity only in the ways that generations of scholars have assumed? Why have some of the most dramatic economic success stories in history—China is only the latest example—occurred in the absence of a rule of law as that term is commonly understood in Western economics and legal scholarship? Can an effective legal system for economic growth be imported, which is the assumption behind a decade's worth of World Bank–generated institutional reforms? Does globalization imply convergence on an efficient model of legal governance for economic activity? Are efforts at legal harmonization such as those in the European Union an effective shortcut to the creation of effective legal regimes?

We do not claim to have definitive answers to all of these big questions, of course. (We may be foolhardy for writing a book about such a huge topic, but we are also sensitive to the limitations of our analysis, a point we explicitly address below.) What we do have, however, is a perspective on the relation between law and capitalism that generates answers quite different from the ones taken for granted in the economics literature and the policy world.

Before summarizing our analytical perspective and its implications, we pause to define a few key terms. The law referenced in our title—and the focus of our analysis—is law supplied by the sovereign. In other words, it is law promulgated by legislatures, government agencies, or courts and enforced by agents of the state. We often use the term "formal law" to distinguish this type of authority from informal governance mechanisms such as social norms, rules promulgated by organizations, and codes of best practice. We do not, however, limit "law" to the sum of legal rules or standards found in statutes and case law. Instead, the focus of our analysis is the formal legal system, including the processes by which formal law is made, contested, and ultimately implemented and enforced. "Capitalism" for our purposes is market-oriented economic activity in a system of declining state control of productive assets. Market-oriented systems are typically associated with private ownership of the means of production, but as is well known, market economies are compatible with extensive state ownership or hybrid ownership patterns. We discuss China and Russia extensively in this book, with the full knowledge that these economies are not completely capitalist in their orientation. Sometimes observers make the same claim as to Japan and Germany—two other countries we examine in depth—though the argument is more rhetorical as applied to them. Nonetheless, it raises an important point that should be made at the outset: just as there are varieties of capitalism,[7] there are varieties of legal support for capitalist activity. China and Russia are particularly interesting to us precisely *because* their economies are unevenly evolving toward, rather than fully possessed of, market institutions in a system of private ownership. The ongoing experience of these countries provides the opportunity to analyze the role of law in facilitating the movement toward markets and the obstacles to this trajectory.

As explained more fully below, the empirical core of the book comprises six analytical narratives of recent corporate governance scandals or controversies. "Corporate governance" is shorthand for the complex system by which firms are structured, financed, and controlled. Our own backgrounds as scholars of comparative corporate law account in part for the book's emphasis on corporate governance. But there are several powerful reasons to focus on corporate governance as a vehicle for better understanding the relation between legal and economic institutions. First, firms are the most important private actors in a market economy. A successful capitalist economy without successful firms is inconceivable. Thus, the legal underpinnings of firm-level governance, as well as the legal responses to firm-level crises, warrant close analysis. Second and more important, as we have learned from experience throughout the world in the recent past, corporate governance is linked to every facet of a country's economic, political, and legal structures. Many of the rules by which firms operate are supplied by the state ("formal law," to use our terminology), but ownership structures, managerial priorities, and relationships with other market actors are also deeply embedded in the political, social, and economic infrastructure. An extended inquiry into corporate governance thus requires venturing deep into the institutional structure of the entire economy. We therefore use corporate governance as a lens through which to view a much larger set of institutional phenomena in a given country and to analyze, as rigorously as possible, the relation between the legal system and the portion of the economic system that is directly related to firms' structures and governance.

Analytical Framework

According to the prevailing view, law fosters economic activity (exclusively) by protecting property rights. A legal system that clearly allocates and protects property rights (a rule of law) precedes economic development and is a precondition to economic success. Once such a system is in place, it constitutes a fixed and politically neutral institutional endowment—an unchanging foundation for economic activity. The formal characteristics of legal systems—in particular, whether they adhere to common law or civil law—determine how well they provide protection of property rights (especially investors' rights). The quality of property rights protections, in turn, determines economic outcomes.

We refer to this view, perhaps somewhat unfairly, as "Weber's legacy"[8] because, like Weber, modern policy makers and economics researchers are attracted to a formalistic and deterministic view of the relation between law and markets. Law drives economic activity; the higher the quality of the legal rules, the better the economic outcomes. We do not mean to downplay the contributions of this literature. It has provided some fascinating empirical results that have provoked an intense and ongoing dialogue between economists and legal scholars. But we believe that the conceptual apparatus widely in use today does not provide very powerful tools for unpacking the important questions we posed above. In our more cynical moments, we caricature the canonical view that has taken hold in the economics literature and policy world with the following simple equation:

good law + good enforcement = good economic outcomes

It is easy to understand why so many economists and World Bank reformers have been attracted to a simple view of law's relation to a liberal market economy. It is clean and straightforward. It depicts law as a kind of technology that can be inserted in the proper places—and imported from abroad when necessary—to accomplish an important task. And the canonical view rests on the hoariest of conventional wisdoms: that a rule of law is a prerequisite to economic growth and political liberalization.[9] As one scholar puts it, the "fullest achievement [of the rule-of-law ideal] is associated with the maturation of capitalism into laissez-faire competition under conditions of political stability."[10]

This view, however, rests on a number of assumptions that do not bear up under careful scrutiny, as we explain in chapters 1 and 2. And it does not explain some of the most important economic success stories of the twentieth century, such as Japan, Korea, and most recently, China. Unfortunately, good law (whatever that means, exactly) and good enforcement (ditto) do not lead inexorably to good economic outcomes. On the other hand, many countries have achieved remarkable economic growth with legal systems that do not live up to the rule-of-law ideal.

This book is an attempt to provide a new perspective on *how* law supports markets. The starting point for this effort is the recognition that law is not an endowment like a fixed capital investment that, once in place, provides a firm foundation for capitalist activity.[11] The vibrancy of a capitalist system hinges on creative destruction in the sphere of governance as well as the economic sphere. Governance structures of all types, including law, must adapt and respond to changes in the economy. Rather than thinking of a legal system as a fixed endowment for the economy, it is more productive to view the relationship between law and markets as a highly iterative process of action and strategic reaction. We call this a "rolling relationship" between law and markets.[12] This is not to say that the relationship is smooth, effortless, or necessarily efficiency-enhancing. Indeed, we will see that it is often edgy and unpredictable. The first point is simply that law and markets react to one another with the mediation of human agents and institutional mechanisms. Viewing the relationship as dynamic rather than fixed is important because it shifts the focus of inquiry from the origin of legal systems to the ways they change and where they are heading.

The second basic recognition motivating our analysis is that not all legal systems—not even all legal systems associated with successful economic development—are organized similarly or perform identical functions in support of economic activity. In other words, there is no single rule of law that maps onto real-world economic success. We will see that, as a historical matter, different types of legal system are conducive to economic success. Each has its own costs, benefits, and vulnerabilities. We are not referring to the canonical taxonomy of common-law and civil-law systems, which looms so large in the literature. We find this distinction to be unhelpful for analytical purposes. Rather, legal systems can be distinguished on the basis of several factors that have not received sufficient attention in the literature,[13] including (1) the organization of the legal system, (2) the functions that law plays in support of market activity, and (3) the political economy for law production and enforcement.

1. *Organization.* Legal systems can be more or less centralized in relation to the law-making and enforcement processes. Centralized systems typically vest law-making powers in the legislative or the executive branch and prefer centralized law enforcement mechanisms of the state to such decentralized law enforcement tools as courts and private litigation. Decentralized systems allocate law-making and law enforcement activities to multiple agents, including private parties who may exercise extensive rights to initiate law enforcement and to participate in law-making processes. Decentralized systems appear to be more adaptive than centralized systems, but they are far more complex, posing challenges in terms of predictability and the capacity to engineer broader social change. By contrast, centralized systems appear to have greater organizational capacity but may be less responsive to particularized demand for change.

2. *Functions.* Law can perform multiple functions in support of market-oriented economic activity. The clear allocation and protection of property rights, which is the exclusive focus of existing literature, is only one possible

function of law. In some legal systems this protective function of law is, indeed, dominant.[14] But in others residual rights of control are allocated to multiple agents, encouraging or even forcing them to bargain over outcomes within the boundaries established by law. In these systems the coordinating function of law dominates. Supplemental to these two basic functions of law are signaling and credibility enhancement. Law can provide important signals to market actors, inducing behavioral change, even if the signals are not universally backed by legal enforcement. Law can also be used to lend credibility to government policies, enhancing their effectiveness. The signaling and credibility-enhancing functions of law are equally prevalent in systems in which the protective or coordinating functions of law dominate. We therefore focus primarily on the differences between the protective and the coordinating functions. In each real-world system, these functions of law coexist and may be balanced differently in different areas of the law. The dominance of one or the other function, however, distinguishes legal systems. There is clearly an affinity between the organization of a legal system and the functions it performs. Centralized systems tend to be coordinating, whereas decentralized systems tend to engender a protective function of law. The question of which will dominate depends on the existence and character of a host of institutions and organizations such as courts, lawyers, law enforcement agencies, labor unions, and business groups that either precede the introduction of formal law or co-evolve with it. Once an entire system for supporting a particular function of law is in place, it is difficult (but not impossible) to change. As our case studies demonstrate, under the right external circumstances, change capable of altering the organization and dominant function of a legal system does occur.

3. *Political economy.* Law, a product of human interaction, obviously does not function independent of the political system. Yet the prevailing view implicitly assumes that legal systems that are conducive to economic activity are politically neutral endowments. Others have noted, of course, that law changes by means of the political process. But the political economy is crucial to the formation and change of legal systems in a way that has not been developed in the literature: the political economy determines whether law is *contestable*. As we use the term, "contestability" is a measure of the extent to which law is subject to a process of creative destruction via the participation of private, social, and governmental actors, as opposed to being an instrument exclusively of political actors with unilateral law-making authority. Contestation of law may occur in centralized and decentralized legal systems, but the identities of the participants in the contestation of law and their interests are likely to differ. A highly centralized legal system

favors state-vetted interest groups and actors. A decentralized legal system favors self-organized groups and individuals.

The final basic recognition is that law is not the only mechanism governing economic activity in capitalist systems, and in some successful economies it is not even the primary mechanism. Any deep understanding of the relation between law and capitalism must therefore account not only for the supply of formal law, which has been the exclusive focus of analysis, but also the *demand* for law, which can vary over time and with changes in the constituencies who participate in market activity. The demand for law and the ability to voice that demand are significantly affected by the organization and functions of the legal system in a country, as described above. Moreover, demand for law will vary from country to country depending on the political economy and the nature of the market. Demand for law increases with changes in the socioeconomic conditions of those who have access to the production of law, with the creation of new market transactions for which nonlegal mechanisms of governance are inadequate, with the introduction of new market entrants who lack access to alternative mechanisms, and with the failure of existing mechanisms to provide effective governance or to respond effectively to changes in the economic or the political sphere.

The organization of legal systems, the functions they perform, and their relation to the political economy, as well as the demand for law, have important implications for any theory of legal change. Explaining legal change (that is to say, how legal systems change as opposed to changes in specific legal rules)—something else the existing literature is not very good at—is crucial because, as we will see, legal change is a feature of each of the diverse countries we study in this book. We show that our analytical framework provides a useful way to think about legal change around the world.

Applying the Analytical Framework: Institutional Autopsies

Thus far we have sketched our framework of analysis in rather abstract terms. In order to put flesh on the framework, we apply it in an approach we call the "institutional autopsy." This entails close examination of a firm-level crisis, problem, or controversial corporate governance event. As noted above, corporate governance is a window into the larger and more complex system of economic governance. We believe that by carefully examining an extraordinary firm-level event and the response it generated among key actors, one can gain a much deeper understanding of the system's structure, its strengths and weaknesses, and the likely direction of future institutional developments. Notwithstanding the aura of demise surrounding the term, we think "autopsy"—particularly in the medical school sense—captures the essence of our methodology: the systematic analysis of a complex system to reveal its inner logic, weaknesses, and prospects for reform. (If readers prefer an engineering metaphor, our case studies examine "stress tests" of the various systems under investigation in the book.) In each case, our goals are to use the single-firm event as a springboard to understanding the role of law in corporate governance and economic growth in each country and to try to provide an intellectual roadmap for thinking about future reforms of each of the systems.

We perform institutional autopsies on six recent corporate controversies from around the world. We begin with the Enron debacle and focus our attention on how the U.S. legal system—which in many respects is an outlier in its decentralized, protective, and contestable features—both contributed to and responded to the crisis. Next we turn to the Mannesmann executive compensation scandal and criminal trial in Germany, with its paradigmatic centralized and coordinative legal system, and its struggle to accommodate nontraditional business practices. We then examine the institutional response to the rise of hostile takeovers in Japan, which offers another example of a centralized, coordinative legal system confronting new challenges. Next we examine the role of law in a foreign institutional investor's challenge to one of the Korean *chaebol,* or business groups. Then we turn to two economies that are making fitful transitions to capitalism: those of China and Russia. For China we use an insider trading and false disclosure scandal at a state-owned firm listed in Singapore to analyze the challenges to legal governance in China and to suggest how an apparent conflict between informal coordination and formal rights enforcement can be resolved in a manner that merges these two alternative modes of governance. The case also gives us occasion to reflect on the operation of the Singaporean governance system and speculate whether it might hold lessons for China. Finally, we examine the use of law in the hands of President Vladimir Putin to "renationalize" Yukos, a major player in Russia's energy market.

In each case, we show how our analytical framework helps reveal the deeper significance of these controversies. We situate the controversy within a much broader (if necessarily succinct) examination of each country's historical use of law to govern market activity, expose the key challenges to legal governance they face, and provide an intellectual roadmap for understanding future legal change in light of those challenges.

A few words about what we are *not* trying to do with this methodology. Contemporary academic and policy research concerning this topic are replete with rankings and indices—rule-of-law rankings, investor protection indices, and so on. These objective measures have proved provocative and useful in many ways. But they also have serious limitations that are often ignored in succeeding waves of scholarship and policy advice. The institutional autopsies presented in this book are not intended to serve as the basis for ranking the countries under study or for side-by-side comparisons of the quality, effectiveness, or efficiency of their legal institutions (to cite some of the more common measures in use today). Indeed, the tendency to place great analytical weight on quantifiable but extremely thin legal variables is one source of our dissatisfaction with the existing literature. Our focus is positive (descriptive), not normative. We have tried to provide theoretically informed descriptions of the separate systems—to understand each on its own terms rather than by reference to an ideal type or another system. Indeed, one of the major messages of the book is that law does not function similarly in every successful economy. Each of the countries we discuss faces its own legal governance challenges going forward, with its own preexisting institutional inclinations to both guide and hinder that process. We make comparisons among the countries wherever such comparisons present fertile analytical ground. But we do so to explore the institutional choices a country has made in the past or that may be open to it in the future, not to keep score.

Limitations of the Methodology

No methodology is perfect, and we want to address the limitations of ours up front. The cases featured in our institutional autopsies were not selected from a random sample of comparable events. We could have selected different cases, different countries, or different time periods as the focus of our study. It is possible that our case selection affected our inferences and conclusions. As noted above, however, we had many reasons for picking these cases. Perhaps most important, each was deemed sufficiently important that people working within the affected system reconsidered its operation in light of the new information revealed by the event.

Another possible weakness in our methodology is that we focus on extraordinary events. Such events may mislead if the objective is to understand the ordinary operation of a system. But we believe that out-of-equilibrium events are often very revealing because they expose features and weaknesses of a system that were beneath the radar when it was functioning smoothly. To use a metaphor suggested to us by Mel Eisenberg, an autopsy reveals more information than an annual checkup. A separate justification for focusing on problematic or controversial events is that, for better or worse, big events have always been important catalysts for lawmaking throughout history. Think of the legal responses to the South Sea Bubble in late eighteenth-century England,[15] the Depression's role in the creation of the federal securities laws in the United States, the impact of the 1997–98 Asian financial crisis on the Korean legal system, or the Enron scandal's role in catalyzing passage of the controversial Sarbanes-Oxley Act in the United States.

An institutional autopsy can be interesting and informative in its own right—and may even have entertainment value. Our goal, however, is to learn from the autopsy about a system, that is, to generalize from a firm-level breakdown to the operation of a system of governance. We have taken care to select the cases so that they reveal system-specific vulnerabilities. We therefore place each case in the broader governance context in which it occurred with the help of secondary literature that has identified key characteristics of these systems.

The final limitation stems from the definition of "law" that we have adopted for this book—state-created (or formal) law. This is obviously a top-down approach to understanding the relation between law and markets. A bottom-up approach would examine the organizing principles that shape market activity and the enforcement actions of the relevant community. We could have examined the grassroots formation of informal norms, practices, and organizational codes that support market exchange in the absence of or in support of formal law. Weber himself was careful to define law in such a way that it included rules created and enforced by agents of the sovereign, as well as rules created and enforced by other groups such as the church, gangs, and merchants.[16] Similarly, Hayek believed that law, in the sense of an accepted set of basic norms that govern society, precedes legislation. There is no question that informal rules of this type are crucial to economic activity. In fact, informal rules and nonlegal mechanisms of governance feature prominently in our analysis. The focus on formal law defines our entry point for the analysis of a particular system of governance. By analyzing the relevance—or irrelevance—of formal law we learn a great deal about the availability and efficacy of alternative mechanisms. The focus on formal law is an attempt to more clearly define the scope of analysis, not a normative preconception about the merits of legal and nonlegal forms of governance.

Outline of the Book

Part I sets the stage for our analysis. In chapter 1 we sketch the building blocks of the prevailing view of the relation between law and markets in the literature from Weber to the present and show how academic research has shaped legal reform efforts around the world at the beginning of the twenty-first century. We expose the assumptions underlying the prevailing view and note some real-world facts that are inconsistent with its basic premises. Chapter 2 is the analytical heart of the book. In place of the prevailing view, we develop a dynamic conception of legal and market development, emphasizing different functions played by law in support of markets, the importance of analyzing the demand for law and the process of legal development, and adaptation of law to the needs of the marketplace.

Part II applies the analytical framework in six institutional autopsies: the Enron scandal and ensuing legal reforms in the United States (chapter 3), the executive compensation trial held in connection with the Mannesmann takeover in Germany (chapter 4), the hostile takeover attempt by Livedoor and contemporaneous adoption of guidelines for takeover defenses in Japan (chapter 5), the scandal at the SK group and insurgency by a foreign institutional investor in Korea (chapter 6), the China Aviation Oil crisis and ensuing resolution of the problem in China and Singapore (chapter 7), and the struggle for control over natural resources in Russia illustrated by the Yukos episode (chapter 8).

Part III extends the analysis by exploring the implications of the institutional autopsies. In chapter 9, we move beyond system-specific analysis to compare the functions and centralization of lawmaking across countries. Because the autopsies reveal legal change to be a feature common to all the systems we analyze, chapter 10 examines the process of legal change and its implications for foreign legal transplants, convergence, and legal harmonization. We end in chapter 11 by stating our key conclusions and describing several fertile areas for future research.

———

The goal of this book is to deepen understanding of law's role in the economy over time and across countries. Along the way, we hope to deepen understanding of what globalization means for domestic legal development today. We bring to this inquiry a lawyer's attention to institutional detail and (we believe) a sophisticated sense of how law actually operates in the world, as opposed to the role it plays in theoretical models and regression analyses. We have no quarrel with theory or empirical research—we use both extensively to inform our analysis. But many who comment on this important question (economists, in particular) fail to see law for what it is—the product of human interaction—and fail to perceive the functions that legal institutions actually play in support of markets, the perpetual (if uneven and unpredictable) process by which those institutions are formed and reformed, and the ways in which every society, from the most to the least highly developed in economic terms, supplies substitutes for legal institutions so that markets can function and economic organizations can be formed.

Alas, the relation between law and capitalism, like many things in life, is far more complex than one would hope for in an ideal world. But in the complexity lie discernible patterns, the perception of which promises to change the way we understand a subject that has, with good reason, occupied generations of scholars.

PART I

From Weber to the World Bank, and Beyond

ONE

The Prevailing View:
Impact, Assumptions, and Problems

The literature concerning the relation between law and market-oriented economic activity is vast and spans disciplines ranging from law, economics, and sociology to political science. Merely outlining the thinking at the level of detail it deserves would fill an entire volume; we hope simply to describe the view of this relation that has become deeply engrained in both the academic literature and the policy world and then step back to expose some aspects of this view that do not bear up under careful scrutiny. Inevitably, this sort of task risks caricature or paper-tiger slaying. To be sure, nuances in the literature exist that extend and clarify the picture well beyond the sketch that we provide (see Trebilcock and Leng 2006 for a helpful survey). But the reality is that a very simple view of the relation between law and markets has taken hold in the minds of many smart people—people whose research and policy advice carry tremendous weight. That simple view, not a deeply nuanced perspective that would follow from a careful reading of the entire body of literature, is repeated in important academic journals and the pages of World Bank publications and animates the legal reforms undertaken in many countries in the recent past.

The prevailing story goes like this: A rule of law to protect property rights and enforce contracts is an essential precondition to economic development because without it, transaction costs (in terms of unpredictability, enforcement problems, and so on) will be prohibitive in many cases. Thus, in the absence of legal order, markets will not grow and economies will falter. The one recent nuance given to this view that gets an occasional nod in the literature is that a rule of law may not be essential in early stages of economic growth but becomes essential to sustaining growth.[1] Following Sabel (2005), we call this view the endowment perspective because it treats a legal system as if it were like a highway or a dam—a fixed investment that must be built before economic development can take off but that once in place determines the path of development without itself being subject to change. We briefly trace the intellectual history of the endowment perspective and examine its implications.

The Endowment Perspective

This perspective on law is indebted to Max Weber, who famously stated that a "rational legal system" is a precondition of the emergence of capitalism (Weber 1981). This conclusion followed from his comparison of industrializing countries of western Europe with countries that were not experiencing the Industrial Revolution. By a process of subtraction, Weber concluded that what industrializing countries possessed and the others lacked was a Protestant work ethic and a rational legal system (Trubek 1972).

A century later, drawing in part on Weber's views, Nobel laureate Douglass North extended these ideas into the realm of institutions. North (1990, 2001) argues that what separates rich and poor countries is the quality of their institutions, which he defines as the rules of the game for economic activity and their enforcement characteristics. According to North, rich nations have managed to form credible, low-cost institutions (in particular, formal, state-backed enforcement regimes) that protect property rights and enforce contracts. Poor countries lack institutions that foster market exchange. Because institutional change is path-dependent, it is difficult for countries with a weak endowment to change the foundations for their future growth. In other words, North sees institutions as playing a role in economic development similar to that of Weber's rational legal system.

Carrying this intellectual legacy a step further, a line of literature pioneered in the 1990s by Rafael La Porta, Florencio Lopez-de-Silanes, Andrei Shleifer, and Robert Vishny spearheaded the empirical investigation into the legal foundations of economic growth.[2] In the original papers (La Porta et al. 1997, 1998), the authors introduced a database that codes legal indicators for the quality of shareholder and creditor rights protection for forty-nine countries.[3] The countries are classified according to their "legal origin," that is, the historical source of their legal system. The categories used are English common law and civil law, with the civil law systems subdivided into those of French, German, or Scandinavian origin. The legal indicators are regressed against economic outcome variables. The methodological approach may suggest that unlike Weber and North, La Porta and colleagues are interested in a particular set of rules rather than broad contours of different legal systems. In fact, the specific legal indicators that enter each regression are interpreted as proxies for more substantive characteristics of the legal system. The original paper investigates the ways in which legal protections (and legal origin) affect the level of ownership concentration of firms (that is, the extent to which large blocks of shares are held by a relatively small number of shareholders), whereas subsequent papers investigate law and legal origin as determinants of external finance of firms as measured by the size of stock and credit markets (La Porta et al. 1997), securities markets (La Porta et al. 2004), and private credit markets (Djankov, McLiesh, and Shleifer 2007).[4]

Regardless of the economic outcome variable being tested, the work suggests that English common-law systems provide better protections and thus produce better economic outcomes than do the civil-law systems, particularly the French system. Shleifer and Glaeser explore the reasons for these remarkably consistent findings[5] in a paper that traces the origins of the common and civil law systems all the way back to the twelfth century, when England first established the jury system (Glaeser and Shleifer 2002). They argue that twelfth-century England's weak central control and powerful local interests led to the emergence of a jury system that insulated adjudication from powerful local magnates, laying the foundation for courts as institutions that protect private interests, in particular, private property rights. By contrast, according to this account, France at the time was already saddled with centralized political control that gave the Crown monopoly power over courts. The courts therefore tended to serve the monarch's interests and were less inclined to serve the interests of private individuals.[6] Other differences between North's work and that of La Porta et al. notwithstanding,[7] this approach to explaining differences in legal systems clearly places the major protagonists of the law and finance literature in the endowment camp.

Although for the most part the law and finance research studiously avoids the larger claim that the quality of legal protections determines economic growth (as opposed to financial market outcomes),[8] other research has investigated this linkage. Mahoney (2001a) finds that the common-law countries grew faster than the civil-law countries, at least in recent decades. Drawing explicitly on Hayek's theory of spontaneous order via bottom-up, decentralized institutional adaptation (Hayek 1944), Mahoney explains the finding as a result of the common law's support for private initiative, as opposed to the top-down governmental control associated with civil-law systems. In other words, the common law trumps the civil law because courts are better suited than legislatures to continuously adapt rules to the needs of market participants (Hayek 1973).[9] Thus, by the end of the twentieth century, the endowment perspective had found powerful empirical support from scholars who shared the unproven assumptions of earlier generations of thinkers about the link between law and market-oriented economic institutions. The endowment perspective, in the modern-day statistical form it takes in the law and finance literature, took academia by storm. A cottage industry was created for economists all over the world, who made use of La Porta and colleagues' legal indicators and legal origin classifications to generate papers buttressing the prevailing view. The quality of law appeared to drive economic outcomes everywhere one looked, and the common-law regime appeared to systematically provide higher quality legal protections than did the civil-law regimes.

The law and finance literature has also been highly influential in policy circles. This is not surprising, because its findings confirm many of the views previously espoused by the World Bank concerning the importance of legal systems to economic development.[10] With the help of La Porta and colleagues, the World Bank established a database that assigns a numerical indicator to each country for a host of institutions ranging from shareholder and creditor rights to labor protections, the operation of courts, and so on.[11] New findings concerning the relation between law and market development are quickly reported as economic laws of nature in World Bank publications. More concretely, the endowment perspective, with the support of the law and finance literature, has driven the legal reform policies of the World Bank and other international organizations. The literature lends a scientific patina to these reform policies, although the authors of these studies would probably distance themselves from the conceptual shortcut made by policy advisors, which identifies changes in specific rules with changes in the nature of the legal system.[12] Once a legal system is reduced to the sum of legal rules found in statutes, it can be treated like a piece of technology. As a result, legal reform is a technocratic endeavor (as reflected in the World Bank's "legal technical assistance programs" [Mathernova 1995]), not a political or social one. This is extremely convenient because the World Bank and most other international organizations have no mandate for political involvement or reform in the countries they advise.

This technical approach is also highly problematic, however. First, the coding of specific legal indicators has not always withstood scrutiny, and the results have not always proved to be robust in the face of recoding efforts (Spamann 2006). Second, legal rules are embedded in a host of other complementary rules and institutions. Without a better understanding of the context in which a specific set of rules has emerged as well as the environment in which they are to be inserted, the simple transfer of law as technology is meaningless. Third, treating proxies as the real thing may confuse symptoms with causes. In fact, legal origins turn out to have little power to explain the effectiveness of legal institutions, a variable that is closely associated with economic growth (Berkowitz, Pistor, and Richard 2003a).

Assumptions and Problems

Having sketched the intellectual history of the prevailing view of the relation between law and capitalism and its real-world impact, we now highlight the assumptions—some hidden, some obvious—on which it rests. First, from Weber to La Porta and colleagues, causation is assumed to run in one direction: from law to economic institutions and growth. Once law is in place it falls out of the analysis.[13] Second and in related fashion, a legal system's position in relation to markets is taken as exogenous and fixed. Law is treated as if it were imposed from somewhere outside markets and economic activity—as a precondition to them, as just noted—and then serves as a stable and unchanging foundation for economic life. From this perspective, which has been firmly reinforced in the law and finance literature, law is heavily path-dependent, in that crucial features of a country's economic structures are dictated by the historical origin of its legal system. According to this view, the development of economic institutions is channeled through law as a result of long-ago events such as colonization or military conquest. Third and more implicitly, the operative function of law vis-à-vis market activity is almost universally deemed to be *protection*—of property rights generally and of investors' rights specifically—in the law and finance literature. No serious consideration is given to the possibility that law might perform *other* key functions in support of economic activity. Finally, the prevailing view is projected as if law were the sole mode of governance in market-oriented societies. Social norms, self-regulatory organizations, best practices, and other rules for market activity that are not legally enforceable have generally found little place in the analysis of the ways law supports an economy, particularly in the law and finance literature and subsequent work.

The role of social norms and other informal mechanisms of governance has been the subject of vast recent research, of course. (Most notably, North's work on institutions contemplates a major role for beliefs and other informal constraints. Aoki [2001] and Greif [2006] define institutions as sustainable systems of expectations and beliefs; this definition does not draw a fine line between formal and informal institutions.) Moreover, few scholars or policy makers would consciously subscribe to a completely law-centric view. Yet the obvious tension between the importance of non-legal mechanisms of governance and the conception of the rule of law as consisting solely of legally enforceable rules has not been addressed head-on (perhaps because nonlegal mechanisms are difficult to observe and incorporate into formal models, regression analyses, and reform programs). Instead, the literature and policy programs suggest that societies either thrive economically with "high-quality law" or falter without it.[14]

Many of these assumptions stem from a deeper underlying assumption: that law is a *politically neutral* endowment. But law is obviously a product of human interaction. This basic fact rarely enters the analysis of the way in which law contributes to economic performance. As we noted above, economists are fond of saying that the rule of law must be put in place as a precondition of economic growth. We recognize that this is rhetorical shorthand, but it is telling that economists—so meticulous about certain aspects of their analysis—seem uninterested in the process by which countries acquire and use law, even when law is the explanatory variable in their analyses. The bulk of the new empirical literature about corporate governance, for example, treats law as completely exogenous to markets (La Porta et al. 1998). This is an important statistical move for the producers of this research, because it deflects criticism of multi-colinearity in the use of legal rules as explanatory variables. The methodology has been justified on the ground that many countries have transplanted their law from abroad during periods of colonization or conquest, so the legal rules used in the regressions are not the products of interactions that could simultaneously affect the dependent variables for economic institutions and outcomes. But it conflicts with a proposition that the same literature makes elsewhere, namely, that the original institutions that gave rise to the emergence of a legal system, in particular the invention of the jury system was determined by political conditions, namely, a weak monarch and powerful local interests in England. If politics matter at the outset, why should politics not matter for the subsequent development of legal systems?

We argue that whatever its original source, in order for law to perform any useful function in support of markets it must fit local conditions and thus must continuously evolve in tandem with economic, social, and political developments.[15] As we explore extensively in chapter 10, exogenously imposed law rarely fits conditions in the host country without considerable adaptation by the local law-making community (Berkowitz, Pistor, and Richard 2003a). But adaptation to create a closer fit is unlikely to occur if nonlegal substitutes are available to perform the needed functions at lower cost or if the legal transplant was motivated by factors not closely related to the functional, social, or political needs of the host country (Kanda and Milhaupt 2003). In other words, the economics literature implicitly considers only the "supply" of law in a given society, completely neglecting the role of demand.[16] This is true even when political analysis explicitly enters the discussion. In a paper that builds on the law and finance literature, Djankov et al. (2003) develop an analytical framework for assessing the likely impact of transplanting common law or civil law to developing countries or transition economies. In this framework, a country's legal system is the intersection of the transplanted legal system with a country's "institutional possibility frontier" (IPF), which in turn is a function of a country's location on a continuum between autocracy and disorder. This framework denies the possibility that the preexisting institutions and the transplanted law both are moving targets and that the dynamic interplay between the two may produce outcomes that are well beyond the schematic predictions of this model. A good example of how transplanted private law can be transformed into mechanisms of state control is Russia's bankruptcy law, discussed in chapter 8.[17] Treating a legal institution as a black box implies that the core of any legal system, in particular the strategic use of law by key players, is ignored. In short, because the economics literature poorly conceptualizes where law comes from, its explanations for variations across countries in the use of law to govern economic activity are not very convincing.[18]

We address the problems with these assumptions in considerable detail throughout the book. For now, simply consider some facts about law and economic growth that are deeply problematic for the prevailing view with its emphasis on institutional endowment. All of the law and finance literature is based on recent economic performance—mostly using data from the 1990s, with the most expansive research based on the period from 1960 to 2000. Viewed through a broader historical lens, however, the link between legal origin and economic growth falls away. Our research shows that origin of a legal system has poor predictive power with respect to high and low rate of economic growth for a large sample of countries over long periods of time. We examined data from 1870 to 2000, and divided it into four widely recognized periods of economic history. In every period, countries belonging to at least one civil law family have grown faster than the common-law countries, and in the three most recent periods, spanning virtually the entire twentieth century, either the Scandinavian or the German civil-law countries have grown faster than

Table 1.1 Legal Originas and Economic Growth

Average annual per capita growth rate	1870–1913 (1)	1913–1950 (2)	1950–1973 (3)	1973–2000 (4)	1870–1913 (5)	1913–1950 (6)	1950–1973 (7)	1973–2000 (8)
Common law	-.00081 (.00289)	.00036 (.00333)	-.00585 (.00937)	.01318 (.00809)	—	—	—	—
Civil law	—	—	—	—	—	—	—	—
English legal origin	—	—	—	—	—	—	—	—
French legal origin	—	—	—	—	.00043 (.00313)	-.00078 (.00319)	-.00354 (.00863)	-.02112*** (.00762)
German legal origin	—	—	—	—	-.00016 (.00427)	-.00721 (.00435)	.06187*** (.01450)	.03078** (.01279)
Scandinavian legal origin	—	—	—	—	.00471 (.00523)	.01403** (.00533)	.00645 (.01823)	-.00670 (.01608)
Constant	.01596*** (.00156)	.01292*** (.00180)	.05023*** (.00523)	.02267*** (.00452)	.01514*** (.00247)	.01328*** (.00251)	.04437*** (.00689)	.03585*** (.00608)
Observations	48	48	77	77	48	48	77	77
R^2	0.0017	0.0003	0.0052	0.0342	0.0202	0.2301	0.2397	0.2289
Adjusted R^2	-0.0200	-0.0215	-0.0081	0.0213	-0.0466	0.1776	0.2085	0.1973
F-test of overall significance	0.08	0.01	0.39	2.65	0.30	4.38***	7.67***	7.22***

Standard errors in parentheses.

***, **, * indicate significance at 1%, 5%, and 10%, respectively.

the common-law countries, at a high level of statistical significance (see table 1.1).

After controlling for a variety of other factors that may influence growth, such as a country's initial GDP in a given period, population growth, and educational attainment, legal origin still has weak predictive power for growth over a long sweep of time. Moreover, our research shows that numerous countries have made the leap from low to high growth, frequently in succeeding periods of economic history, suggesting that the origin of a country's legal system does not pose a significant constraint on its prospects for growth. This research is consistent with the findings of Hausmann et al. (2005), who find more than eighty "growth accelerations" in countries around the world after World War II. Few of these accelerations have been sustained. Most important, existing economic theories only weakly predict when growth accelerations are sustained and when they fizzle out.

China's recent rise as an economic power poses another major challenge to the prevailing wisdom (F. Allen, Qian, and Qian 2005; Clarke, Murrell, and Whiting 2006). China's GDP has grown at an annual rate of more than 9 percent for two decades, yet its legal system is highly underdeveloped, its corporate governance is problematic, and its capital market is small. As Clarke, Murrell et al. (2006, 26) conclude, "[T]he experience of the reform era in China seems to refute the proposition that a necessary condition for growth is that the legal system provide secure property and contract rights." Yet China is simply the most recent and most dramatic illustration of the fact that numerous high-growth economies throughout the twentieth century lacked the type of legal protections associated with economic growth according the prevailing view. If the prevailing theory cannot explain some of the most remarkable growth stories in history (which, as we will see, include the experience of Korea and arguably Japan as well as China), it may be time to readjust our thinking about the relation between law and capitalism.

TWO

Rethinking the Relation between Legal and Economic Development

In this chapter we outline the framework of analysis that animates the remainder of the book. Our framework responds directly to the problems with the prevailing view uncovered in chapter 1. We are the first to acknowledge the simplicity of the insights that motivate our analysis. But as we will see, these insights have not made their way into the literature and policy advice that we have surveyed, and these simple insights, when assembled into a cohesive perspective, have major implications for the way we understand legal systems, legal change, and the impact of globalization on law around the world today.

The starting point for our analysis is the recognition that in reality, law is not a fixed endowment in the sense of an unchanging foundation for market activity. As Schumpeter famously noted, a crucial source of the vitality of capitalist systems is "creative destruction"—a response to challenges that arise from competitive pressures or exogenous shocks. It is hardly surprising, then, that the sustainable development of capitalist systems should depend in part on the continuous development of new governance structures to support capitalist enterprise. Law, like capitalism, is constantly evolving. Max Weber realized the potential tension between a "rational" legal system (one that generates stable expectations) and the need for legal adaptation within a rapidly developing economy, but he never fully resolved this tension in his work. The ongoing relation between economic *and legal* change has always existed and has to some extent been recognized by close observers, but the full implications of an iterative process of legal and market development have escaped sustained analysis.

We believe that a better way to approach legal and economic development in capitalist systems is to view the relationship as a highly iterative process of action and strategic reaction. Historical experience in a diverse range of countries suggests that the path of development is something like this: Market change occurs, typically because of the introduction of new technology, the entrance of new players, a shift in consumer demand, or a scandal that reveals damaging new information about the operation of the market or its participants. Market change of any type raises new questions about, for example, the right to use new technology, the ability of new entrants to participate in the market, or the need for new rules to govern market conduct. In order to mitigate uncertainty and restore equilibrium in the market, these questions must be answered by someone. In most developed economies, many of these questions are answered by legal actors, be they legislators, bureaucrats, judges, or some combination thereof.[1] Virtually every legal response, in turn, creates new incentives (and often new uncertainties) for market players, who adapt their conduct to the new rules and push at the margins of the new legal order. These market reactions raise new questions of their own, and the process repeats itself. In short, there is a *rolling relation* between law and markets,[2] which serve as two points in a continuous feedback loop.[3]

The way in which a given legal system responds to market change, however, is likely to vary depending on how it is organized and the nature of the dominant functions it performs. We can expect that countries vary significantly along these dimensions. Understanding these differences is the next step in our analytical framework.

Organization of Legal Systems

Not all legal systems associated with economic success are organized similarly. Some are highly concentrated, with few actors involved in the lawmaking and enforcement processes. Others are more decentralized, with greater opportunities for a range of actors to participate in lawmaking and enforcement. These differences can affect both the substance and the enforcement of law. To understand how organization affects substantive law, consider a brief example from the production of corporate law. Continental European countries tend to insulate the process from directly affected actors. The European Union closely follows this model when it assembles a "High Level Group of Company Law Experts"[4] for developing the principles for a new takeover directive or a "Committee of Wise Men on the Regulation of European Securities Markets" for developing a new framework for securities market regulation in the Union.[5] Committee members are almost exclusively drawn from academia. By contrast, drafting and reform committees in the United Kingdom and the United States typically include practitioners from the fields of business and law—people with not only practical expertise but also a direct stake in the outcome.[6] It would be naïve to suggest that by giving academics the primary role in lawmaking continental European jurisdictions effectively insulate that process from political influence. In fact, the pool of professors recruited into the process tends to vary with shifts in political power, and draft proposals are often substantially revised in enacting a new law.[7] Nevertheless, these different law-making processes help account for the fact that there is remarkably little overlap between the directives composing the bulk of European company law and provisions typically found in state-level corporate statutes in the United States (Carney 1997).

Moreover, the content of the law may be affected by the absence or exclusion of certain constituencies from the law production process. An informative example is provided by the state of Delaware. Despite its small size and diminutive stature in virtually all other areas of the U.S. political economy, it is the most attractive jurisdiction for incorporation among Fortune 500 companies. The absence of strong labor constituencies may have given Delaware the edge over such states as New Jersey and New York in the competition for incorporation at the beginning of the twentieth century (Arsht 1976),[8] a lead Delaware has maintained in part by producing corporate law that is favorable to managers and investors rather than other organized constituencies, which still have little input into the revision or development of Delaware corporate law.

The interpretation, application, and enforcement of law also are affected by organizational factors. Some of this influence is captured in the stereotypical distinction between common-law and civil-law systems. In the usual rendition, judges in civil-law systems do not make law but merely interpret the codes. In formal terms, courts are not bound by precedent, suggesting that the legislature has a mandate to monopolize legal innovation. Although there is some truth in the stereotype,[9] the operation of real-world legal systems is much more complex. Contrary to the caricature, civil-law codes are not highly specific and thus cannot be outcome-determinative in most cases. In fact, they were written to last indefinitely, and their drafters were well aware of the fact that societies change. Indeed, at the time the Napoleonic codes were enacted, France had just experienced a series of political and economic revolutions. Not surprisingly, therefore, in practice the interpretive function of courts in civil-law systems is often indistinguishable from lawmaking.[10] Moreover, though there is no formal precedent, judges are well aware that their decisions might be overturned if they are contrary to the standards set by the highest court. Consistently rendering decisions that are overturned by higher courts is not only disruptive to the legal system but is also a poor career strategy for judges, so lower courts are highly conscious of prior rulings. In short, there are functional equivalents between the features of common-law and civil-law systems that are often said to be most characteristic of their differences.

In our view, more important than these formal characteristics are the incentives a given legal system generates to invest in innovation and adaptation of governance over time and the way this process is influenced by access to the legal system at the law-making and law enforcement stages. Some legal systems encourage litigation by providing access to law enforcement apparatus by individuals who have been adversely affected by state or private action. Others encourage participation in lawmaking by involving well-organized constituencies in the formal legislative process or by consulting them informally at the implementation stage. Some do both. Once we look beyond the caricature of civil law and common law and analyze the way legal systems are organized, we find configurations that are more varied and do not map neatly onto the legal origin hypothesis as presented in the law and finance literature.

In fact, there is often substantial organizational variation *within* countries belonging to the same legal family. The U.K. legal system, for example, is much less accessible to a decentralized process of litigation than is the U.S. legal system. The United Kingdom has no contingency fees for attorneys, and class-action suits are much more tightly restricted than in the United States. As a result, there is no interest group comparable to the American bar that constantly mobilizes adversarial litigation. Similarly, Germany and Japan differ substantially in the organization of their legal systems although both originate from the German civil-law system. On the whole, Germany is much more litigious than Japan (Ietswaart 1990)— itself a fact that is difficult to square with a strong-form hypothesis about the effects of legal origin. In key areas such as labor disputes and issues related to corporate governance, however, access to the courts in Germany has been constrained by legal rules that create entry barriers to decentralized dispute settlement in order to protect cooperative bargaining among organized stakeholders. In the Japanese system, important governance and regulatory issues were typically resolved via informal bargaining between bureaucrats and the business elite, often through more direct channels between the public and private sector than was the case in Germany. Only after the costs of litigation were reduced did litigation become an important component in the resolution of corporate governance disputes in Japan (West 2001). This has allowed Japan to shift from an economic system that was arguably more centralized than Germany's to one that is allowing more decentralized access to law and greater contestation through litigation brought by parties to a conflict than is presently the case in Germany.

Although this trend is remarkable for what it signifies about changing attitudes toward law in the postwar period, it is not inconsistent with earlier trends. Japan has experienced considerable variation in litigation rates since it began industrializing in the late nineteenth century, with substantially higher rates of litigation prior to World War II than at any time thereafter until very recently (Haley 1978). Such dramatic changes in the use of law over time can hardly be explained by legal origin theories. Indeed, if anything, a legal origin story would predict higher litigation rates in the immediate postwar period given the influx of U.S. law during the occupation. The point is that a focus on legal origin masks more than it illuminates as a signifier of how real-world legal systems differ among themselves and change internally over time.

The Multiple Functions of Law

Just as legal systems in capitalist countries vary in organization, law can perform a variety of functions in support of economic activity. The endowment perspective suggests that law's only role in an economy is protection of (individual) rights.[11] But this is misleading. Law, of course, does play a major role in the protection of property rights in capitalist systems. Rights need to be protected against abuse by holders of political power and by other market actors to promote saving, investment, and creative endeavor. Indeed, the clear delineation, protection, and transferability of property rights are typically deemed to be the key to economic development (for example, Hoskins 2002). Similarly, third-party contract enforcement via the courts is often viewed as key to economic performance (North 1990).[12] This protective function of law is often the justification provided for lawmaking and enforcement activity. And as we have seen, the protection of investors' rights (a specific type of property rights) lies at the heart of the law and finance literature.

But the rights protection paradigm overstates what legal systems can possibly achieve. In a Coasian world without transaction costs, legal entitlements could be clearly allocated so that parties can bargain over the optimal allocation to achieve efficient results. But as Coase himself noted decades ago (Coase 1960) and a large number of economists have come to realize in the meantime (Johnson, Glaeser, and Shleifer 2001), the real world is characterized by substantial transaction costs. The implication is that the legal system itself is at the center of balancing conflicting interests, not only at the time of the initial allocation of rights but whenever their exercise conflicts with rights of others—neighbors, passers-by, new market entrants, or members of society at large. The allocation of rights involves value judgments and political bargains at each juncture. Not surprisingly, the nature and proper subjects of property rights protection can differ widely across societies. Important social science research has sought to identify the causes of these observed variations and has frequently traced them to the structure of the economy and the nature of economic activities. For example, societies that depend on a common pool of resources (Ostrom 1990) develop different governance structures than do those that pursue trading activities (Greif, Milgrom, and Weingast 1994; Greif 2006) or farming (Allen 2001). The extensive literature about varieties of capitalism has documented differences in the value placed on social as opposed to individual goals across systems (Hall and Soskice 2001), which may affect the nature of the protections provided.[13]

Given the limitations of rights protection in real-world legal systems, our goal is to identify the actors and interests that find protection in the legal systems of the countries we examine, particularly as markets change, and to highlight how often the protective function of law is overshadowed in importance—in reality, if not rhetorically—by other functions. For example, in chapter 3 we argue that the legal reform adopted in the wake of the Enron scandal in the United States, though publicly justified as a means of protecting investors, might more insightfully be viewed as an attempt to partly centralize legal governance over corporate activity and to signal a higher governmental priority on combating white-collar crime.

In addition to protection of rights, markets also require coordination of activity. Markets are essentially made up of relationships, which must be managed in some way in order for markets to function properly. Laws help manage relationships in a variety of ways. For example, they allocate endowments among incumbents, set the terms of access by new entrants, and determine which actors have the authority to answer questions raised by market change. Consider laws relating to defenses against hostile takeovers, which we explore in our institutional autopsy on Japan. Unsolicited ("hostile") takeovers pose genuine risks for the shareholders of a target company, who face collective action and information problems in evaluating whether to transfer control to the bidding company. Thus, in many systems, hostile takeovers are regulated in order to protect shareholders. But hostile takeovers also raise a fundamental question for the economy: Who—the bidding company, the incumbent directors of the target company, the shareholders of the target company, or others such as employees or governmental actors—should decide whether control over the target should be transferred to the bidder and on what terms? As they have developed in Delaware, the takeover rules cede the basic authority to accept or resist a takeover bid to the board of directors of the target company, subject only to very broad constraints imposed by courts. In the United Kingdom, the rules allocate that authority primarily to the shareholders of the target company. Disputes that arise in the context of takeovers are resolved by an institution—the Takeover Panel—that has been established and is staffed by representatives of financiers, investors, and members of the legal profession. By developing general rules of behavior and enforcing them by means of consultation, the U.K. system stresses coordination rather than litigation. By contrast, in the United States, takeovers are highly litigious events, with attorneys playing a key role in developing takeover practices through contractual innovation.[14]

The rules recently developed in Japan blend the two approaches but more closely resemble the Delaware rules in permitting incumbent managers to resist unwanted bids by means of a powerful legal technology developed in the United States and colloquially known as the poison pill. Thus, although takeover rules ostensibly are designed to protect investors from coercive bids, coordination of economic activity—the allocation of power and the management of relations between shareholders and the board of directors—is either the intended result (as in the United Kingdom) or an unavoidable by-product (as in Delaware) of any such rules. Other countries' laws erect or facilitate barriers to entry by permitting pre-bid defenses such as multiple voting rights or golden shares. Rules that were either designed for or could be used as pre-bid defenses were at the core of the European battle over the future of the takeover directive, as we discuss in chapter 4.[15]

As the above examples suggest, law can be consciously structured to achieve coordination among key players by ensuring that they share decision-making powers. A major example is the German co-determination regime. By mandating employee representation on the supervisory board, which appoints the management board, the law forces shareholders and management to bargain with employees over corporate strategies, not merely specific measures that might affect employees at their workplace. Like law with a protective function, a law that seeks to coordinate may well give rise to legal arbitrage or be used primarily as a signaling device rather than for ensuring effective coordination. In the case of German co-determination, for example, the introduction of the law appears to have reduced the power of the supervisory board and enhanced that of top management (Gerum, Steinmann, and Fees 1988; Pistor 1999). Moreover, as the analysis of the Mannesmann case (chapter 4) reveals, the interests of employee representatives are not always perfectly aligned with those of their base. Still, the critical point is that the design of legal systems can be used to reflect social and political preferences for collective bargaining and coordination as opposed to individualized rights enforcement.

Although we stress the importance of protection and coordination as characteristics of different legal systems, we recognize that the tasks of law in any society cannot be reduced to these two functions. Law also supports economic activity by playing auxiliary roles such as signaling and credibility enhancement. Quite apart from its direct consequences, law sends a signal or makes a statement about the type of conduct lawmakers desire (Sunstein 1996). Such a statement may be an effort to manage social norms or to bring about behavioral change in other ways. Signaling is an important function of any economic governance regime because markets rely on information. Law not only helps set the rules by which market activity takes place, but it also makes a larger statement about governmental priorities, the future direction of policy, the relative strength of interest groups concerned with a specific issue, and other information that may be useful to market actors. Often, the signals sent by law may be more potent or novel than the legal provisions themselves. This is one of the major conclusions we draw from our study of the Enron scandal. The Sarbanes-Oxley Act, passed in response to the scandal, appears to have energized law enforcers and reassured investors by signaling a more proactive governmental stance toward financial crime and poor corporate governance, but the law itself is largely a mixture of preexisting or arguably ineffectual legal concepts that may have added little to existing investor protections (see Romano 2005). It also signaled to courts and lawmakers in Delaware that the federal government was ready to step in and further centralize legal governance of the corporate sector unless state institutions took up the task (Roe 2002). We will argue that much of the legal development that has taken place in China since the early 1980s falls into this category: it is of little protective value but is salient to market actors for the signals it sends about government policy and the future direction of reforms.

A signal often can be sent by important actors taking measures that fall short of legally enforceable statutes or regulations—what legal scholars somewhat ambiguously call "soft law." An example is the voluntary adoption of a code of conduct by an international organization, governmental actor, or firm. The announcement of such adoption alone may trigger behavioral change by the recipient of the signal (at least if the signal is perceived to be credible, a factor we consider below). We will explore a recent example of this phenomenon in Japan, where two government ministries in 2005 jointly promulgated guidelines for corporate takeover defenses endorsing the poison pill. Although the guidelines lack the authority of law, they immediately triggered a host of responses in the private sector because they signaled the policy views of important governmental actors. Courts immediately took note of the signal as well, incorporating the guidelines into their judgments and ensuring that the "soft law" would influence development of the "hard law."

Signaling works only if the signal is credible. Another important function that law performs in the economy is enhancing the credibility of state-supplied governance structures. This reduces the overall cost of governance and enhances its effectiveness by mitigating a major source of political uncertainty (Maxfield and Schneider 1997). According to Schneider and Maxfield, "[c]redibility in this context means that capitalists believe what state actors say and then act accordingly" (11). In the absence of such governance structures, each outcome must be bargained for and implemented anew. Moreover, even optimal ad hoc solutions to economic problems may be subject to time or dynamic inconsistencies (Kydland and Prescott 1977). That is, without credible hands-tying measures, state and private agents may adjust their behavior over time in ways that undermine government policy.

Several features of law make it well suited to the role of credibility enhancement. Law is an *authoritative* statement about desired or required behavior, backed by formal sanctions for noncompliance. It is also generally more difficult to change than other governmental pronouncements, in part because legal change typically requires the coordination of several state actors, a point that we return to below. Backing a policy or norm with law reinforces the signal that society (or at least a powerful subset thereof) deems a given type of behavior to be important, deterring conduct that could undermine the policy or erode the norm. Germany's approach to executive compensation provides a powerful illustration. For reasons we discuss below, lavish executive compensation like that in the United States is inconsistent with postwar German social and corporate governance institutions. Although those institutions are now under considerable stress as a result of the greater interdependence of financial markets and the infusion of different practices into the German system, German criminal law provides an avenue by which legal actors—prosecutors and courts— can intervene to resist movement toward U.S. compensation practices.

German norms and policies about acceptable levels of and motives for executive pay have greater credibility and stickiness than they would in the absence of legal backing.[16] And the prosecution of an executive for approving "unreasonable" compensation sends a powerful, credible signal about the continued viability of social norms.

We have separately analyzed four roles that law can play in support of economic activity, in contrast to the usual focus on property rights protection alone. Of course, a given law may have all, some, or none of these functions. At the same time, the four functions are interrelated and may be mutually reinforcing. For example, coordination provides a form of protection for those whose actions are coordinated via legal authority, because they are at least assured a seat at the bargaining table. Conversely, protective law might play an important coordinative function by serving as the focal point around which negotiations or strategic adaptations to the law take place. The important point is that we lose considerable analytical traction when law's many contributions to markets are lumped under the heading of "property rights protection." Most important, it obscures our ability to see that some of these functions may be in tension with other crucial attributes of a successful economic system, such as adaptability and innovativeness.

———

So far we have argued that understanding the organization of legal systems and distinguishing the various functions of law provide a powerful way of understanding the *varieties* of legal systems associated with capitalism in the real world. Figure 2.1 provides an illustration of this concept. The graph is two-dimensional and thus cannot fully account for the multiple functions of law that we have described. We explore these other functions and how they map onto the two dominant functions in our case studies. In Part III we show how this matrix helps explain their quite different institutional trajectories in the relation between law and capitalism in each system.

We are not the first to develop an organizing concept that is an alternative to the conventional divide between civil law and common law. Analyzing differences in criminal procedure across countries, Mirjan Damaška has developed a model that links features of the legal system to structures of authority (Damaška 1975). He distinguishes between "hierarchical" and "coordinate" models for organizing the criminal justice system, which he links directly to different ideas and practices of state authority. He argues that classic English liberalism gives rise to diffuse government control and a preference for a coordinative as opposed to a hierarchical model. By

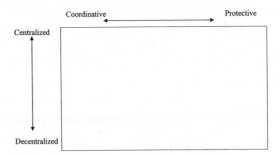

Figure 2.1. Legal systems matrix

contrast, hierarchy became the dominant organizing principle in Continental Europe after the centrifugal forces of feudalism had been overcome. Our distinction between centralized and decentralized legal systems bears obvious resemblance to this model. The main difference is that our focus is on the organization of legal systems as it relates to market activities. Embracing principles of market-based economic activities by definition implies that direct state control plays a less prominent role. The spectrum of governance that we describe therefore begins with coordination and ranges all the way to decentralization, where the making and enforcement of law depend on the willingness of private parties to mobilize the legal system.[17]

Our model also differs from a more recent attempt to link legal systems to political structure. In "The New Comparative Economics," Djankov et al. (2003) argue that any system faces the challenge of designing institutions that effectively protect property rights and creating a strong state capable of enforcing property rights, while constraining the temptation of a strong state to infringe on these very rights. They describe this as the "conflict between the twin goals of controlling disorder and dictatorship" (597). The design of legal systems, in their view, is directly related to the political challenges that a given system faces. Where disorder is the actual or perceived major challenge, a legal system that prefers regulation to litigation is the answer. Conversely, where dictatorship is the threat, (decentralized) litigation will trump (centralized) regulation. In our view, the Hobbesian dilemma may indeed have been relevant in determining certain early choices in the evolution of legal systems. The model has little traction, however, in explaining the continuous evolution of law in capitalist systems today as most countries find themselves somewhere in the middle between disorder and dictatorship. Moreover, the model internalizes law and political processes, but it treats law as exogenous to the process of economic change. By contrast, in our model law is an integral part of adaptation and change as depicted in the rolling relation between law and markets.

Our attempt to reconceptualize different legal systems in response to the outpouring of law and finance literature bears some resemblance to the trajectory of the "variety of capitalism" debate (Hall and Soskice 2001; Streeck and Thelen 2005). As in the legal origin literature, the proponents of a particular classification system—corporatist models as opposed to market models—first sought to identify indicators that could be used to classify and map countries once and for all. This proved to be futile, however, because few countries actually displayed the precise indicators that were identified in the literature, or the mapping did not generate the results that the theory or classification system predicted.[18] The next step in the debate, therefore, was to characterize the differences between systems using a broader brush. Thus, the literature about varieties of capitalism introduced the notion of "liberal" and "coordinated" market economies (Soskice 1990; Hall and Soskice 2001) by identifying essential characteristics without attempting to enumerate specific expressions thereof. In a similar vein, we want to move away from the law and finance literature's reliance on specific indicators to differentiate common-law from civil-law countries and instead explore the organizational features of legal systems irrespective of their origin.

But we have a broader goal as well. We intend to push the analysis beyond descriptive categories of legal systems. The purpose of the institutional autopsies in Part II is to analyze systems at a moment of great challenge or crisis that could be system-transformative. When analyzing the relevant players and their use of law or alternative governance structures prior to the crisis or in response to the crisis, we observe the microprocesses by which different systems are reorganized, adapted, or reinvented. We propose that these *processes* of change—rather than static indicators—are critical for understanding the relation between legal and economic development.

Substitutes for Law

If we disaggregate the functions of law and internalize the processes of legal, economic, and political change, we not only deepen understanding of the way law supports markets but also help illustrate why law is often *not* used to support economic activity, even in successful markets. In any economy, nonlegal substitutes are potentially available to perform each of these functions. There is a substantial literature about the central role of nonlegal rules (for example, norms)[19] in the governance of a vast array of human activity. Exactly why most people abide by norms most of the time is not well understood, but several theories exist, and these theories dovetail nicely with our discussion of the functions of law above. One theory is that compliance with norms signals cooperative behavior, which is beneficial to the complier because it triggers cooperation by the other party (Axelrod 1984). Another is that, as with law itself, compliance or noncompliance is rewarded or punished in ways that people find meaningful. It is evident that norms, like law, evolve over time and often in tandem with stimuli that bring about market change (Ellickson 2001).

Historical experience suggests that a priori, law is not superior to such "nonlaw" as a device for governing economic activity, at least across all stages of development and all markets.[20] The high growth experienced by many countries—including South Korea and Japan in the 1960s and 1970s and China today—indicates that norms and other extralegal devices can serve as a foundation for economic success, at least to a point. Although the Asian cases are often treated as enigmas or exceptions to the conventional wisdom (Trebilcock and Leng 2006), they simply provide the most dramatic illustration of the point that nonlaw can sometimes perform the roles of law at lower cost. The illustrations, however, are not limited to "catch up" economies. The experience of Silicon Valley in the United States in the 1990s, for example (Saxenian 1994), is equally supportive of this point.

We elaborate on these historical experiences in subsequent chapters. At this stage, we simply note that alternative development models, elaborated in a growing body of literature, confirm the intuition that both law and nonlaw can support economic activity. Ongoing relationships and repeated deals can provide protection for economic interests. Coordination and credibility enhancement can occur via pacts between political leaders and business groups (North and Weingast 1989) or among members of a network based on ethnicity or kinship (Greif, Milgrom, and Weingast 1994; Greif 2006; Rauch 1999). These pacts simultaneously help facilitate information flow and policy transmission throughout the economy. Guidelines and best practice codes can send signals about desired behavior to targeted communities of market actors. As exemplified by the high-growth East Asian economies, political leadership can engender credibility in economic policy and enhance compliance with its goals. Elite bureaucracies such as that of Japan in the postwar high growth period can also generate credibility and foster coordination.

The Political Economy: Supply and Demand for Law

Recall that one of our criticisms of the endowment perspective is its fixation on a rather simplistic view of the supply of law and complete neglect of demand-side factors. In order to understand why some countries and some markets rely more heavily on law as a mechanism of governance than do others, and to better understand how legal systems change, the supply and demand for law must be considered in greater depth. This, in turn, requires stripping away another assumption of the endowment perspective: that law—though its original form and substance might have been shaped by politics—is a *politically neutral* endowment.[21] Contrary to its typical portrayal in the economics literature and the policy world, law is a political product not only at its inception but in the way it affects and is shaped by the interests of political, social, and economic actors.[22] It is impossible to understand where law comes from and where it is going without venturing into the realm of the political economy.

On the supply side, many commentators now recognize the obvious point that enforcement, not simply the law on the books, must be taken into account. But it is important to expose the major reasons for the frequent divergence between formal law and law as enforced. One reason is related to the division of labor on the supply side of the legal system. Two largely (though not completely) distinct groups of actors are involved in the separate processes of enacting rules and enforcing them. Legislators and bureaucrats make ex ante rules in the form of statutes and regulations, and legal professionals (judges, prosecutors, and lawyers) interpret, apply, and enforce them ex post. In order for law to play a role in support of markets, different actors must coordinate their activities in the law production process. But coordination may fail. The actors whose coordination is required may not share similar interests with respect to the law or may understand the law differently. Even if the interests and understandings of the actors are aligned, other constraints (for example, budget limitations, higher priorities) may reduce the scope of action of an essential actor.

The demand for law as a device for governance in the economy is a function of many factors, of course, including the structure of government, the nature of the political system, and the level of educational attainment in the society. We focus on three factors that are directly relevant to our discussion. First, all else being equal, the existence of effective, lower-cost nonlegal alternatives will reduce demand for law. (By "effective" we mean "capable of protecting or coordinating the interests of those with veto power over the contents of law and access to legal enforcement mechanisms.") This is why it is so crucial to account for nonlegal alternatives in any model of the interaction of law and markets. However effective the legal system may be at performing market-supporting functions, actors can be expected to opt out of the legal system whenever nonlegal alternatives are available at lower economic or social cost to them. Although in the postwar period Japan's legal system was highly developed (no insurmountable supply problems existed), demand for law was dampened by the highly relational structure of the dealings between Japanese business groups and bureaucrats (Milhaupt 1996). Interests were protected and market activity was coordinated by repeated interactions between the public and the private sectors. Credibility was enhanced by the central role of elite bureaucrats and by the very fact of economic success under the informal model. The state successfully signaled its policy goals through "administrative guidance."[23] Law was not irrelevant to this system—indeed, many of the nonlegal mechanisms of governance were facilitated by the legal structure, so law played an important coordinative function in the economy (Milhaupt 1996). But overt and extensive reliance on the legal system for protective purposes could be avoided in many areas of economic activity.

Second, not only is the supply of effective law influenced by demand, but conversely, the demand for law is affected by supply. Some countries, particularly those experiencing rapid transitions toward economic growth, simply lack the technical capacity or political inclination to produce a legal system that performs crucial governance functions. In these systems, market actors have no choice but to pursue nonlegal alternatives. In today's world a late developer seeking to catch up with economically more advanced countries has at its disposal *legal* technology as well as commercial technology developed elsewhere. Legal solutions, like other technological solutions, can often be borrowed at lower cost than they can be developed from scratch, although the effectiveness of this form of legal development is open to question (see chapter 10). Nonetheless, the low-cost supply of standardized legal solutions to governance problems helps explain the increasing outward similarity of law in market-oriented economies around the world today.

Supply can affect demand in a more profound way: the relative influence of different agents (legislators and bureaucrats, bureaucrats and courts) in the law-making and law enforcement processes may change over time. From 1960 to 1990, the period that has come to be known as the East Asian Miracle, for example, policy guidance announced and enforced by a highly regarded bureaucracy, not legislation, was dominant (Pistor and Wellons 1999). Courts were sidestepped to an important degree because bureaucrats used their own enforcement devices to achieve policy goals, as in the case of Japan's administrative guidance. By contrast, during the 1990s Japan launched large-scale institutional reforms to create a more flexible and "participatory" legal system consistent with the maturation of its economy. For example, barriers to the use of courts for enforcing investor rights were lowered, triggering a substantial increase in litigation rates (West 2001). The bureaucracy lost credibility owing to a series of policy mistakes and scandals, while legislation enacted via the parliamentary process and judicial decisions gained in importance. Thus, a shift in the relative power of the bureaucracy and of political and judicial actors in the law production and enforcement processes coincided with and was influenced by a major shift in the demand for law (see Milhaupt and West 2004). Changes in the relative power of economic actors may have similar effects. As our case studies demonstrate, the increasing importance of foreign investors has put substantial pressure on domestic constituencies and the ways in which they resolved problems in the past. The uncertainties created by these new configurations have created a greater demand for law—not only by new entrants but also by incumbents.

Third, as markets grow in size and complexity and as market actors become more heterogeneous, demand for law appears to increase. Social theorists including Karl Marx and Adam Smith long ago noted that changes in economic systems, including growing economic complexity, coincide with changes in the ways in which economies are governed. A simple explanation is that as markets increase in size and transactions take place beyond the reach of informal governance structures based on mutual monitoring, trust, and reputation, formal law may be needed to fill the vacuum.[24] In particular, actors who lack access to informal mechanisms of governance seek legal tools with which to participate fully in economic markets.[25] But this explanation says little about types and functions of law for which there might be increasing demand. Our institutional autopsies reveal the importance of the allocation of enforcement power in shaping the law. The targets of enforcement activity, the choice of criminal or civil action, and the use of procedural mechanisms to encourage mass private enforcement actions by investors are all politically charged. As we will see, countries vary enormously in their approaches to these questions, with major implications for the role that law plays in their respective economies. Occasionally, as in the Yukos case, law enforcement is blatantly used in service of political ends. More often, the political choices underlying enforcement decisions take more subtle forms but have equally important consequences. To cite another example, procedural roadblocks to investor lawsuits in

China—reflecting not only limited institutional capacity but also concerns for social stability and the ambiguous role of the courts in the communist government's regulatory hierarchy—limit the universe of responses to the acute corporate governance problems posed by existing ownership structures in China. The United States, with its plethora of activist attorneys, incentive fee arrangements that encourage suits, procedures for facilitating mass litigation, and multiplicity of forums (state and federal) for law production and enforcement, stands at the other extreme.

As elaborated in many of the succeeding chapters, global market development has increased demand for *protective* law, particularly in systems in which informal relationships have largely supplanted widespread enforcement of legal rights. Contrary to the Weberian perspective, however, legal systems at the forefront of this development appear to be moving away from detailed rule making in favor of open-ended, flexibility-enhancing standards, thereby modifying the nature of protective law. For example, in corporate law, there has been a movement (at least among developed market economies)[26] away from highly regulatory or mandatory law toward a more "enabling" approach epitomized by Delaware law.[27] With this approach, essentially any deviation from the state-supplied set of default rules is permitted, subject only to policing of outrageous conduct by the courts at the behest of aggrieved investors. Related examples are the replacement of rule-based accounting practices with standards-based practices in the United States and the endorsement of the open method of coordination as an alternative to top-down legal harmonization in the European Union (Scott and Trubek 2002).

Why do we observe this movement? The reason is that law's ability to provide stable and predictable solutions to future contingencies declines as economic complexity increases. Put differently, socioeconomic and technological change renders law incomplete (Pistor and Xu 2003b). A major role of legal systems in a world of incomplete law is to allocate lawmaking and enforcement functions to the agents that are best able to resolve disputes over unforeseen and unforeseeable contingencies, thereby facilitating continued change. Thus, a growth in economic complexity increases demand for law that provides flexibility and adaptability at the expense of predictability.

Viewing law as a neutral (protective) institutional endowment also masks the political realities of law's impact on those it affects. Whatever the motivation of the producers of law, it often has disparate impacts on incumbent stakeholders and challengers in the economy. Law may reallocate control and decision-making rights from one constituency (for example, management) to another (for example, investors or employees). Legal change may also signal a change in policy direction with potentially redistributive effects, triggering a host of responses by those who expect to benefit or lose from the change. The responses do not depend only on the purpose and language of the statute. Equally important is the way legal change is perceived by relevant constituencies (Sunstein 1996). Thus, law potentially shapes demand for legal governance even when little attempt is made to control outcomes for specific constituencies, which are often unforeseeable or unintended.

Bringing our analytical perspective full circle, the demand for law as a governance device is likely to be affected by the extent to which potentially affected constituencies are allowed to participate in lawmaking and law enforcement. Centralized legal systems by definition do not provide as many ports of access for participants, and outsiders who lack access must find nonlegal governance devices to order their affairs. By contrast, decentralized legal systems foster mechanisms of legal enforcement. The courts, as the ultimate demand-driven law producers, are likely to play a more important role in decentralized than in centralized legal systems. Similarly, the demand for law is likely to be greater where law plays a predominantly protective function in the economy. Where law is used principally to coordinate relations among insiders, actors are more likely to resort to nonlegal governance mechanisms to advance and protect their interests.

PART II

Institutional Autopsies

We use the analytical framework outlined in chapter 2, coupled with a methodological device we call the institutional autopsy, to investigate different countries' responses to the challenge of globalization. This phenomenon is a particularly useful reference point for understanding the link between law and capitalism. Globalization has palpably affected the supply and demand for law in many countries and highlighted the fact that law has different functions in different countries. The supply side is affected because formal law has become a highly fungible and widely traded commodity. The IMF, the World Bank, and the World Trade Organization, to name only a few international organizations, promote standardized legal reforms to further economic development. Similarly, major international law firms seek to expand the use of standardized private legal models for transactions around the world. Moreover, governments often conduct comparative analyses of foreign laws when embarking on major reform projects to inform themselves about available solutions, legitimize their action, or attract foreign investors. The demand for law is also affected, because globalization puts pressure on different constituencies within a given system that may benefit or lose from market integration and capital flows. It also adds new constituencies, in particular, foreign strategic and portfolio investors, whose demand for formal legal solutions to governance issues may differ from that of domestic constituencies. The variety of motivations for the increased supply and demand for law in a global environment confirms the multiplicity of roles that law plays in capitalist societies. If we analyze these motivations, it quickly becomes apparent that protecting property rights of investors—the typical focus of analysis—is not the only or necessarily the most important role of law in economic and closely related political markets.

Our point of departure in each case is a crisis or major event at the firm level that exemplifies how an exogenous shock such as foreign entry into a capital market or other market change affects a preexisting system of governance. We identify a relevant firm-level crisis and conduct an institutional autopsy. In medicine, an autopsy is an important strategy for learning about the operation of a complex system in the hope of gaining deeper insights into its strengths and vulnerabilities. Like the human body, economic and legal institutions are complex systems that defy simple mechanical analysis (Auyang 1999). The process of a differential diagnosis is therefore a useful metaphor with which to capture the kind of analysis that is required for understanding the operation of these systems.

This method allows us to identify relevant constituencies on the demand side of law. They will invariably include investors, employees, and management, but depending on the country they may also include bureaucrats and politicians as direct stakeholders in the firm. Once these stakeholders and the level of their relative power in the pre-crisis firm are identified, we can reconstruct the governance structure of the pre-crisis firm. Moreover, we can analyze the way each of the major stakeholders responds to the crisis and ultimately how they fare in the post-crisis environment. The institutional autopsy as applied to firms is thus not a simple postmortem; rather, it allows us to project our analysis backward and forward and to analyze a system in motion.

A severe crisis or major event may trigger a broader response, including the supply of new mechanisms of governance to resolve the crisis and prevent future ones. Law may not be the only remedy applied, but given the ubiquity and perceived fungibility of formal law today, it is highly unlikely that a reform package will lack a legal component. Therefore, the mere use of law as a remedy for a firm-level crisis is less interesting than the purpose for which law was (and was not) chosen, the parties who advocated for legal reforms, and those who potentially benefitted from legal change.

As suggested by our analysis of the determinants of the demand for law, the efficacy of legal change in a governance regime will depend significantly on how the law's consumers respond to it. A complete institutional autopsy will therefore also involve an assessment of the demand for the new governance structures, if any, that have been put in place. For the specific case studies we present in this book, such an analysis is bound to be preliminary because changes that were introduced to respond to these crises are too recent to allow a full assessment of their effectiveness. In Part III, however, we discuss how similar events in the history of capitalism have affected consumers and suppliers of the law in the long term.

THREE

The Enron Scandal:
Legal Reform and Investor Protection
in the United States

It seems appropriate to begin our institutional autopsies with the collapse of Enron and its aftermath. Enron's breathtakingly rapid unravelling in 2001 threw a good deal of cold water on the perception that the United States had reached the zenith of legal and corporate governance. This perception had been building throughout the 1990s, propelled in part by the law and finance literature. We opt for a simple rendition of the crisis, because the precise mechanics of Enron's accounting fraud are less important for our purposes than situating the event in the contemporary U.S. market and legal structures.[1]

As we will see, the Enron saga vividly underscores several major themes of this book, not the least of which is that all market-oriented economies, however highly developed, require constant regulatory recalibration; the legal infrastructure for a capitalist economy is always under construction. We will also see how a decentralized and highly protective legal system helps give rise to and responds to a corporate crisis. The legal response to the Enron debacle and other U.S. scandals in the name of investor protection has proved to be almost as controversial as the underlying events. Thus, the reverberations from these scandals promise to affect the U.S. legal system and corporate governance structure for years to come.

The Story

On 16 October 2001, an energy and commodities trading company called Enron announced that it was taking a $544 million after-tax charge against earnings and causing a $1.2 billion reduction of shareholders' equity. Both actions were related to transactions between Enron and a partnership called LJM2, which was created and managed by Andrew Fastow, Enron's CFO.

Less than a month later, Enron announced that it was restating its financial statements for the period from 1997 through 2001 because of accounting errors relating to transactions with two other Fastow partnerships, LJM1 and Chewco. The restatement reduced Enron's reported net income for the period by about $500 million, reduced shareholders' equity by a total of about $1.5 billion, and increased reported debt by about $2.5 billion. Enron also disclosed for the first time that Fastow had received $30 million from LJM1 and LJM2. Enron filed for bankruptcy in December 2001.

At its founding in the mid-1980s, Enron was a staid natural gas drilling and pipeline company operating in regulated markets. Within a decade, it had effectively turned itself into a financial institution, shifting its focus to trading in the substantially unregulated markets for energy-related financial instruments. The concept was simple: there was more money to be made in energy brokering, trading, and risk management than in owning and operating physical assets such as pipelines and storage tanks. This was the "asset light" strategy of CEO Jeff Skilling. By the late 1990s, Enron was being regularly celebrated as the most innovative company in United States. It quickly grew to be the seventh-largest company in the country. Skilling and Ken Lay, Enron's CEO for most of its meteoric rise, were deified in the financial press.

It all came crashing down with Enron's filing for bankruptcy in the immediate wake of the earnings restatements. Almost overnight, about $68 billion in market value evaporated, while thousands of employees lost their jobs and their retirement assets. Arthur Andersen, Enron's auditing firm, would be convicted of obstruction of justice in connection with investigations of Enron's reporting practices, leading to its demise.[2] Confidence in corporate America suffered its most serious blow in decades. A February 2002 report by a special investigative committee of the Enron board (known as the Powers Report) found serious failures on the part of literally every actor involved, from the CEO to Enron's auditors and attorneys.

As with most crashes, getting to the bottom of what caused the Enron disaster is a complex task, because the wreck was caused by a chain of failures rather than a single shock or the breakdown of a single part of the enterprise. Several contributing causes are clearly discernible, even if the magnitude of the separate contributions cannot be calculated with precision. The most important factors include the following.

First, Enron engaged in accounting fraud. Enron used a variety of unlawful techniques to enhance its financial statements. For example, in some instances generally accepted accounting principles (GAAP) permit assets shown on a balance sheet to be revalued ("marked to market") where a market price for the assets can be established. Enron abused this accepted accounting methodology by "selling" assets to ostensible third parties that were actually affiliated with Enron and thereby establishing inflated market prices against which to revalue similar assets still held on its balance sheet. Moreover, Enron engaged in sham hedging transactions with counterparties under its control. These transactions were designed to conceal losses it had sustained in its trading operations by making it appear as if a creditworthy third party was obligated to pay Enron the amount of those losses. In reality, however, Enron had contributed most of the capital that the counterparty was obligated to pay pursuant to the hedging agreements. Enron was hedging with itself.

Second, Enron abused special purpose entities (SPEs) to obtain favorable accounting treatment. As Enron transformed its business into risk trading, it relied heavily on SPEs to insulate the company's financial statements from the risks and price fluctuations inherent in its trading activities. Use of SPEs for this purpose is legitimate and widespread, provided that the SPEs are established according to criteria designed to ensure that risk has in fact been transferred to an *independent* entity. A company that does business with an SPE may treat it as if it were independent (and thus avoid consolidating the SPE on its own accounting statements) if an independent party invests at least 3 percent of the equity in the SPE and the independent party controls the SPE. The point of these rules is to ensure that the risk associated with the assets has actually been transferred to the SPE. To keep these transactions off its balance sheet, Enron widely flouted these rules by transferring assets to SPEs affiliated with Andrew Fastow and other Enron officers and by cheating on the 3 percent independent equity rule. This became the favored mechanism by which Enron achieved the improper accounting treatment for the asset sales and hedges described above. As the Powers Report explained, "Many of the most significant transactions apparently were designed to accomplish favorable financial statement results, not to achieve *bona fide* economic objectives or to transfer risk. Some transactions were designed so that, had they followed applicable accounting rules, Enron could have kept assets and liabilities (especially debt) off of its balance sheet; but the transactions did not follow those rules" (Powers, Troubh, and Winokur 2002, 4).

Third, executive compensation schemes provided perverse incentives to engage in this conduct. Although perhaps an extreme example, Enron highlights the trend toward equity-based pay that accelerated dramatically in the United States in the 1990s. Compensation of Enron's top executives, like that of their corporate counterparts elsewhere, was heavily tied to performance, with "performance" defined principally as shareholder wealth creation. In 2000, total executive compensation for the two hundred highest-paid employees of Enron was $1.4 billion. Of this amount, almost $1.1 billion was attributable to stock options and bonuses (Joint Committee on Taxation 2003, 13–14). As the variable (performance-based) component of executive compensation increased, executives had ever more powerful incentives to "make their numbers" by meeting analysts' expectations for quarterly earnings. For some executives, the personal financial rewards of reporting false earnings were simply too tempting to resist. Even for many who steered clear of outright fraud, the incentive to "manage" earnings by the use of accounting gymnastics was very powerful. In many instances, SPEs, derivatives, and complex financial transactions provided the vehicles by which performance was achieved.

Fourth, Enron's board failed in its oversight function. On paper, Enron had a model board. The 2001 board had fifteen members, some of whom had more than twenty years of experience on the board of Enron or the boards of its predecessor companies. Many served on other boards as well. A Senate report found the directors to "have a wealth of sophisticated business and investment experience and considerable expertise in accounting, derivatives, and structured finance" (Permanent Subcommittee on Investigations 2002, 8). In practice, however, the directors performed dismally. The board waived in-house conflict-of-interest rules to authorize some of the most problematic of the transactions with the Fastow partnerships. Having approved the transactions, it then ignored warning signs of serious problems with their accounting treatment and failed to be vigilant in monitoring the risks they presented to Enron. Both the Powers Report and a subsequent Senate report concluded that although some information was concealed from the board, it bore a share of responsibility for Enron's collapse. At bottom, the board failed to fully understand Enron's labyrinthine transactions or to appreciate the risks they presented to the company, relying instead on the assurances of Arthur Andersen.

Fifth, outside professionals acquiesced in Enron's accounting fraud, if they did not actively assist it (see Coffee 2007a). The complex transactions at the heart of Enron's misleading financial statements required the participation of outside experts. Lawyers established the Fastow partnerships that served as accommodation parties for the welter of transactions that Enron kept off its balance sheet and issued legal opinions to investors certifying that risk had been transferred from Enron to the SPEs. Banks designed and invested in many of these entities. Enron's auditor approved the accounting treatment accorded the transactions. Yet as within Enron itself, conflicts of interest clouded the judgment of independent actors. Arthur Andersen's conflicts of interest in its role as auditor are well known. In the year the scandal hit, Arthur Andersen was generating more revenue in consulting fees from Enron than in auditing fees. David Duncan, the Andersen partner in charge of Enron audits (who stood to lose the most by alienating the client), consistently deflected concerns from within his own firm about the aggressive accounting treatment accorded the Enron transactions. Duncan eventually pled guilty to obstruction of justice for orchestrating the destruction of tons of Enron documents when the firm was under investigation. After Sherron Watkins, vice president of corporate development at Enron and a former Andersen employee, sent a memo to Ken Lay expressing her concerns about the accounting treatment of various transactions with the Fastow partnerships, the prominent Houston law firm of Vinson & Elkins was retained to investigate. But this firm was Enron's regular outside counsel, the very firm that had assisted in structuring and providing legal opinions concerning many of the suspect transactions. Vinson & Elkins concluded, after a brief investigation, that "facts disclosed through our preliminary investigation do not, in our judgment, warrant a further widespread investigation by independent counsel and auditors" (Hendrick 2001, n.p.). After Enron collapsed, the Powers Report found "an absence of . . . objective and critical professional advice by outside counsel at Vinson & Elkins, or auditors at Andersen" (Powers, Troubh, and Winokur 2002, 17).

Sixth, underlying all of these factors was a high-tech stock market bubble in the United States that caused many market participants to let down their guard and retain confidence in Enron's financial statements, despite many warning signs that they were too good to be true. As one government report put it, "Enron . . . excelled at making complexity an ally" (Joint Committee on Taxation 2003, 16). Efficient capital markets are supposed to see through complexity and accurately price the risks associated with a business. Yet for years, Enron's dazzling performance seduced market players, including large institutional investors, into accepting—without understanding—Enron's byzantine transactions or aggressive accounting practices. Faith-based investing helped undermine the integrity of stock market prices.

Enron and Late Twentieth-Century U.S. Capitalism

What light does the Enron debacle shed on contemporary U.S. capitalism and law? The precise cause of the crisis is the subject of considerable debate,[3] and our aim is not to evaluate the different hypotheses that have been advanced. In any event, most hypotheses incorporate the factors set out above and differ principally in the weight they attach to a specific factor. More important from our perspective is how this constellation of factors is linked to the institutional environment for corporate governance in the United States and how Enron's collapse and its aftermath highlight the interactions among market shifts, legal rules, and changing expectations.

To understand the broader context in which the Enron debacle occurred, it is necessary to step back several paces and view U.S. corporate governance from a distance. With the partial exception of the United Kingdom,[4] the structure of corporate ownership in the U.S. is unique. Publicly traded corporations in the United States have widely dispersed shareholding; elsewhere, ownership is typically lodged in an individual, family, or corporate group (Gilson 2006b). This is significant because although all systems of corporate governance present agency problems, the locus and severity of those problems vary depending on the structure of ownership. In a system of widely dispersed shareholding, the agency problem is most severe as it relates to the officers and directors of the firm, on one hand, who actively participate in running and monitoring the business, and the investor-shareholders, on the other, who seek a financial return but generally do not have a meaningful say in the firm's operation. The severity and contours of the agency problem have changed over time—principally with a shift in the shareholding population from individuals to institutions during the latter part of the twentieth century—but it has been the focus of U.S. corporate law and governance since the 1930s.

Attempts to mitigate the agency problem explain many developments in twentieth-century U.S. corporate law and governance. For example, the United States is an outlier in the extent to which it provides legal rights and enforcement mechanisms to shareholders. As Shleifer and Vishny (1997) argue, dispersed shareholders rely heavily on legal protection because they lack other means of ensuring a return on their investment. The most dramatic example is the passage of the federal securities laws in the 1930s. These laws drew intellectual support from the notion, first articulated by Berle and Means (1932), that the separation of ownership from control requires *legal* intervention to ensure that shareholders are not misled or abused by distant managers. Shareholder derivative litigation, class-action lawsuits for securities fraud, the notion of the "private attorney general" to police misconduct in the market, and the use of high-powered attorney incentive compensation mechanisms that facilitate and encourage their use were developed in the United States and are all directed at the agency problem. The result is a highly complex and decentralized system of corporate and securities law enforcement, with many of the most powerful tools in the hands of private investors (and their lawyers) rather than government agencies. In this system, the courts play a prominent role, deciding the suits brought by private attorneys general. In short, the distinctive pattern of dispersed share ownership contributes to another distinctive feature of the United States: the organization of its legal system.

Key market developments in recent decades can similarly be explained as responses to agency costs. The conglomerate mergers of the 1960s and 1970s grew from the agency problem: managers wasted free cash flow in empire-building acquisitions that reduced share value. The market responded to the problem with a wave of breakups and hostile takeovers in the 1980s. When the hostile takeover boom waned in the late 1980s, stock options took center stage in the 1990s in the fight against agency costs. The theory, which seemed unassailable at the time, was that directly linking significant portions of managerial compensation to stock price would align the incentives of managers and shareholders.

Apart from law, a dispersed shareholder regime such as that in the United States also relies heavily on the liquidity and valuation functions provided by a robust stock market. Liquidity provides an exit option for dissatisfied shareholders, and in an efficient market, price signals provide valuable corporate information to investors. But robust securities markets capable of performing these functions require a host of institutional supports that may be difficult for a country to develop and maintain (Black 2000). Outside professionals such as accountants, underwriters, lawyers, and stock analysts (commonly referred to in the post-Enron environment as "gatekeepers") play a major role in the healthy functioning of securities markets by lending their expertise and reputation to publicly traded firms in order to enhance the integrity of information produced for the benefit of investors.

As Coffee (2004) has argued, sensitivity to stock price as a means of alleviating the agency problem and the role of gatekeepers collided with unhappy results in the Enron debacle. Takeovers, the growing use of equity compensation, the increased activism of institutional investors, and a move toward deregulation that allowed managers to sell their firm's shares at inflated prices all worked to heighten managerial sensitivity to stock price. Simultaneously, however, the market and legal environment in which gatekeepers operated was undergoing transformation, creating potential conflicts of interest and lowering the perceived risk of liability for allowing misleading financial disclosures by their corporate clients.

Ironically, law—the bedrock of investor protection in the United States—played a large role in placing these two strands of corporate governance on a collision course. For example, decisions of the Delaware courts approving measures such as the poison pill and the "just say no" defense had a major impact in slowing the hostile takeover market in the early 1990s (Kahan and Rock 2002). Equity-based executive compensation got an unintended boost from Congress. Concerned with "excessive" executive compensation, Congress amended the tax code in 1992 to eliminate corporate deductions for cash compensation greater than $1 million unless it is tied to performance goals that are established and monitored by independent directors. In hindsight, it is not surprising that corporations responded to the change in tax law by loading up on bonuses, stock options, and other forms of variable pay. Although stock options and other forms of variable compensation were touted at the start of the decade as powerful antidotes to the agency problem of shareholders and managers, by the early twenty-first century their potential as powerful means of *expanding* that problem was painfully exposed. The vigilance of gatekeepers in the Enron crisis and similar scandals may also have been eroded by a series of legal developments in the 1990s. Congressional dissatisfaction with class-action securities fraud litigation (largely sparked by lobbying by Silicon Valley entrepreneurs and venture capitalists) resulted in the passage of the Private Securities Litigation Reform Act (PSLRA) of 1995. The PSLRA raised a number of procedural hurdles (such as more difficult pleading requirements) for plaintiffs seeking to bring class-action securities fraud suits. The law may have partly dissipated fear of liability for securities fraud.[5] In 1994, in a separate ruling, the Supreme Court held that there is no aiding-and-abetting liability in private suits brought under the federal securities laws. This ruling insulated accountants, auditors, and lawyers from secondary liability for fraudulent corporate disclosures. Together, these developments reduced the probability that important market actors involved in the securities offering process would face liability for misleading financial disclosures, arguably contributing to a decline in the deterrence environment for corporate fraud.

In broad terms, then, Enron's collapse was facilitated by a simultaneous breakdown in key mechanisms designed to alleviate the agency problem of shareholders and managers. The mechanisms failed during a perfect storm of misaligned market and legal incentives, abetted by Enron's own hyper-competitive ("rank and yank") internal corporate culture in which target chasing and earnings manipulation took over. Executive compensation arrangements and market expectations created a single-minded focus on stock price at exactly the time when the incentives of market actors to exercise vigilance in ensuring that financial results were accurately reported to investors were being degraded. In several major cases including Enron, the high-powered incentives to engineer fictitious financial results simply overwhelmed the enfeebled watchdogs. In this capitalist storm, the stock market euphoria of the late 1990s played the role of warm ocean water in a hurricane: providing the energy that transforms an atmospheric disturbance into a devastating disaster.

Other factors in the U.S. political economy at the time appear to have contributed to the degradation of the corporate governance environment and loss of confidence in the integrity of the market. Although the Securities and Exchange Commission (SEC) is an independent agency, its chairman and four other commissioners are all political appointees.[6] The SEC chairman during the Enron debacle and its immediate aftermath, Harvey Pitt, was appointed by President George W. Bush. Shortly after his appointment, Pitt famously promised an audience of accountants a "kinder and gentler SEC."[7] Previously, Pitt had spent almost twenty-five years as a private attorney representing corporate clients and the accounting profession, often in matters that came before the SEC. Pitt's predecessor as chairman, Arthur Levitt (appointed by President Bill Clinton), had advanced an aggressive reform agenda. But one of Levitt's major reform initiatives—to prohibit auditors from doing consulting business for the firms they audit—was blocked by the accounting lobby, which had hired Pitt to resist the SEC's proposed regulation. Pitt's perceived conflict of interest as head of the SEC contributed to the climate surrounding the Enron scandal. Even the conservative editors of the *Wall Street Journal* concluded that Pitt "isn't restoring trust in American capitalism."[8]

A legal system that is decentralized and highly responsive to market demand has many advantages for capitalist activity. But this episode highlights two of the major potential vulnerabilities of the U.S. system of massive decentralization and extensive private participation in the lawmaking and enforcement processes. The first is capture. As we will see, the perception (real or imagined) that the SEC had been cowed into quiescence by the financial industry in the years leading up to the corporate scandals of the early twenty-first century affected the post-Enron legal environment. The second vulnerability is that sometimes major governance problems require coordinated solutions, not individualized initiatives to protect rather narrow interests. Yet the U.S. legal system is far more conducive to the latter type of response.

The Response

Initially, the political response to Enron's implosion was muted. The Bush administration deflected regulatory impulses with a "bad apple" explanation—any system, however robust, is subject to exploitation by those bent on perpetrating fraud. According to this view of events, Enron was an aberration whose rarity actually served to confirm the soundness of the U.S. corporate governance structure. But this view was shattered by the World-Com scandal, which broke in the spring of 2002. As with Enron, massive accounting fraud perpetrated by senior executives went undetected by the board or external watchdogs. The U.S. system of corporate governance was thrown into crisis, and a governmental response could not be avoided.

Congress responded with the Sarbanes-Oxley Act (commonly known as SOX), which was passed in the summer of 2002 without dissent. It was called the most sweeping reform since the enactment of the securities laws in the 1930s. Briefly, SOX (1) places oversight of the accounting profession under a new regulator called the Public Company Accounting Oversight Board (PCAOB), (2) increases criminal and civil liability for securities fraud, (3) restricts the ability of accounting firms to engage in certain nonaudit services on behalf of their auditing clients, (4) requires CEO and CFO certification of a firm's financial statements and internal controls, (5) requires extensive disclosure of off-balance-sheet activities and "real-time" disclosure of information about the issuer's finances and operations, (6) requires firms to audit their internal controls, (7) requires that firms have an audit committee composed entirely of independent directors, at least one of whom is a "financial expert," and charges this committee with responsibility for the "appointment, compensation and oversight" of the firm's auditor, (8) prohibits corporate loans to directors and mandates disgorgement of certain CEO and CFO compensation if "misconduct" results in a restatement of the firm's financial statements, and (9) establishes reporting requirements for securities lawyers who suspect that their clients have violated the securities laws.

Return to our analytical framework to examine this law. The first point to note is that SOX plainly represents a major departure from the usual approach to investor protection in the United States. That approach is to provide investors (and their attorneys) with enforcement tools and to limit the direct involvement of the government in substantive regulation of corporate conduct. The act, by contrast, contains no mechanisms of private enforcement. Only the SEC (possibly working with the stock exchanges) and the criminal justice authorities have standing to enforce the law. Starting with the first article of the statute, which creates a new oversight agency for the accounting profession (the PCAOB), the law's approach is highly regulatory and mandatory, and it substantively intrudes into corporate structures.[9] What explains this departure from the norm? Like the last major regulatory initiative of the federal government in corporate governance—the securities laws of 1933 and 1934—SOX was born of scandal and extraordinary levels of distrust in the integrity of the stock market. In the United States, major economic crises often evoke a more centralized *regulatory* response by lawmakers. Moreover, to the extent that Congress accepted gatekeeper failure as the cause of the Enron scandal, responding to the scandal by leaving enforcement in the hands of the very same gatekeepers would have been unjustified. Thus, within our framework, SOX represents a significant shift in the legal environment for corporate governance toward the centralized, coordinative (regulatory) end of the spectrum.

Yet for all its significance, SOX is only one statute, not a fundamental realignment of the U.S. legal system for economic activity. The underlying infrastructure of private rights enforcement, interest group alignments, and political dynamics still exerts tremendous centrifugal force on lawmaking and enforcement for market activity. The law temporarily jolted those dynamics with a major regulatory shift toward the center, but as we will see, in the years following enactment of SOX, centrifugal forces reasserted themselves in a major way.

It is also instructive to ask what function SOX performs. Ostensibly, the protective function is paramount. The act is full of provisions designed to protect the property rights of shareholders by improving the accuracy of financial disclosures and limiting conflicts of interest that could affect such accuracy, both within the firm and with respect to the outside audit. Most controversially, section 404 of the law requires firms to audit their internal controls and provide management's comments on the adequacy of those controls.[10] Compliance with section 404 has cost some firms in excess of $20 million and has led some smaller publicly held firms to opt out of the SOX requirements by delisting from the stock exchanges. It has also deterred a number of foreign firms from listing their shares in the United States. An SEC advisory committee set up to study the problem recommended exempting small public companies (which make up about 80 percent of all listed firms) from these requirements, but the SEC rejected this approach.

Protection of shareholders, however, is not the only or the most important function of SOX. This becomes clear on examination of several related characteristics of the law. First, SOX is not a coherent reformulation of U.S. corporate governance laws and policies by the federal government but a motley assortment of rules governing a wide swath of corporate activity. The reforms "have a somewhat random quality" and "appear to have been taken off the shelf and put into the mix, not so much because they would have helped to prevent the recent scandals, but because they filled the perceived need for far-reaching reform and were less controversial than other measures more clearly aimed at preventing similar scandals" (Chandler and Strine 2003, 957). As a result, the law is composed of regulatory mandates that will absorb large amounts of directors' time and energy regardless of whether they improve the accuracy of financial reporting or investor protection at a given firm.[11] Surveying studies of the accounting profession and audit quality, scholars suggest that "many of the 'solutions' embodied in SOX are not only unlikely to solve the [accounting] profession's alleged problems; they may well have serious unintended negative consequences." (DeFond, Francis, and Carcello 2005, 5). Second, rhetoric aside,[12] many of the law's provisions are not really new. Rather, SOX federalized or reenacted a number of provisions that already existed, such as civil and criminal liability for fraudulent financial disclosures, and legislatively mandated certain practices that were already common among public firms, such as having independent audit committees that included financial experts (See Cunningham 2003). As one pair of commentators asked, "So what has the new legislation accomplished? The provisions of SOX deal both directly and indirectly with the deficiencies of U.S. corporate governance. But many U.S. companies would have instituted these changes anyway. The law already punished fraudulent reporting, including the misreporting in Enron" (Holmstrom and Kaplan 2003, 21).

Sarbanes-Oxley largely sidestepped the issue of executive compensation. The law prohibits insider loans and requires disgorgement of equity-based compensation in limited circumstances, but Congress did not more directly touch the political hot potato of executive compensation. If, as our exposition of the Enron case suggests, executive compensation arrangements formed the primary motivation for accounting fraud, then SOX focuses squarely on the symptoms rather than the disease.

Given the law's features and subsequent history, signaling appears to be the major function of SOX. There appear to be several distinct audiences for the signals sent by the legislation. Most directly, it signals to top executives that the government has taken a more aggressive stance toward enforcement of financial fraud laws. The act signals to corporate boards that they need to monitor their firms' operations and, in particular, financial reporting. It signals to prosecutors that investigation of white-collar crime is better supported politically. It signals to external gatekeepers such as accountants and lawyers that they play a crucial role in the integrity of the corporate governance system. Most generally but perhaps most important, it signals to the investing public that the stock market is again worthy of its confidence. Even commentators who are very restrained in their evaluation of the substantive merits of SOX exhibit optimism about the signaling function of the law. For example, Holmstrom and Kaplan (2003, 22) concede that "SOX has probably helped to restore confidence in the U.S. corporate governance system."

Events subsequent to the passage of SOX underscore the limited nature of the protections actually provided by the legislation and also call into question the power of the signals it sent. The most glaring example is the fall 2005 collapse of Refco, a huge commodities and futures trading company, just six weeks after its initial public offering (IPO) on the New York Stock Exchange. Like Enron, Refco used transactions with entities controlled by an insider (in Refco's case, CEO Robert Bennett) to keep an undesirable entry (a $450 million debt) off its balance sheet. As in the Enron case, actors within and outside the firm missed or ignored warning signs that the financial statements did not add up. As with Enron, all actors pointed to someone else as bearing responsibility for the failure of the financial reporting system: the outside attorneys who structured the transactions absolved themselves of responsibility for accounting issues, the auditor deflected blame on the ground that it is difficult to detect intentional falsification of accounts, and the board claimed that critical information was withheld from it, disabling its monitoring abilities. In fairness, the CEO and CFO certifications of SOX did not yet apply to Refco. By the terms of the legislation, they do not apply to IPO registration statements, and because Refco had become a public company only a few weeks prior to its collapse, it had not yet issued a regular report to which the certifications apply. But had they applied, it is hard to imagine that Refco's CEO, at the center of the fraud, would have hesitated to certify the accuracy of the financial statements.

Aftereffects

In many ways, the most interesting aspect of this saga is what came next—a period, still ongoing, of intense activity by a diverse set of players to reach re-equilibrium in the regulation of corporate governance in the United States after the jolt provided by SOX. In this section, we draw upon our analytical framework to analyze the post-Enron corporate governance environment in the United States.

We suggested above that SOX represented both a centralization of corporate governance regulation and a powerful signal of the seriousness with which the federal government approached corporate governance. Developments in the years following passage of SOX suggest that the law has energized the federal investigation and prosecution of corporate and securities fraud. Although there have been criminal investigations of corporate crime for decades, the complexity and resource-intensiveness of these cases generally did not make them a high priority for prosecutors, particularly outside of a few large cities such as New York. The law changed this, although it changed very little in a strictly *legal* sense.[13] The federal securities laws have provided for criminal liability for "willful" violations since their enactment in the 1930s. Mail and wire fraud statutes have also long been available to those prosecuting white-collar crimes, along with a host of other statutes.[14] Rather, SOX signaled a new *political and career* climate for investigation and enforcement. At nearly the same time the law was enacted, President Bush formed the Corporate Fraud Task Force, composed of high-level law enforcement officials and financial regulators, "to provide direction for the investigation and prosecution" (U.S. Department of Justice 2004, 12) of significant financial crimes committed by corporations, their directors, officers, and professional advisers. The task force's annual reports indicate that it views its mandate in fairly blunt terms: investigating and prosecuting as many cases as possible. The *Second Year Report* highlights the fact that the task force has obtained more than five hundred corporate fraud convictions or guilty pleas and charged more than nine hundred defendants and more than sixty CEOs with a corporate crime (ibid., iii). Corporate fraud is now the FBI's top priority within the financial crimes area. This increased emphasis is an explicit response to the Enron bankruptcy (U.S. Department of Justice 2005, 52).[15] Resources for these complex investigations are now available, and prosecution of corporate crimes is highly beneficial from a career perspective. The climate has changed so significantly that there is now competition among federal prosecutors, state attorneys general, and other regulatory actors for cases to prosecute.

In part, the justification for this shift was premised on the argument, alluded to above, that owing to resource and staffing limitations as well as the vagaries of politics, the SEC is incapable of serving as the sole governmental watchdog over the securities markets. This was the key argument advanced by Elliot Spitzer, the attorney general of New York, for his aggressive investigation and prosecution of corporate crimes following the Enron scandal.[16] As the legal basis for this unprecedented foray by a state official into a field dominated by federal law enforcers, Spitzer relied on an obscure New York statute from 1921 that had been largely dormant for decades.[17] Wielding this statute in a manner his critics described as a "blank check" or "weapon of mass destruction,"[18] Spitzer brought proceedings against many high-profile targets, including Merrill Lynch, executives of WorldCom, Citicorp's Jack Grubman, and major New York brokerage firms. Regardless of one's views about Spitzer's post-Enron activities, they provide a vivid illustration of how the U.S. legal system begets ever greater complexity and decentralization of the law enforcement process in the name of investor protection.

Despite the new enforcement climate, however, after Arthur Andersen's conviction only one *firm* has been indicted for corporate, accounting, or securities fraud. Perhaps it is telling that the indicted firm is a law firm, Milberg Weiss, the bête noire of corporate America known for its representation of plaintiffs in class-action securities fraud litigation. Federal prosecutors instead have entered into "deferred prosecution agreements" with numerous corporations including AIG, Computer Associates, and Merrill Lynch. These agreements grew from a 2003 Department of Justice policy concerning principles of federal prosecution of business organizations (widely known as the "Thompson memo" after its author, Deputy Attorney General Larry Thompson). This policy permitted prosecutors to forgo prosecution of a corporation if it acknowledged responsibility, agreed to cooperate with the government in the prosecution of the individuals responsible, and instituted controls to prevent reoccurrence of the problem. This policy vested prosecutors with enormous discretion in working out the terms of the agreement without supervision by courts or an opportunity for appeal to higher Justice Department authorities. Terms of the agreements varied widely and sometimes required the suspect corporations to engage in a range of activities unrelated to the nature of their alleged offenses, such as making mandatory charitable contributions or maintaining required levels of in-state employment.

The rise of deferred prosecution agreements can be viewed both as part of the new post-Enron law enforcement climate and as a partial reaction against it. On one hand, these agreements provide a way to obtain more and faster convictions and guilty pleas from individual defendants. In many cases, the target corporations have waived the attorney-client privilege to provide information to prosecutors that can be used against the firm's officers and employees. But deferred prosecution agreements also represent a partial retreat from law enforcement efforts that result in the death of major corporations. Fallout from the Arthur Andersen conviction, which brought down a household name and a force in the U.S. economy that employed thousands, is clearly relevant to the Justice Department's change in policy. Acknowledging the "collateral consequences" of criminal prosecution of corporations, prosecutors have pulled back from utilizing every enforcement weapon at their disposal. As one U.S. attorney put it, "When that company [under criminal investigation] comes to the government and says, 'Don't destroy a great American company,' that's a very appealing argument" (Blum 2005, n.p.). Instead, law enforcers cleverly adapted their arsenal to increase convictions of individuals in corporate fraud cases. Not surprisingly, they found a way to increase their own discretion and power in the process.

The Thompson memo's history is itself a telling illustration of the centrifugal law-making and law enforcement forces at work in the U.S. legal system. The Department of Justice, following SOX's regulatory signals, took an aggressive stance against corporate crime with the Thompson memo. The memo identified a corporation's (1) willingness to waive the attorney-client privilege and (2) "promise of support of culpable employees and agents . . . through the advancing of attorneys' fees" as factors that may be considered by federal prosecutors in assessing the adequacy of a corporation's cooperation, which in turn is a factor that must be considered in deciding whether to indict the corporation. Hence corporations in the post-Enron environment began to waive the attorney-client privilege and to limit the circumstances under which they would advance attorneys' fees for employees facing criminal investigation. These practices grew increasingly controversial, prompting the introduction of a Senate bill to overturn the Thompson memo[19] and spawning litigation by private parties whose interests were jeopardized by the policy. In 2006 a U.S. district court judge held that the government had violated the constitutional rights of employees whose payment of legal fees had been cut off by the accounting firm KPMG in an accounting fraud investigation.[20] The judge found that "KPMG refused to pay because the government held the proverbial gun to its head." In response, the Justice Department retreated. In late 2006 the Thompson memo was replaced by a new set of principles for federal prosecution of business organizations (dubbed the "McNulty memo," after its author, Deputy Attorney General Paul McNulty.) The McNulty memo provides that "[p]rosecutors generally should not take into account whether a corporation is advancing attorneys' fees to employees or agents under investigation and indictment"; nor may prosecutors negatively weigh a company's refusal to waive the attorney-client privilege in making a charging decision.[21]

Judges (in particular, members of the Delaware judiciary) also responded to the signals sent by the passage of SOX. For years, a persuasive line of scholarship has argued that Delaware is the winner in the lucrative state-level competition for corporate charters in the United States because its judiciary is sophisticated and the flexible, enabling structure of its corporate law allows for adaptation to changing business circumstances.[22] But the passage of SOX was a significant *federal* incursion into corporate governance, signaling a potential consolidation of corporate lawmaking at the center and a corresponding erosion of Delaware's dominant position in the production of corporate law in the United States (see Roe 2005). Public statements by current and former Delaware judges indicate that they take this risk very seriously (see Chandler and Strine 2003; Veasey and Guglielmo 2005). Some scholars have suggested that the Delaware judiciary bears some of the blame for the current problems with executive compensation, because its case law presents significant procedural and substantive obstacles to shareholders seeking to challenge executive pay awards (Gordon 2002b). Accurate or not, the *perception* that SOX was passed in response to shortcomings in state corporate law makes the risk to Delaware courts of federal action highly salient.

A shareholders' suit in the Delaware courts concerning Michael Ovitz's termination as president of the Walt Disney Corporation illustrates the way SOX has altered the landscape of corporate law production in the United States.[23] The shareholders of Disney, a Delaware corporation, sued Michael Eisner and the board of directors for approving a $140 million severance payment to Ovitz per his employment contract, after only one highly troubled year as president. The litigation bounced back and forth between Delaware's Chancery Court and Supreme Court because of a procedural issue for almost ten years before a trial was held on the substantive issue: Did Eisner and the board members breach their fiduciary duties to shareholders by failing to properly inform themselves before approving Ovitz's contract and then terminating him in the most expensive way the contract allowed?[24] The plaintiffs presented evidence that the compensation committee of the board was deferential to Eisner and was poorly informed and passive with respect to the negotiation of Ovitz's contract and the subsequent decision to terminate him in the most expensive way possible.

Although the Chancery Court (the trial court) found that Eisner surrounded himself with a "supine board" (40, n. 487) and "enthroned himself as the omnipotent and infallible monarch of his personal Magic Kingdom" (41), the court ruled that it would be improper to hold Eisner and the board to post-Enron, post-SOX standards because the conduct at issue took place in a different corporate governance climate. Thus, the court found no liability on the part Eisner or the board.[25] Chancellor William Chandler wrote:

> [T]here are many aspects of defendants' conduct that fell significantly short of the best practices of ideal corporate governance. Recognizing the protean nature of ideal corporate governance practices, particularly over an era that has included the Enron and WorldCom debacles, and the resulting legislative focus on corporate governance, it is perhaps worth pointing out that the actions (and the failures to act) of the Disney board that gave rise to this lawsuit took place ten years ago, and that applying 21st century notions of best practices in analyzing whether those decisions were actionable would be misplaced (1).

The case illustrates the dilemma into which the post-Enron legal environment threw the court. It knew that Delaware corporate law must be responsive to the signals sent by SOX. Failure to do so may risk further federal incursions into Delaware's dominant position in the market for corporate law production. Yet finding for the plaintiffs in this case not only would have penalized the directors for failure to comply with a higher standard of conduct than was common at the time of their actions but it also may have created a liability crisis in corporate boardrooms around the country, encouraging firms to reincorporate in other states. The court responded to this dilemma with a substitute for law: a shaming sanction. Rather than finding the directors liable to investors, it excoriated the Disney board in a highly formal manner and at least suggested that, going forward, the legal standards would be raised to match the expectations of the current corporate governance climate. In so doing, the court sent its own signal to investors, corporate directors, and perhaps the U.S. Congress.

The Disney case also highlights one of the asserted benefits of a common-law system of corporate law: flexibility in adapting to changed market circumstances. In contrast to legislation, which provides a relatively brittle, one-shot response to the problem it addresses, courts can respond incrementally over time by refining the standards of conduct and liability applied to corporate actors. As we have noted, the Disney case may signal heightened scrutiny of board independence and oversight with regard to executive pay awards. Quite possibly, this result, however modest, is superior to any direct regulation of executive pay that Congress could devise.

Clearly, one can imagine situations in which sweeping change is desirable, but as the Disney case suggests, a case-law system may make such far-reaching change difficult.

As the above discussion indicates, the post-Enron era in corporate governance in the United States has been a time of considerable flux. As the fifth anniversary of SOX approached, debates about the direction of U.S. regulatory policy and its impact on the competitiveness of U.S. capital markets reached a higher pitch. The law's regulatory approach to issues of corporate governance had provoked a backlash in the corporate community. A high-level group of business and finance leaders calling itself the Committee on Capital Markets Regulation issued a report in late 2006 calling for major reforms to the corporate regulatory environment.[26] The report presented evidence indicating a loss of competitiveness of U.S. capital markets compared to foreign stock markets and financial centers. John Thornton, president of the New York Stock Exchange and the committee's co-chair, voiced the fear that "[t]here are clear signs that global confidence in our capital markets has been diminished."[27]

Two aspects of the committee's report are particularly interesting from our perspective. First, the committee stressed "investor protection and shareholder rights as bedrock principles of U.S. capital markets" in calling for enhanced shareholder rights and more efficient regulation.[28] Note the rhetoric of rights protection in which all major regulatory moves in the United States are couched, even when they seek to *roll back* the impact of legislation heavily steeped in the rhetoric of investor protection. Implicitly, at least, the committee appears to suggest that the reality of SOX's investor protections did not match the rhetoric. Second, and more telling, the committee emphasized the need for better coordination of activity by the plethora of enforcement agencies operating at the federal and state levels in the area of corporate governance, and it expressed concern about overenforcement, especially private litigation. In this respect the report echoes a major theme we have attempted to develop in our rendition of the Enron saga: the tradeoff between the traditionally decentralized rights enforcement model of law prevailing in U.S. markets and the ability to provide coordinated solutions to severe governance problems.

We cannot predict whether future reforms will be enacted or precisely how the pendulum will continue to swing in the debates about U.S. regulatory policy. But in the aftermath of the corporate crises of the early twenty-first century, we can clearly see how actors in the U.S. legal system are still struggling to find the equilibrium point between centralization and decentralization of the legal system for corporate governance in the post-Enron world.

Conclusion

Several interrelated points about the Enron scandal and its aftermath bear emphasis. First, the episode vividly illustrates the iterative nature of the relation between law and capitalism in the United States and the need to go beyond an analysis of one law in isolation to reach a complete understanding of the way law supports markets. The scandal motivated production of law by legislators, acting quickly on limited information and within a politically charged environment. Other actors in the law production process interpreted and enforced the law in ways that maximized and protected their own interests, at least to the point at which law production and enforcement threatened other important interests of the system, such as the continued viability of major business enterprises and the attractiveness of the U.S. capital markets to smaller public companies and foreign issuers. These new law enforcement efforts—such as Spitzer's actions and the use of aggressive tactics in the negotiation of deferred prosecution agreements—generated their own legal controversies and subtle realignments in the balance of power between private and public actors and within the law production process. The United States has now entered a period of reevaluation and recalibration of the post-SOX legal environment for corporate governance. The act was only the starting point for the construction of new institutions of corporate governance. The end point is not yet in sight.

The second point, closely related to the first, is that the United States stands at one extreme in the use of law for protection of investor and property rights. (See chapter 9 for further discussion.) The legal response to the Enron crisis provides insight into how and why this is so. Although Congress responded with an uncharacteristically regulatory approach to corporate governance following the Enron scandal, SOX immediately triggered a host of adaptive and strategic reactions among other lawmakers, law enforcers, and private actors. Federal prosecutors, the SEC, the Delaware courts, and state attorneys general, among others, all responded to the signals sent by the law, as least as they perceived them. In the process, the legal environment for corporate governance in the United States became even more complex and decentralized. Calls are now being made to once again reverse the trend—to coordinate, to simplify.

Third, the Enron episode suggests that legal protection for investors in the United States—the subject of vast empirical and theoretical work in the past decade—is a far more complex edifice than the literature suggests. Although the literature focuses on shareholder rights provided by corporate law as the foundation for dispersed share ownership and robust capital markets, this is only one element, and perhaps not the most important one, in an extraordinarily elaborate set of constantly evolving institutions that foster investor confidence in the United States. And at least if our evaluation of SOX is accurate, some of the most important work of law in this institutional setup is performed by signaling rather than the substantive protections provided by the law itself.

Finally, because elements of SOX have now been adopted in many countries around the world, it is important to see that the act was a legal response to the distinctive features and vulnerabilities of late twentieth-century *U.S.* capitalism. Indeed, the entire legal approach to investor protection in the United States may be a response to the defining quality of U.S. corporate structure—dispersed share ownership—rather than the cause of it, as the economics literature suggests. Decentralized lawmaking and enforcement parallel and arguably complement a decentralized system of incorporation, share ownership, and capital-raising in the United States. If the Enron disaster was an outgrowth of the vulnerabilities of this distinctive economic structure, and if SOX was an unusual regulatory countermove against decentralized investor protection in the United States, then transplanting SOX in foreign soil is a highly questionable exercise.

FOUR

The Mannesmann Executive Compensation Trial in Germany

Germany has the third-largest economy in the world,[1] yet the features of German capitalism stand in stark contrast to the American system. As we will see, the role that law plays in the economy differs also, as vividly illustrated by the recent criminal trial of corporate executives for deciding to award a key manager a large bonus in connection with the successful completion of a merger. In this story we can observe how a social system and a legal regime organized along very different lines deemed scandalous conduct that in the United States is considered business as usual.

The Story

In February 2000 a merger agreement joining Mannesmann, a German firm, and Vodafone, a British telecommunications company, was signed. Mannesmann had traditionally focused on the coal and steel sectors but had diversified into telecommunications in the 1990s. The friendly merger capped a heated and widely publicized hostile takeover battle that began with Vodafone's unsolicited bid for Mannesmann, which fought to defend its independence. After failing to mobilize the French company Vivendi as a white knight and facing increasing shareholder support for the Vodafone offer, Mannesmann's management conceded defeat. The companies agreed that Vodafone would acquire Mannesmann for the equivalent of €360 per share paid as a combination of shares in Vodafone and cash; the telecom operations of Mannesmann would be placed directly under Vodafone management, and other parts of the company would be spun off. The price Vodafone agreed to pay in February 2000 was €63 billion (€125 per share) more than its initial hostile offer in the fall of 1999.

As merger negotiations were being finalized, the Presidium, an executive committee of Mannesmann's supervisory board, resolved to pay Klaus Esser, the chairman of the company's management board, a £10 million (or roughly €15 million) "appreciation award" for his efforts to enhance shareholder value.[2] According to the minutes of the Presidium meeting, Mannesmann's largest shareholder, Hutchison Whampoa, had initiated this move. At first, Canning Fok, group managing director of Hutchison Whampoa, had offered to pay this award from his firm's own coffers.[3] Esser, however, rejected that offer. He insisted that he would only accept an appreciation award paid by Mannesmann, the company he had served. He also requested that his entire management team share in the award. Fok contacted the CEO of Vodafone, who reportedly supported the payment of appreciation awards for Esser and other members of his team.

The Presidium's resolution stated: "Dr. Esser shall, at the request of the major shareholder, Hutchison Whampoa, and following an agreement reached between Hutchison and Vodafone, be paid an appreciation award of GB£10 million. The Presidium consents. The appreciation award shall be paid when Vodafone acquires a majority of the shares."[4] Another £10 million was made available for appreciation awards to the other managers.

The Presidium was made up of four members: Joachim Alexander Funk, the previous chairman of Mannesmann's management board; Josef Ackermann, the top manager of Deutsche Bank, a major holder of Mannesmann shares; Klaus Zwickel, the chairman of the German national labor union for the steel sector, IG Metall; and Jürgen Ladberg, the representative of Mannesmann's employees. The decision, made by simple majority vote, was supported by Ackermann and Funk. Ladberg had excused himself on account of illness, and Zwickel, who participated via conference call, abstained. A subsequent company memorandum stated that Zwickel and Ladberg "took note of the decision"[5] but were unable to support it because they found it difficult to explain to their employee constituencies.

The decision caused a major public outcry when it was reported in the press. The general perception was that top managers of Mannesmann had taken advantage of the sale of a German flagship company and enriched themselves before departing the scene. To make matters worse, Mannesmann had lost its independence to a foreign firm and was now obligated to spin off some of its core operations.[6]

Legal action was initiated by the state prosecutor's office in Düsseldorf, where the company is headquartered, but only after a small law firm (Binz and Sorg) in southern Germany challenged the decision not to launch a criminal investigation.[7] The alleged crime was breach of trust on the part of the Presidium members who approved of the decision (Ackermann and Funk) or acquiesced in it (Zwickel and Ladberg) as well as the beneficiaries of the payments.[8] After lengthy pretrial investigations, court hearings began in early 2004. In July the trial court acquitted all of the accused.[9] The prosecutor's office appealed the decision,[10] and Germany's highest criminal court, the Bundesgerichtshof (BGH), reversed, arguing that the lower court had misinterpreted the requirements of criminal breach of trust.[11] In November 2006, the court of first instance in charge of retrying the case finally terminated the trial with the approval of the prosecutor's office and the accused on the ground that there was no longer a "public interest" in criminal prosecution.

At this point, some readers no doubt are wondering what made the Mannesmann episode a corporate scandal or crisis. Is it the fact that the top management pocketed the appreciation award? That the payment was approved without much debate by the Presidium with only half its members present in person? Or that top managers who had increased shareholder value to the tune of €63 billion found themselves in a criminal court?

For the German popular press and the public at large, as well as for the prosecutor's office, the scandal clearly lay in the behavior of Mannesmann's corporate insiders. In pictures appearing on Web pages and in journals, men in dark suits were depicted stuffing cash into their pockets.[12] Headlines such as "*Aberwitzige Vereinbarung*" (A Crazy Deal)[13] and "*Wie auf einem Basar*" (Just Like in a Bazaar)[14] were common in the general press. The proceedings against Esser, his colleagues, and the members of the Presidium who approved the payments were depicted as the most important legal actions taken against prominent figures in Germany since the party finance affairs of the 1980s.[15] Law professors were invited to provide their legal opinions to the press. Some suggested that the payment of the awards was legal and that the prosecutor's complaint contained only broad allegations without substantiation.[16] Others argued that the appreciation awards violated corporate law and corporate governance principles. According to them, the takeover battle may have increased shareholder value, but it did not improve the corporation's finances. Thus, Fok had the right intuition when he offered to have Vodafone pay Esser's bonus. Using Mannesmann's funds was deemed inappropriate.[17]

The German and international business press took quite a different position. A *Fortune* headline declared, "In Germany High Pay Is a Crime."[18] From this perspective, the true scandal was Germany's resistance to internationally accepted corporate practices, including the standard U.S. practice of giving a "golden parachute" or "golden handshake" to a departing executive. Commentators argued that the criminal indictment and the length and outcome of the adjudication created uncertainties that endangered Germany's standing as a center of international business and finance. This view was supported by Angela Merkel, the leader of the Christian Democratic Party, who became chancellor in the fall of 2005.[19] In the words of Josef Ackermann, one of the accused, "Germany is the only country where those who are successful and create value are tried in criminal court."[20] The extent to which the episode divided public opinion is best reflected in the opening statements of trial judge Brigitte Koppenhöfer on the day she pronounced the verdict. Never before in her twenty-five years on the bench, she said, had she experienced as much pressure, which ranged from "telephone terror to open threats." She claimed to be particularly dismayed by the desire of prosecutors and the defense team to "instrumentalize the press" in order to influence the outcome.[21]

Germany's corporate law (*Aktiengesetz*, or AktG) provides that the compensation of the members of the management board, the top managers of the corporation, shall be determined by the supervisory board. The law also provides that compensation shall be "reasonably related" to the tasks the management board members perform and the circumstances of the corporation (section 87, AktG). This provision is noteworthy because unlike U.S. corporate law, which is largely silent on the question of executive compensation and leaves it to the business judgment of the board of directors, German statutory law sets the outer limits of compensation packages. Obviously, the term "reasonable" and the proportionality requirement are ambiguous terms requiring interpretation. Prior to the Mannesmann case, not a single case had applied section 87, so there was no preexisting legal gloss on these terms. As explained below, German lawmakers have been reluctant to give shareholders the right to sue management. Moreover, the Mannesmann case notwithstanding, criminal courts have not been very active in enforcing corporate law. The provisions of the law are enforced by social norms, not legal mechanisms.

When the trial court acquitted the defendants, it held that they had breached corporate law (in particular, section 87) but that this breach was not sufficiently severe to justify criminal punishment.[22] It reasoned that the appreciation award was not reasonably related to managerial tasks because when it was granted all such tasks had already been performed. In particular, the court concluded that the German word *Aufgabe* ("task" in English) required that compensation be promised for future, not past, efforts. But Esser and his team had already agreed to leave the company within a few months. The appreciation award could therefore hardly be justified on the ground that it would create the right incentives for management performance. Nor was the compensation appropriate in light of the overall situation of the company, which had just been sold and was in the process of spinning off valuable assets. Despite the violation of section 87, however, the court found no criminal liability. The appropriate corporate decision makers had acted, and they had followed proper formal procedures in making and reporting their decision.

On appeal, the state prosecutor was joined by the federal prosecutor's office. The latter's task is to screen any appeals lodged with the BGH and pronounce its support for or reservations against the appeal. According to the prosecutor, €30 million had been paid out by the company without any corresponding benefit accruing to it. This constituted a breach of trust under the law without any further consideration of the severity of the breach required. The main argument put forward by the prosecution was that finding breach of trust under Germany's criminal code requires a *severe* breach in cases where the trustees are allowed to exercise judgment in making their decision but not in cases where the decision was not within their discretion and therefore constituted a per se breach.[23] The Presidium's decision to pay an appreciation award was deemed a per se breach of trust. The trial court's conclusion that this decision did not reach the threshold of a criminal breach of trust was therefore misplaced.

In its verdict, the BGH followed the argument of the prosecutor's office and reversed the trial court's decision.[24] The high court concluded that "a bonus payment not called for in the employment contract, as compensation for an effort already owed by the employee under the contract, which is paid as a mere reward to the officer and without any prospect of future benefits to the company (payment of acknowledgment without compensation), must be considered squandering the company's property in breach of fiduciary duties. It is per se illegal, requiring no assessment as to whether the amount might be justified under Section 87 AktG."[25]

The BGH gave little weight to the fact that Vodafone's chief executive, Christopher Gent, was consulted before the Presidium approved the payment and supported the plan. Although the appreciation award had not been approved at a shareholder meeting, under German law a trustor (in this case the shareholders) can agree to an action that damages its property interests, thereby eliminating criminal liability. But the BGH found that Vodafone held only 9.8 percent of Mannesmann's shares on the day the decision was taken in February 2000, and the court concluded that it was "merely" a majority owner with 98.6 percent of the shares in March 2001, when the payments were actually made. The remaining shareholders were bought out in 2002. German criminal law, according to the BGH, does not recognize a retroactive approval of an act or decision that damages the interests of a beneficiary.[26]

The reversal sent the case back to Düsseldorf for retrial. Shortly after the start of the retrial the defense lawyers for Josef Ackermann asked the court to terminate the proceedings. Under German law, a criminal case can be halted prior to a final court ruling if, in the opinion of the court, there is no longer a public interest in pursuing the trial and both the prosecutor and the accused agree to end the trial (section 153a StPO, Germany's Code of Criminal Procedure). Such a decision may be accompanied by obligations such as performing social services or contributing money to public-interest organizations. In terminating the criminal trial on 29 November 2006, Stefan Drees, the new judge presiding over the retrial of Esser, Ackermann et al., explained the lack of public interest in continuing the trial by pointing out that the allegedly wrongful acts had taken place more than six years earlier, none of the accused had been previously charged under criminal law, they had already endured years of legal proceedings, and the underlying factual and legal issues remained complex. He also stressed that the critical legal issues had been resolved by the BGH in the decision that reversed the acquittal. The court conditioned the termination of the trial on the accuseds' paying a total of €5.8 million to various public-interest organizations.[27] Josef Ackermann, who had been central to approving the appreciation awards in February 2000—but had not received any material benefits personally—was charged €3.2 million; Klaus Esser, who had received €15 million, was required to pay one-tenth of what he had received, or €1.5 million; Joachim A. Funk was obliged to pay €1.0 million. The two labor representatives who had neither supported nor opposed the decision received "tickets" of €60,000 and €12,000, respectively. All defendants denied that the decision to request an early termination of the trial amounted to an admission of guilt.[28]

German Capitalism

The Mannesmann episode differs from an ordinary corporate crisis. There was no major clash among stakeholders with conflicting interests or different views of how the firm should be run. Vodafone, the new parent, had no objection to the payment. Those on the side of "capital" (that is, shareholders and creditors),[29] represented by Ackermann, approved the payment. Labor, represented by Zwickel and Ladberg, passively acquiesced. No shareholder filed suit.

Rather, Mannesmann was a battle over the future of the German model of capitalism, pitting new corporate practices against the normative foundations of the old order. For observers unfamiliar with this model, the fact that a labor union representative (Zwickel) and an employee representative (Ladberg) sat on the Mannesmann Presidium might seem surprising. Yet this has been common practice since the introduction of codetermination in 1976.[30] Under the codetermination law, all corporations with two thousand employees or more must reserve 50 percent of the seats on their supervisory board for employee representatives. The seats are filled by employee elections in a scheme that gives some representation to white-collar employees and the majority to blue-collar workers. In addition, one seat is reserved for a representative of the relevant national labor union. Codetermination at Mannesmann dates back even further because the company's core business prior to its expansion into telecom was steel. As such, the company was subject to a special codetermination regime for the steel industry enacted in 1951.[31]

German capitalism has been described as a corporatist system wherein key stakeholders—shareholders, workers, and the state—bargain for outcomes that maintain a balance between the profit motive of shareholders, labor interests, and broader social concerns. This cooperation was institutionalized by a set of legal rules that emerged over the course of the past century to give employees access to information as well as decision-making rights in the governing bodies of the corporation. The origin of firm-level participation dates back to the last decade of the nineteenth century (Hopt 1994; Pistor 1999). In July 1891, an amendment to the law governing entrepreneurial activities (*Gewerbeordnung*) provided that workers' councils could be established within companies on a voluntary basis. During World War I, labor unions and the Social Democratic Party took advantage of a law governing support services for the fatherland (*Gesetz über den vaterländischen Hilfsdienst*), which was primarily designed to force the males who were not actively involved in warfare to participate in military production, to include provisions mandating the creation of workers' councils and workers' arbitration bodies.

After World War I, Germany's new constitution gave workers' councils recognition at the firm level. It also declared workers' councils to be political organizations representing the interests of labor and called for the councils to play a political role in state administration at the regional as well as the federal level. Subsequent legislation, however, realized the potential of this provision only at the firm level. These laws were annulled during the fascist period as the overriding *Führerprinzip*—the principle of an undisputed central leader—ruled out participatory models.

The development of codetermination after World War II was strongly influenced by the experience of fascism. The alliance between powerful private capital—in particular, the coal and steel industries, concentrated in the Ruhr valley—and the political regime was seen as one of the major pillars of the fascist regime. The prevailing view at the time was that political democracy must be combined with social constraints on the use of private capital, a concept that has been termed *Wirtschaftsdemokratie* (economic democracy). The 1949 constitution explicitly provided for the possibility of nationalizing industries. Moreover, it established a constitutional link between the protection of private property and the social context in which private property rights are realized. Article 14 of the 1949 constitution guarantees the right to private property and inheritance but stipulates that "the contents and scope of property rights shall be determined by law." In addition, section 2 of the same article explicitly states that property is not only a right but also an obligation and that the exercise of private property rights shall benefit society as a whole.[32]

The institutional basis for workers' participation in the postwar era was created with the enactment of legislation concerning corporate codetermination in the coal and steel industries (Montan-Codetermination Law of 1951)[33] and concerning the internal organization, or "constitution," of the firm (*Betriebsverfassungsgesetz* of 1952), which revived firm-level employee participation of the sort that had existed in the Weimar Republic. The 1951 Montan-Codetermination Law established equal presentation of employees on supervisory boards in the coal and steel industry, and the 1952 law gave employees in other industries (if the companies had more than five hundred workers) the right to delegate employees to the supervisory board, where one-third of the seats were reserved for them. Finally, in 1976 the Codetermination Law was adopted, which extended equal employee representation on the supervisory board to all of the largest companies in Germany irrespective of the industry sector.[34]

The evolution of mandatory codetermination exemplifies the importance of situations of deep political or economic crisis in shaping the path of legal development. As noted in our analytical framework, reform legislation is often enacted in response to events that galvanize political actors. World War I and II were such events in Germany. The most far-reaching reforms, however, were introduced only after the Social Democrats together with the liberals gained power in 1972. There was no crisis that triggered the enactment. Instead, the earlier developments were now brought to what, in the eyes of the Social Democrats and the labor unions, were their logical conclusion. The Codetermination Law has remained in place ever since, notwithstanding the fact that from 1982 to 1998 the more conservative and traditionally more pro-business Christian Democrats were in power and have been again since 2005 (albeit in coalition with the Social Democrats). This suggests that codetermination and the social consensus about the nature of German capitalism have been "institutionalized" (Huntington 1965), making future change difficult.[35]

Another core feature of Germany's capitalist system is highly concentrated ownership, even of the largest corporations, in stark contrast to the U.S. model (Roe 1993). According to data compiled by La Porta et al. (1998) the three largest shareholders of the top ten listed corporations in Germany hold, on average, 48 percent of the outstanding shares.[36] Becht et al. (1999) present similar results regarding the concentration of voting power.[37] In Germany, banks often hold voting powers far in excess of the actual amount of stock they own in a given company, because they are the major custodians for shares held by small investors (Baums 1997). Even when excluding banks as custodians, Becht et al. find that the median largest voting block in Germany is 50.2 percent, but it is only 11 percent for the largest firms listed on the DAX 30.[38]

Mannesmann had historically displayed many of these features of German capitalism, but the structure and composition of the firm's ownership had changed considerably prior to the takeover. At the time of the Vodafone bid, however, neither Deutsche Bank nor any of its subsidiaries held a substantial stake in Mannesmann. Publicly available data suggest that Deutsche Asset Management, an investment fund controlled by Deutsche Bank, held 1.8 percent of outstanding shares in Mannesmann. The largest shareholder of Mannesmann in late 1999 was Hutchison Whampoa with a stake of 10.2 percent. In one departure from the standard model, besides Hutchison Whampoa's stake, at the time of the Vodafone bid Mannesmann's shares were widely held.[39] In comparison with international standards, however, Mannesmann's ownership remained fairly concentrated, with the ten largest shareholders holding 25.7 percent of outstanding shares. Only three of the top ten shareholders were German entities; all others were based in the United States, the United Kingdom, or Hong Kong.[40] Nonetheless, the key stakeholders of the German governance model—capital and labor—were represented on its supervisory board and the Presidium. Josef Ackermann of Deutsche Bank (which is one of Mannesmann's original shareholders, owning shares since 1890)[41] had a prominent place as chairman of the supervisory board as well as the Presidium, charged with determining executive compensation. The continuing influence of Deutsche Bank over Mannesmann most likely stems from the bank's representing small investors.

Vodafone's Bid: An Attack on the German Model

The German model of capitalism has been challenged by the forces of globalization. The Vodafone bid marked the first time that a foreign company launched a hostile takeover bid against a flagship German firm. Although foreign acquisitions of German companies were not unknown, they had been conducted as friendly deals. Among German companies, hostile takeovers were essentially nonexistent; the first case came in 1997 when the steel giant Krupp launched a hostile takeover bid against its rival Thyssen. After worker protests and a public outcry over a conflict of interest at Deutsche Bank, which advised Krupp on the takeover even though the bank was also sitting on Thyssen's supervisory board, Chancellor Schroeder intervened. He reminded the parties that a hostile transaction was contrary to Germany's implicit norms of behavior and successfully encouraged the firms to form a joint venture (Höpner 2001). Although they still cannot be considered a common feature of Germany's corporate governance model, occurrences of hostile transactions began to rise in 2006.[42]

Moreover, the ownership structure of German firms is changing. Blockholders have begun to sell some of their stakes in response to tax reforms enacted in 2002 that eliminated capital gains tax for such transactions. The tax previously was 53 percent (Edwards et al. 2003). This has resulted in a decrease in the size of block holdings, in particular, those held by banks. According to Wójcik (2002), banks reduced their holdings from an average of 29 percent in 1997 to 24 percent in 2001 (ibid, table 5, p. 32). Legal reform is another element in the changing landscape. Germany introduced a number of corporate governance reforms in recent years. In 1998, for example, a law aimed at promoting transparency and shareholder control in corporations was enacted that, among other things, eliminated multiple voting rights for listed companies.[43]

Vodafone's hostile bid for Mannesmann demonstrated the likely implications of these trends for Germany's corporate elite as well as for the German governance system more generally. Without the changes in Mannesmann's ownership structure throughout the 1990s, Vodafone could not have hoped to acquire a controlling stake in the company in a public tender offer. Instead, it would have been forced to negotiate with the controlling shareholders. Moreover, Vodafone was not an insider in the German system, so it was free of social norms or political pressure that might have prevented it from launching a hostile bid.

Thus Vodafone's bid exposed the threat that globalization poses to the German model of capitalism. This is well illustrated in the interplay between the defendant, Deutsche Bank's Ackermann, and the trial court judge. Ackermann adamantly supported the payment of a bonus to Mannesmann's departing executive team. He repeatedly stated in court and in the media that he believed the payments were justified in light of the extraordinary service that Esser and his team had provided to the company and its shareholders.[44] He also noted that such payments were common in international markets and that the amount was well within the usual range for the type of transaction in question. In other words, Ackermann behaved as a player in the international marketplace would behave. Germany happened to be where Mannesmann and Deutsche Bank were located, but the business standards for such transactions originated elsewhere. In his view, Germany had to adapt to global standards, not the other way around. The trial court judge explicitly disagreed with this point of view. In opening remarks given on the day she announced the court's ruling, Judge Koppenhöfer lectured Ackermann that Germany was not a "law-free" environment, asserting that this in fact was one of the country's strengths as a host for business.[45]

The confrontation between the international banker—a Swiss national whose appointment as top manager of Deutsche Bank signaled the bank's international aspirations—and the German judge reflects the broader conflict between domestic norms and those of the international marketplace. Accepting the latter would clearly undermine the German model of capitalism as developed in the postwar period. Rejecting international business practices, however, might affect Germany's attractiveness to international business and capital.

The behavior of the two labor representatives was highly revealing as well. Although Jürgen Ladberg had not attended the meeting called to decide on the appreciation award, he was nonetheless accused of aiding and abetting the criminal breach of trust because he did not protest the decision. The participation of Klaus Zwickel was critical for securing the quorum (three of four members) needed for the Presidium to take binding decisions. He was clearly uncomfortable in this pivotal role. In abstaining, he had explained that as union representative he could not support the decision but did not wish to block it, either. This led to his indictment for aiding and abetting the criminal breach of trust.

Why did the two labor representatives not join forces and reject the proposal? Should we not expect labor to safeguard social norms that favor egalitarianism in the workplace instead of glorifying the CEO and other top managers and multiplying their pay, as the court and the prosecutor's office argued, for tasks that any person in a similar position should have fulfilled?

It is unlikely that labor was playing a cooperative game with the investors, hoping for reciprocal favors later on. The merger with Vodafone created an endgame for the blue-collar workers because Mannesmann's remaining steel assets were slated for sale. It is more likely that labor deferred to capital with respect to issues that, in their view, did not directly affect employee interests. This interpretation is consistent with the statement by the two employee representatives that they found it difficult to explain the bonuses to their constituencies and thus took note of the payments but did not protest them. Taken together, the key pillars of the German capitalist system—banks and labor—did not defend the system's principles when they came under attack. The bank representative, himself not part of the German corporate insider culture, clearly sided with the Anglo-American model. For the labor representatives, on the other hand, the stakes were not high enough to openly resist the importation of practices that challenged the norms on which the postwar model of Germany's social market economy had rested.

Legal Response

Did the Mannesmann case with all its implications (in particular, the signal it sent about the vulnerability of large German firms to takeovers and the increased exposure to international corporate practices including radical changes in executive compensation) trigger any broader institutional response in an attempt to either defend or reform Germany's capitalist system? One immediate response, widely attributed to the fate of Mannesmann, was Germany's role in blocking the adoption of the European Takeover Directive in June 2000. German representatives in the European Parliament voted down the adoption of the Takeover Directive, which had been in the making for more than a decade.[46] The goal of the directive was to lower the barriers to takeovers within the European Union and to establish common standards for such transactions. The draft directive borrowed heavily from the U.K. system, which imposes strict neutrality on the board of a target company once a takeover bid has been made.[47] Defensive measures taken after a bid has been made require shareholder approval. Although Germany's representatives were not alone in opposing this rule, most observers attribute the failure to adopt the directive to a change in the position of the German government (Gordon 2002a; Hertig and McCahery 2003). It argued that the strict neutrality rule was too rigid and that it contradicted the goal of creating a level playing field for companies throughout the European Union. Instead, the directive was said to disadvantage firms in countries that had weak prebid defenses. Because Germany had eliminated most prebid defenses in its corporate law reform of 1998, its firms were said to be more open to a takeover threat than were firms from France or Scandinavian member states that continued to have multiple voting rights in place that constituted strong postbid defenses.[48]

With the European directive sent back to the drawing board, the German parliament was free to adopt its own version of a takeover law, which it did in January 2002.[49] The new law created a modified neutrality rule. Rather than requiring shareholder approval of defensive measures taken after a takeover bid is made, it required only the approval of the company's supervisory board. This, of course, is a less costly procedure, and, given the likely bias of employee representatives against a takeover, it increases the chances that such measures will be approved. It is not obvious whether an earlier adoption of this law would have changed Vodafone's takeover of Mannesmann. Yet the law sent a clear signal that Germany would allow (if not encourage) its companies to defend themselves against hostile takeovers.

A revised E.U. Takeover Directive finally became effective in May 2006.[50] It is a considerably watered-down version of the one voted down in 2000. Thus the clash of systems in the Mannesmann experience appears to have affected the development of takeover law, not only in Germany but throughout the European Union. The new directive requires board neutrality in principle[51] but allows countries to opt out of this provision. If a country generally imposes board neutrality on all listed companies, it may nevertheless exempt companies targeted by bidders from the board neutrality requirement if the bidder is not subject to similar rules.[52] All member states of the European Union were required to enact the directive into national law by May 2006. The German takeover law enacted in the wake of the Mannesmann case therefore had to be amended. But Germany chose to grant its companies the utmost flexibility permitted by the directive in responding to a takeover. German law now provides that shareholders may empower the board to take defensive measures before any takeover bid has been made.[53]

Another legal response to the Mannesmann case was the enactment of a law concerning the disclosure of executive compensation in the summer of 2005.[54] The law requires that listed companies disclose the compensation package of each individual member of the management board. Previously, only the combined compensation package for all members had to be disclosed, making it difficult to determine the pay of individual members, particularly the chairman of the board. The law is modest compared to some proposals that favored a legally prescribed ceiling for top executive compensation. Instead, the law leaves it to corporate stakeholders to assess and respond to the compensation packages that are set by the companies themselves. Finally, a law designed to enhance the integrity of corporations and strengthen shareholders' ability to hold managers liable for violating the interests of the corporation (the "Law concerning Enterprise Integrity and the Modernization of Avoidance," or UMAG) was adopted in 2005.[55] The law seeks to strike a new compromise between the desire to strengthen the monitoring role of shareholders, in particular minority shareholders, and the fear that extensive litigation powers might be abused. The default rule in German corporate law had been that the supervisory board determines whether to bring litigation to recover damages when executives harm the corporation and that shareholders could mount such an action only if they represented a substantial stake in the company. Because supervisory boards tend to be dominated by shareholders who own large blocks of stock, minority shareholders had little chance of mounting a legal challenge against executive action. Recently, Germany has repeatedly lowered the threshold for minority shareholders to demand that the supervisory board take legal action against directors.[56] In 1998 the threshold was set at either 5 percent of outstanding shares or shares representing at least €100,000 of the company's market value. The 2005 UMAG lowers this threshold to 1 percent of outstanding shares or €100,000 of the par value. Moreover, minority shareholders may now bring actions on behalf of the corporation in their own name. The previous rule that only a court-appointed representative could do so has been abolished.

The trend toward empowering shareholders to sue management and thereby decentralize enforcement in the area of corporate law has been further strengthened by yet another law, adopted in the fall of 2005, that facilitates "model case proceedings."[57] These are not U.S-style class actions, but they have been inspired by the U.S. system. Plaintiffs or defendants may initiate proceedings to certify a model case proceeding in cases related to insider trading, securities regulations, and takeovers. The filing temporarily suspends all similar cases brought until a regional court has certified the case.[58] Once a court has heard a duly certified model case, the ruling is binding on other courts trying the same matter.[59]

These changes appear to signal that the lawmakers have shifted from a position that was highly skeptical of uncontrolled litigation power for shareholders to one that allows the judicial process to play a greater role in the enforcement of principles of corporate governance. While not fully decentralizing law enforcement and certainly stopping short of empowering attorneys (by means of contingency fees) to be proactive in pursuing such cases,[60] the new legislation nonetheless marks a watershed in the development of the German corporate governance system.

Law's Functions in German Capitalism

In the traditional model as it evolved in the postwar period, law in Germany played a coordinative role in corporate governance. Key legal rules were designed to ensure bargaining and coordination among actors rather than to supply a substantive solution.[61] Multiple constituencies are legally empowered to partake in strategic decision making, yet none has sufficient power to dominate the bargaining process. This forces each constituency to seek compromise through bargaining. It also ensures that the state retains a role as ultimate arbiter by changing the balance of power by legislative intervention or by punishing constituencies that deviate too far from the socially accepted path.

During Germany's rise to economic strength, a corporatist system placed employers, labor, and the government in a position to bargain among themselves to determine wages and other aspects of corporate policy. This system was supported by legal institutions that allowed employers as well as labor to organize, promote bargaining between the two groups, and gave the government the power to extend the outcome of a bargain over wages to entire industrial sectors, including companies and employees that have no union or employer association organization.[62] The law created only the framework within which bargaining and decision making took place. It accomplished this coordinating function by vesting multiple constituencies with competing rights rather than allocating final decision-making powers to only one constituency. At times the system might have been skewed toward one group, as in the case of quasi-parity codetermination.[63] Nonetheless, that employee representatives were (and still are) sitting on the supervisory board ensured that shareholders and managers need to recognize their interests, if only to arbitrate around them—or at times bribe union officials to overcome resistance against management strategies, as the recent scandal at Volkswagen suggests.[64]

The coordinating function of law was not limited to the provisions of the law on codetermination. German corporate law has traditionally rejected the protective approach centered on rights enforcement. Shareholders have always had recourse to the courts in extreme cases, but only after their concerns had been mediated either by the supervisory board or by a court-appointed representative of shareholder interests. As we have noted, recent legal change has taken a more protective and decentralized view of shareholder rights and may trigger more extensive use of such rights (Noack and Zetsche 2005). Even so, the prevailing view in Germany that the interests of the corporation may trump shareholder interests might militate against convergence toward the U.S. model of value maximization for shareholders. The BGH clearly illustrated the philosophical difference in the Mannesmann ruling, in which it argued that Vodafone, with its 98.6 percent stake in Mannesmann at the time the appreciation awards were paid, could not effectively validate the payment because unanimous approval would be required for such a decision, which was contrary to the interests of the corporation. Earlier on in the proceedings, the trial court judge pointedly reminded Ackermann that shareholder value creation is not a justification for overstepping the boundaries established by law.

Conclusion

One of the most important and lasting effects of the Mannesmann trial could be the role of courts as agents of Germany's traditional model of capitalism. After having been passive bystanders to corporate affairs during Germany's rise to economic prominence, they may become the bulwark against change, upholding the traditional norms of the German corporate governance system. As the public response to the acquittal suggests, these norms reflect those held by the public at large.[65] But tensions seem unavoidable. Our dissection of the case has shown that critical stakeholders in the old governance model have either switched sides and now endorse a more Anglo-American model (German banks) or have passively acquiesced in actions that appear contrary to their interests (labor), as suggested by the voting behavior of the two labor representatives in the case.

It will be interesting to see how the courts' newfound role will mesh with the rise of the more protective, decentralized function of law apparent from the series of legal reforms meant to enhance shareholder power (Noack and Zetsche 2005). These changes are likely to increase the number of cases brought before the courts. The Mannesmann episode suggests that the courts will not necessarily enforce the shareholder wealth maximization principle without considering other stakeholders' interests. Within the context of the social norms that make up the fabric of Germany's postwar capitalist system, empowering shareholders via procedural devices is unlikely to transform the system into one based on the maximization of value for shareholders.

Still, the changes currently under way may ultimately trigger a broader transformation of German capitalism. The increase in globalization implies that the key constituencies of the systems are no longer predominantly insiders, that is, German corporations, management, and labor. Instead, foreign ownership of German companies has increased and foreign management, though still not common, is on the rise. Most important, corporations have found ways to opt out of the German legal system, thus weakening the governance structure it prescribes. European law, especially recent cases decided by the European Court of Justice, has dealt a severe blow to the seat theory, on which mandatory application of German law to corporations operating in Germany was thought to rest.[66] Meanwhile, a new regulation concerning what constitutes a European company facilitates cross-border mergers between companies located in two member states.[67] This regulation may be used by companies in one member state (say, Germany) to merge with a company governed by the law of a different member state of the European Union. A complementary directive to the regulation requires that workers of the two merging companies agree on the nature of the codetermination regime.[68] In practice this has meant that when a company from a different member state merges with a German company, the mandatory codetermination regime can be softened considerably. The first company to make use of the new regulation was Allianz, the large German insurance company, which merged with its Italian subsidiary. Allianz remains incorporated in Germany, but the merger has opened up the possibility of renegotiating the codetermination regime and has resulted in fewer board seats overall and a greater proportion of employee seats reserved for employees from outside Germany.[69]

Finally, as suggested by the Mannesmann case, German firms participating in global markets have adopted business practices that differ from Germany's social variant of capitalism. Deutsche Bank's major strength today is bond trading on global markets, not nurturing firms back home.[70] It has reorganized its management structure to resemble more closely the Anglo-American system, in which the CEO is the central and most powerful agent of the corporation. (German law, by contrast, depicts the board as a collective decision-making body.) As a global player that generates much of its revenue outside Germany and is run by a Swiss CEO, there is little reason to believe (as evidenced in the Mannesmann case) that Deutsche Bank will protect the German governance system when the two systems collide. The immediate winner seems to be capital as represented by shareholders and corporate management. For the most part, labor has witnessed these changes passively. The powers of unions have already been eroded by years of high unemployment rates. There are also signs that the broad social consensus about the benefits of codetermination is cracking, with some voices—for the first time in thirty years—calling for its abolition (Adams 2006). Recent legal reforms appear to embrace these changes by allocating more powers to shareholders to fend for their own rights, even at the cost of breaching social harmony, the objective that has long been used to fend off demands for stronger legal rights. Though the Mannesmann episode was hardly responsible for setting each of these trends in motion, it is illustrative of how these trends may affect German capitalism and law.

FIVE

The Livedoor Bid and Hostile Takeovers in Japan: Postwar Law and Capitalism at the Crossroads

Postwar Japan shares many economic and social traits with Germany, including the remarkable success of its institutional structures in promoting economic growth, at least until very recently. Likewise, many of the forces of globalization examined in connection with the Mannesmann case are also buffeting Japanese capitalism and law. As with that case, our institutional autopsy from Japan involves a hostile takeover bid. But in this case, the bidder was a domestic player who represented the "outside" world of aggressive, market-oriented capitalism. Perhaps to an even greater extent than in Germany, the old structures are changing, and new rules seem to apply to economic activity.

In this chapter we consider a hostile takeover bid by Livedoor, a brash Internet company, for Nippon Broadcasting System, Inc., a radio broadcaster affiliated with a major Japanese media conglomerate.[1] As we will see, the bid—in a country where hostile takeovers have been rare and tainted with social stigma—caused enormous controversy and exposed major fissures in Japanese capitalism. It also added momentum to a series of important changes in governance structures in Japan, including the use of formal law (in the form of judge-made rules) in the transfer of corporate assets. It is striking that the dénouement of the episode includes a major transplantation of U.S. (specifically Delaware) corporate law into a set of nonbinding guidelines to help govern corporate responses to hostile takeovers in Japan and the subsequent arrest of Livedoor's president on charges of securities and accounting fraud. This rapid series of events reflects important shifts in expectations about the role of law in the Japanese economy. In the framework of our book, our institutional autopsy reveals a relatively centralized, coordinative system of law and capitalism shifting in response to external pressures and new domestic dynamics.

The Story

Nippon Broadcasting is a subsidiary of Fuji Television Network, Inc. (Fuji TV), Japan's largest media company, and the virtual headquarters of the prominent Fuji Sankei media group. Somewhat anomalously, however, as of early 2005 Nippon Broadcasting held 22.5 percent of the outstanding shares of Fuji TV, and Fuji TV held only 12.4 percent of Nippon Broadcasting's shares. In part to rectify that situation, on January 17, 2005, Fuji TV announced an all-cash offer for all of the outstanding shares of Nippon Broadcasting. The bid was approved by the directors of Nippon Broadcasting, with the four board members who were affiliated with Fuji TV abstaining.

In the midst of the tender offer period, on February 8, 2005, an Internet service provider called Livedoor (formerly called Livin' on the Edge) made the startling announcement that it had just acquired about 9.7 million shares, or 29.6 percent, of Nippon Broadcasting. In combination with shares owned previously, these purchases gave Livedoor 38 percent of the shares of Nippon Broadcasting. The share purchases, which were financed by an issuance of convertible bonds underwritten by the U.S. investment bank Lehman Brothers, were made on an after-hours, off-exchange trading system operated by the Tokyo Stock Exchange. (As such, they fell outside a provision of the securities laws requiring any acquisition of more than 33.3 percent of a company's shares to be made via a tender offer open to all shareholders.)[2] On the same day, Livedoor informed Nippon Broadcasting of its intent to acquire all of its outstanding shares. Livedoor's CEO, a thirty-two-year-old college dropout named Takafumi Horie, held a press conference to announce the expected synergies of turning Nippon Broadcasting's Web site into a portal site and his desire to enter into a business cooperation agreement with the Fuji Sankei group.

In response, on February 23, 2005, Nippon Broadcasting announced that its board had decided to issue warrants to Fuji TV exercisable into 47.2 million shares of Nippon Broadcasting stock. If exercised, the warrants would give Fuji TV majority control and dilute to less than 20 percent Livedoor's stake, which by that time had increased to about 40 percent. This type of warrant (known as *shin kabu yoyaku ken*), authorized in a 2002 Commercial Code amendment, allows directors to issue the instrument without shareholder approval at a price determined by the board, as long as the price is "fair."[3] The Nippon Broadcasting warrants were exercisable at 5,950 yen (about $53), the price offered in Fuji TV's tender offer, but less than the then-current trading price of Nippon Broadcasting stock. Nippon

Broadcasting announced that the warrants were issued for the purpose of ensuring that it remained within the Fuji Sankei group, which would provide long-term benefits to its shareholders.

Livedoor sued to enjoin the issuance of the warrants. The Tokyo District Court enjoined the warrant issuance as "grossly unfair," finding that its main purpose was to maintain control of the firm by incumbent management and affiliates of the Fuji Sankei group. The High Court affirmed. In the face of these rulings, Nippon Broadcasting and Fuji TV abandoned the warrant issuance. Livedoor eventually obtained a majority of the shares of Nippon Broadcasting, whose president announced his resignation, ostensibly to shoulder the blame for "failing to protect the company from a hostile bid."[4]

In the end, the contest for Nippon Broadcasting ended civilly. On April 18, 2005, Livedoor agreed to sell its Nippon Broadcasting shares to Fuji TV at 6,300 yen per share, about the average price it paid for the shares. In return, Fuji TV obtained a 12.5 percent stake in Livedoor for a capital infusion of about $440 million, and the three companies established a joint committee to explore related ventures.

The ultimate outcome of this nearly unprecedented transaction for Livedoor and Horie, however, was disastrous. In January 2006, Horie was arrested on charges of securities and accounting fraud. The prosecutors alleged that Livedoor had released misleading financial statements and engaged, with affiliates, in a series of improper stock trades in the course of acquiring other technology firms. The "Livedoor Shock," as it came to be known in Japan, led to a rapid unraveling of Horie's mystique and a plunge in Livedoor's stock price, resulting in its delisting from the stock exchange. Only eight months after shaking up corporate Japan with the bid for Nippon Broadcasting, Livedoor had virtually vanished overnight, along with its leader's reputation. In March 2007, Horie was found guilty of securities law violations and sentenced to two and a half years in prison.

The Livedoor Bid in Postwar Japanese Law and Capitalism

Although the facts of this transaction may strike readers familiar with U.S. hostile merger and acquisition activity as rather prosaic, it would be difficult to overstate the controversy Livedoor's bid stirred in Japan. To be sure, colorful characters played a role in the public's fascination with the episode. Horie was telegenic, brash, and blunt—in stark contrast to the geriatric blandness of most corporate executives in Japan. Some of the celebrities on Fuji TV programs threatened to resign if Livedoor gained control of their media group. But the hostile bid struck a deeper chord in the Japanese consciousness, not only on a corporate level, but in political and social terms as well. In order to understand why, as with our other institutional autopsies, we need to back up for a moment and explore the contours of the postwar Japanese institutional setup. Only by seeing the background against which this transaction occurred can we understand its jarring repercussions for the country's future.

In postwar Japan, the actions of key actors have been monitored by informal social and economic institutions. One major institution of Japanese corporate governance was the main bank system. The main bank was the largest single lender to a given corporate client as well as one of its principal shareholders. As the central repository of information about the borrower, the main bank played an important role in monitoring the firm's management and rendering assistance, at least in times of distress. Because corporate management was often replaced by bank personnel in difficult situations, the main bank system was said to substitute for the missing takeover market in Japan (Sheard 1989).

The second prominent feature of postwar corporate governance and organization in Japan was the practice of mutual shareholding among firms and financial institutions. Although, as we discuss below, cross-shareholding arrangements have declined in the recent past, in the early 1990s approximately two-thirds of all corporate shares were held for the long term by "stable" shareholders who were generally friendly toward incumbent management. This practice reached its apex in the form of the *keiretsu*. The *keiretsu* are historically derived clusters of affiliated firms held together by stable cross-shareholding, interlocking directorates, extensive product-market linkages, and other links that enhance group identity and facilitate information exchange and risk-sharing. In the heyday of postwar Japanese corporate governance, a main bank was at the center of each of the six principal *keiretsu* corporate groups. Today, mergers among the main banks at the center of several *keiretsu* have weakened the identities of the corporate groups.

The *keiretsu* system and other, less cohesive corporate groupings were means of encouraging asset-specific investments (including investments in human capital). Although cross-shareholding increased the cost of acquiring a controlling block of shares, thus virtually disabling the market for corporate control, the long-term relationships embedded in Japanese corporate shareholding, which were traditionally based on ongoing financial and product-market transactions, encouraged noncapital forms of monitoring. These relationships, in effect, provided an alternative to the disciplining and risk-bearing functions played by the capital markets in some other countries, most prominently the United States and the United Kingdom. The relative immobility of labor in postwar Japan, in part a corollary of a legal regime that was highly protective of employees, complemented the stable group structures by providing incentives for firms to make major firm-specific investments in employee training and development.

Supporting these institutions was a highly informal, interactive relationship between firms and officials in the economic ministries. Much regulatory activity in postwar Japan was the antithesis of the decentralized, court-centered, private-rights-enforcement model found in the United States. Instead, the bureaucracy was engaged in an ongoing process of accommodation with regulated actors, shaping and enforcing compromises rather than directing policy outcomes or formally enforcing statutes and regulations. Regulated actors participated actively, if informally, in the regulatory process. Law stood in the background, available to coerce recalcitrant parties into cooperation and compliance, but it was not the first-order tool used to regulate economic activities.

Now consider the Livedoor bid against this backdrop. The bid came toward the end of Japan's long period of economic malaise, in which the institutional features of Japan's postwar success came under serious and prolonged stress. Several closely related factors explain the controversy caused by this transaction. First, the contest for control was an allegory of "old" and "new" Japan. Livedoor was an Internet firm run by a college dropout in T-shirt and jeans who had made a name, and a billion dollars, for himself buying up small technology companies. The target of his latest ambition was a radio broadcaster (and indirectly, its parent company) in a bloated media conglomerate, steered by starched-shirted sixty-somethings. Livedoor's target selection was all the more striking given the postwar economic structures described above. Although the Fuji Sankei group was not one of Japan's leading postwar *keiretsu*, the Livedoor bid represented an unprecedented assault by an outsider on a firm clearly identified as a member of a corporate group.

Second, the players in this deal, as in several other bids that preceded Livedoor's, used previously unheard-of tactics to pursue their objectives. Livedoor's unsolicited bid, along with its strategic use of litigation to invalidate Nippon Broadcasting's attempt to strengthen ties with its de facto parent company, marked major departures from the norm in the world of Japanese takeovers. As such, it generated a welter of controversy by creating the impression that a new, sharp-elbowed brand of "American" capitalism was infiltrating Japan. In the midst of Livedoor's hostile bid for

Nippon Broadcasting, for example, Fuji TV's chairman remarked, "I wonder if this sort of thing is called American style. I wouldn't know because I am Japanese" (Karube 2005, n.p.). More reflective commentators questioned whether Japan is ready for the wholesale introduction of the U.S. system of corporate governance, with its extensive reliance on freedom of contract, robust capital markets, ex post judicial review, and private enforcement backed by a number of incentives (Uemura 2005). Some in Japan now view hostile bids as part of the standard corporate governance tool kit, with potential to help revive the Japanese economy by moving assets to their most productive uses; others see an undesirable foreign practice inconsistent with Japanese sensibilities and subject to exploitation in Japan's comparatively underdeveloped corporate and capital markets regime.

Closely related to the impression made by the tactical novelty of the transaction is the larger sense (whether genuine or strategically motivated) that corporate Japan is now vulnerable to a wave of foreign acquisitions. For years, some public firms in Japan have traded below their asset values, and the market capitalizations of major Japanese firms are often only a fraction as large as those of their U.S. peers. This anxiety bubbled to the surface during the Livedoor contest, though all the principal players were Japanese. Much critical attention in media and government circles was focused on Lehman Brothers' role in financing Livedoor's bid. Keidanren, a powerful big business lobby, issued policy papers calling for Japan's business community to devise measures to deter "foreign predators." In response to these anxieties, in the midst of the contest for Nippon Broadcasting, the Japanese government postponed a planned corporate law amendment that would permit foreign firms to do cross-border acquisitions in Japan using triangular mergers and stock swaps, even though this mechanism is not particularly well suited to hostile acquisitions. As illustrated by contentious debate in Europe about the Thirteenth Directive,[5] crafting an official response to hostile takeovers touches deep chords of nationalism, protectionism, and fear of the unknown. These forces were also at work in Japan.[6]

Perhaps most important, the Livedoor bid and other contests for control have brought Japanese corporate governance into uncharted territory. The emergence of a market for corporate control in Japan, if nascent, has the potential to significantly change the incentive structure for Japanese managers. Surveys taken in the wake of the Livedoor bid indicated that managers at 70 percent of large Japanese firms were concerned about the "threat" of hostile takeovers.[7] Previously, Japanese managers had few direct incentives, short of financial crisis, to take major steps to enhance the value of their firms,[8] and they prided themselves on working to advance the interests of all corporate stakeholders—prominently including employees—rather than shareholders alone. If these managers are no longer secure from the threat of hostile acquisition or other unwelcome shareholder advances, they ignore shareholder returns at considerable peril to their own futures. Though the number of unsolicited bids in Japan is still very low by any measure, and no bid thus far has been an unqualified success, the trend is upward, and it is not the number but the existence of hostile bids that matters from a corporate governance perspective.

The Response

Two immediate responses to the Livedoor bid require analysis. The first and more direct response is the litigation spawned by the bid. The second, less direct but of more far-reaching import, is the endorsement of nonbinding takeover guidelines by a powerful Japanese ministry. We take up these responses in turn. We then briefly discuss the possible ramifications of Horie's arrest and successful prosecution.

As noted above, hostile takeovers in Japan have been an exceedingly rare phenomenon in the postwar period, at least until the past few years, largely because of the stable and friendly shareholding patterns of Japanese corporations during the period. In the rare case in which a bid was launched, the target board would issue a new block of shares to a friendly shareholder. Owing to the paucity of bids, the Japanese courts were rarely involved in contests for control. The only rule they had formulated up to the time of the Livedoor case was a "primary purpose" test. That is, the court would ask whether the primary purpose of a new share issuance to a white knight was to raise capital. If the answer was plausibly yes, the share issuance would be deemed proper. If, on the other hand, the primary purpose was to dilute the shares of the bidder, the new share issuance would be invalidated. But note the limitations of the rule. First, it is inherently difficult to determine the primary purpose of a corporate transaction by a legal proceeding. Moreover, the rule is not well suited to judging the reasonableness of other types of defensive measures, including the U.S.-style poison pill, that have no corporate finance function. These limitations can be directly tied to the infrequency of litigation regarding takeovers and the extremely limited range of defensive measures used in postwar Japan. In a system in which corporate relations are heavily regulated via relationships and informal monitoring, courts play a less prominent role. And if the courts are rarely asked to resolve a governance issue, they have little opportunity to craft workable rules.

In the Livedoor litigation, however, the court was forced to decide a question that is at the heart of any takeover law: When is it permissible for a target company's board to erect a virtually impenetrable barrier to an unsolicited bid? In invalidating the defensive measure, the District Court noted the preclusive nature of Nippon Broadcasting's warrant issuance, echoing Delaware jurisprudence. (That is, once the warrants were issued to Fuji TV, it would become virtually impossible for a dissident shareholder of Nippon Broadcasting to wrest control of the board away from the favored shareholder.) On appeal, the High Court acknowledged the general applicability of the business judgment rule in the board's determination of how to respond to an unsolicited bid.[9] Yet it affirmed the District Court's decision to enjoin the warrant issuance as "grossly unfair," enunciating the following rule:

> In principle, where a contest for corporate control has emerged, it constitutes a grossly unfair issuance (Commercial Code sec. 280-39(4); sec. 280-10) to issue warrants, the primary purpose of which is for existing management or a specific shareholder who exercises influence over management to retain control, by diluting the holdings of another shareholder. However, where the hostile bidder (1) intends to make a target company or its affiliates repurchase the shares for a premium after the stock price increases (is engaged in greenmail); (2) intends to transfer intellectual property, know how, corporate secrets, key business transactions or customers, which are vital for the management of the company, to the bidder or its affiliates (is engaged in "scorched earth" policies); (3) has acquired the target company's shares so that after acquiring control, the bidder can liquidate assets to secure or pay off bidder's debts or those of related companies; or (4) obtains temporary control of management to sell off valuable assets unrelated to the core business such as real estate or securities in order to pay a one-time dividend from the proceeds, or sell the stock after having driven up the stock price due to the high dividend—in other words, where there is an abusive motive of exploiting the target—then it is not appropriate to protect the bidder as a shareholder, and if it is clear that the interests of other shareholders will be harmed, issuance of warrants may be permitted as appropriate in order to preserve or protect management's control rights, within the limits of necessity and appropriateness as to method of resistance.[10]

Finding insufficient evidence that any of these abusive motives were present in Livedoor's bid, the court concluded that Nippon Broadcasting's board had issued the warrants with the primary purpose of preserving management's control.

In this passage from the High Court's opinion, U.S. lawyers will note a resemblance to the famous *Unocal* case, decided under Delaware law. *Unocal*, decided in the late 1980s at the height of the U.S. takeover boom, remains the basic test used by the Delaware courts in deciding whether to invalidate a target board's defensive measures. The case provides that in order for a defensive measure to be valid, the board must identify a threat to corporate policy and effectiveness posed by the hostile bid, and the defensive response must be proportionate to the threat. The resemblance of the *Livedoor* ruling to this famous Delaware case is probably not coincidental. The courts in *Livedoor* were briefed on how the issue would be resolved under Delaware law, and the recent takeover contests in Japan generated a large body of academic commentary about how rules applied in Delaware would have applied in the cases.

Although the *Livedoor* case is important for its development of judicial rules governing takeovers in Japan, an even more important response to hostile takeovers came in the form of nonbinding guidelines adopted in the immediate aftermath of the Livedoor bid. Before it created the storm of controversy described above, a small number of mostly unsuccessful hostile takeover attempts early in the twenty-first century had roiled business and political circles. Declines in stable shareholding and cross-shareholding patterns during the previous decade had increased the vulnerability of Japanese firms to hostile takeover. In August 2004, "in light of concerns about the steady rise of hostile bids" (Corporate Value Study Group 2005, 2), Japan's Ministry of Economy, Trade, and Industry (METI) established the Corporate Value Study Group, composed of legal scholars, lawyers, and business representatives, to consider an appropriate policy response to hostile takeover activity. Such consultative committees (referred to as *shingikai*) have a long history of involvement in the policy and law-making processes in Japan. Formed under the auspices of a ministry and typically composed of scholars, members of the media, labor representatives, lawyers, and businesspeople, these groups facilitate public-private interaction and policy coordination. They serve as listening posts for ministry officials in charge of drafting bills and give affected interests—at least, those invited to the table by the ministry in charge—a voice in the policy and law-making processes. Typically, the report prepared by the consultative committee serves as the basis for the new law or policy drafted by the ministry. Note the centralized, coordinative role of such groups in crafting public policy. Once policy has been shaped in such a process, ex post litigation concerning the resulting policy—a common phenomenon in the United States—is extremely rare in Japan.

The Corporate Value Study Group's work was based on four key principles: enhancement of corporate value, global standards, prohibition of discrimination between foreign and Japanese firms, and expansion of choice. The study group's report, issued in March 2005 in the midst of the Livedoor controversy, followed extensive research and consultations with experts regarding Anglo-American takeover defenses and legal precedents. It is remarkable for its approval of Delaware takeover jurisprudence. The report begins by noting that no Western country completely lacks corporate defensive measures, because reasonable defensive measures can enhance corporate and shareholder returns. It then provides an exhaustive analysis of Delaware's experience with defensive measures, in particular, the poison pill, focusing on the *Unocal* rule and its progeny. The report also suggests incorporation of doctrinal refinements made in the wake of *Unocal* that emphasize the importance of the shareholder franchise as the ultimate protection against defensive measures that seek to entrench corporate management. Accordingly, the report emphasizes, as a line of Delaware cases has done, that the key inquiry is whether, in spite of the defensive measures, shareholders retain a realistic possibility of unseating the incumbent directors in a proxy contest. Finally, the report discusses incorporation of a rule, such as the famous *Revlon* rule developed by the Delaware courts, essentially requiring the board to auction the corporation to the highest bidder if, after reaching a decision to sell or transfer control of the firm, the board is faced with competing bids (Corporate Value Study Group 2005).

The report notes that the establishment of defensive measures in Japan has been hampered by uncertainty about their legal effect, a paucity of precedents and experience, and a lack of consensus about what constitutes reasonable defensive measures. It then favorably cites an opinion of the Ministry of Justice that "[i]f adjusted for Japanese circumstances, most defensive measures recognized in the U.S. and Europe can also be implemented in Japan" (Corporate Value Study Group 2005, 18). Specifically, the report concludes that warrants of the type Nippon Broadcasting tried to issue discriminately to Fuji TV can be used to implement a shareholder rights plan (poison pill). Again drawing heavily on Delaware jurisprudence, the report discusses ways in which to ensure and enhance the reasonableness of defensive measures, including retaining the ability of replacing the board via a proxy contest, participation of independent directors and advisors in the formulation of defensive measures, the use of "chewable pills" that are cancelled automatically in certain circumstances, and shareholder approval. In short, the report represents a major endorsement of Delaware takeover jurisprudence in the formulation of Japanese policy.

On the basis of the study group's report, takeover guidelines were jointly issued by METI and the Ministry of Justice in May 2005. The takeover guidelines are "modeled after typical defensive measures that have been developed elsewhere" (Ministry of Economy 2005, n.p.) and reflect the heavy influence of Delaware jurisprudence, although they place more emphasis on shareholder approval of defensive measures as a means of ensuring fairness than does Delaware doctrine. Specifically, the guidelines require that defensive measures adopted in response to a possible takeover threat be necessary and reasonable in relation to the threat posed, and they endorse the use of poison-pill-like instruments that make it virtually impossible to accomplish a takeover that is not approved by the target's board of directors.

The takeover guidelines, though technically nonbinding, had an immediate effect on Japan's institutional environment for corporate governance. The Tokyo Stock Exchange altered its listing requirements and a major pension fund association changed its proxy voting guidelines, in both cases to incorporate the principles of the guidelines. As with the endorsement of the poison pill by the Delaware courts two decades ago, promulgation of the takeover guidelines is leading to a wave of adoptions of (or at least keen interest in) the poison pill in the Japanese market, as firms avail themselves of a powerful defensive measure that has been officially sanctioned by two prominent ministries. In the June 2006 shareholder meeting season, the first real test of the poison pill's popularity among Japanese managers, about 150 firms adopted some version of a rights plan. A year later, about 400 firms had adopted a poison pill.

Apart from these institutional responses to the Livedoor bid and other takeover attempts, Horie's arrest adds another important dimension to this episode. Even in this dimension, however, the Livedoor episode has parallels to the United States in the 1980s. Michael Milken, inventor of the "junk bond," which revolutionized takeover financing in that era, was prosecuted for and convicted of securities fraud after the takeover boom had ended. Like Horie, Milken was a maverick who pushed the envelope of acceptable conduct in his business world, making many enemies in the process. It can be argued that both men became targets of prosecution in part because they refused to play by the unwritten rules governing market conduct. This is not to say that either was blameless; the point is that both men simply made high-profile and (at least in the eyes of some powerful segments of the community) unsympathetic targets of prosecutorial zeal.[11]

Perhaps it is too early to reach a judgment about the prosecution and conviction of Horie, but two quite different interpretations are possible at this time. If it signals a heightened emphasis by law enforcers on fairness and transparency in the Tokyo stock market, the move complements other recent measures in Japan that suggest institutional transition from protection of informal corporate relationships to protection of investors. If, on the other hand, the case primarily constitutes selective prosecution of a maverick—not for violation of Japanese law but for violation of Japanese business culture—it indicates that market innovators still risk punishment, despite all the changes that have taken place in the past decade. Even this would signify a move toward law, however, because in the past incumbents have used informal industry relationships and contacts with ministry officials much more extensively than they have used the legal machinery of the state to maintain or strengthen their market positions, punish rivals, and shape the rules of market conduct.

The Players and the Transplantation of Delaware Law

Return now to the new rules governing takeovers, and consider why Japan transplanted Delaware takeover jurisprudence in formulating its guidelines. The first step in the process, at least implicitly, was rejection of an "indigenous" response to hostile takeovers in favor of "global" standards. An indigenous response could have provided robust protections to nonshareholder constituencies, particularly employees, who have been a primary focus of Japanese management in the postwar period. Precedent for such an approach exists in the first German Takeover Code,[12] which permitted adoption of any postbid defenses, essentially without limitation, as long as they were approved by a majority of the supervisory board, half of whose members represent labor. The Corporate Value Study Group's implicit rejection of the German approach is particularly salient given that Japanese corporate law was originally modeled after the German Commercial Code—Japan's corporate law is classified as being of German civil law origin in the law and finance literature—and the two countries shared considerable institutional and social affinities in the postwar period.

As with most transplantations of foreign law,[13] the decision to adopt a global standard rather than formulate an indigenous response is fairly easy to justify on practical grounds. Time was of the essence, at least if one credits the argument that market developments left Japanese firms unduly vulnerable to unsolicited takeovers, particularly via potentially coercive bids. Moreover, the transaction cost environment for the adoption of defensive measures was very high, given the legal uncertainty about the validity of defenses and lack of experience with such measures, which prevented the formation of market consensus about what constitutes fair and enforceable measures, a point repeatedly emphasized by the Corporate Value Study Group. In such an environment, adoption of a respected, market-tested foreign code or practice may have been viewed as the only viable response. Moreover, the process followed in this episode—forming a committee of experts under the auspices of an influential ministry to study foreign systems and recommend a solution to a Japanese policy problem—has a long history in Japan.

But why Delaware? The law and finance literature might suggest that the choice reflects the acknowledged superiority of Delaware law in protecting shareholders. But another Anglo-American standard was available in the form of the City Code on Takeovers and Mergers, by which mergers are regulated in the United Kingdom.[14] The City Code has served as the model for the takeover codes of several other countries, including Singapore and Malaysia. The City Code represents a very different approach to takeovers than Delaware law, mandating "strict neutrality" of target boards in the face of a takeover bid and prohibiting directors from installing defensive measures without shareholder approval. In return for board neutrality, takeover bids are regulated, principally by means of a mandatory offer rule, to prevent unfair or coercive tactics. A takeover panel composed of industry and legal experts engages in a variety of interpretive and disciplinary activities designed to enhance compliance with the code. Arguably, the City Code represents a more attractive candidate for transplant into Japan than Delaware takeover law. Its relatively straightforward rules may be much simpler to replicate and enforce than a complex body of foreign judicial doctrine. And the quasi-administrative role of the takeover panel is more consistent with traditional Japanese approaches to economic regulation than is Delaware's court-centric approach.[15]

Without discounting the role that the comparative intellectual appeal of Delaware law played in the decision to embrace Delaware jurisprudence instead of the City Code, several other factors appear to have influenced the choice. As with any transplant, familiarity with the foreign law among the experts responsible for interpreting and enforcing it appears to have played a role in the adoption of the takeover guidelines. Delaware corporate law is familiar to many Japanese lawyers, economic bureaucrats, and judges, many of whom have studied in U.S. law schools. More specifically, as lawyers or corporate law scholars, at least one-third of the Corporate Value Study Group's members had extensive exposure to Delaware corporate law. The City Code is far less familiar to the Japanese legal community. At the same time, implementing a United Kingdom–style mandatory bid rule was perceived as disadvantageous because it prevents potentially efficient partial bids and would require major changes to the tender offer provisions of the securities law, which may have been politically problematic given the lack of cooperation between METI and the financial supervisory agencies.[16] Perhaps most important for the ministries that endorsed the takeover guidelines and the political constituencies to which they respond, Delaware takeover jurisprudence is more protective of management than is the City Code. Adoption of the City Code, therefore, would have run counter to the strong tradition of concern for nonshareholder constituencies in Japan and exacerbated fears of a wave of foreign takeovers of Japanese firms, alleviation of which is expressly cited by the Corporate Value Study Group as a reason for formulating the guidelines. Thus, Delaware takeover law provided the METI and Ministry of Justice planners with the best of all possible worlds: a familiar and politically attainable global standard that is simultaneously protective of management.

Adoption of Delaware standards and validation of the poison pill in the takeover guidelines also have fascinating parallels to the interest-group explanation for the development of Delaware law (see Macey and Miller 1987). The enormous potential business opportunity presented by METI's undertaking was not lost on the lawyers and financial advisors (Japanese and American) who were directly involved in formulating and promoting the guidelines. Selection of the City Code approach would have sharply limited the role of U.S. advisors in Japanese contests for corporate control and elevated the position of U.K. firms in what appeared at the time to be a large new market for legal services in Japan. Instead, Japan conferred a major potential benefit on U.S. law firms, which have maintained a presence in Japan for the past two decades. Literally overnight, a new market of more than three thousand public companies was created for the poison pill, a sophisticated piece of legal technology developed and market-tested in the United States. Although the U.S. version of the poison pill cannot be adopted as is under Japanese corporate law, the accumulated experience of U.S. law firms with hostile takeovers and defensive measures will be highly salient to Japanese corporations now that Japan's institutional environment for takeovers has taken on a distinctly American cast. For elite Japanese corporate lawyers as well, most of whom received graduate legal education in the United States and are members of the New York or California bar, the transplantation, in particular the need to adapt the poison pill to the domestic legal regime, presents a substantial new business opportunity. In fact, major

Japanese law firms quickly began marketing their own signature pills, utilizing different structures designed to overcome technical hurdles presented by Japanese corporate law.

The point is not that METI caved in to special interests or that the selection of Delaware law was a disingenuous cover for protectionism. The point is simply that Japan's choice was the product of multiple motivations, and as such, is highly ambiguous with regard to the signal it sends about ideological convergence on the shareholder primacy norm or the superior shareholder protections provided by Delaware corporate law.

Implications

What are the implications of these developments for Japanese corporate governance, and more broadly, for its postwar system of capitalism? Three potential scenarios appear possible at this stage. First, consider the possibility of strong-form convergence with the U.S. system of corporate governance. If Japan follows the United States, its reform trajectory is clear. One likely change is that independent directors would take on a much higher profile in Japanese corporate governance. The number of independent directors serving on boards would increase, and they would become central players in structuring and negotiating acquisitions because their involvement would enhance the probability that a court, deciding ex post, would find the installation or retention of a poison pill to be a fair and proportionate response to a hostile bid. Independent directors would thus come to play a key role as arbiters of newly competing constituencies, including shareholders, managers, and employees, in a world of contests for control.[17] This would mark a big departure from postwar practice, under which high economic growth and stable shareholding in friendly business alliances allowed managers substantial leeway to pursue the interests of "the corporation" (which essentially meant employees, creditors and trade partners, and shareholders, in that order of priority). Thus, hostile takeover activity might foster the development of the independent board committee as a new locus of power in the Japanese firm.

These adaptive responses by corporate management would likely trigger strategic countermoves by other market actors. The widespread existence of poison pills could invite increased use of the proxy fight, heretofore little used in Japan, as a means of unseating incumbent management and thereby removing defensive measures. Perhaps most important, recent Japanese experience suggests that the incidence of corporate litigation may increase significantly as market actors test the validity of defensive measures. Indeed,

Japan's first poison pill was immediately tested in the courts by a foreign institutional shareholder. The generation of corporate law doctrine would accelerate as the courts are confronted with a myriad of new questions resulting from steady market innovations at the margins of existing legal rules.[18]

In this scenario, the Japanese legal system, featuring a new degree of flexibility and susceptibility to shareholder monitoring, becomes "supercharged" by changes in the surrounding capital markets and distribution of shareholders. Substantive change is brought about by dynamics that are external to formal corporate governance institutions, as actors such as Livedoor's Horie promote the erosion of corporate norms that stigmatize redeployment of corporate assets to higher-value uses as signaling failure or social disharmony. Ultimately, the ensuing transformations force senior managers to abandon their attachment to existing institutions. As recounted by Ronald Gilson (Gilson 2006a), this is essentially the story of the United States in the 1980s. Similar developments outside the formal corporate governance framework created forces for change so powerful that those favoring existing institutions, particularly senior managers, could not contain them. The result was a dramatic transformation in American corporate governance from a system that served largely to protect value-destroying decisions by insular groups of senior executives to a model whose attributes animated international reform proposals.

But it is also possible to envision a very different set of implications for Japan. Current developments may not trigger adaptive and strategic responses that supercharge Japan's corporate governance institutions. To the contrary, the takeover guidelines may simply increase managerial entrenchment. By validating adoption of the poison pill, the guidelines may simply lock insular boards in place and provide a perfect substitute for the disappearing institutions of stable shareholding and cross-shareholding. As Gilson (2004) has pointed out, to the extent that the poison pill has worked in the United States as a negotiating tool for the benefit of shareholders rather than simply as a means of blocking bids that threaten incumbent managers, it has worked because of the surrounding infrastructure of independent directors, judges capable of discerning proper from improper motivations for adoption of a pill, and capital market pressure (Gilson 2004). If much of this infrastructure is missing in Japan—and it is certainly possible to identify important gaps in the infrastructure—the pill may freeze market actors in their tracks. In the scenario of path dependency, adoption of Delaware takeover law *reinforces* rather than transforms the existing institutional setup.

Yet in all likelihood, neither the strong convergence nor the cryonic suspension effects of the pill outlined in the scenarios depicted above will come to pass in precisely the supposed fashion. This follows from a basic truth: Delaware takeover jurisprudence will operate differently in Japan than in the United States. Legal transplants are always tenuous experiments, and this particular transplant may be especially unpredictable. Japan has borrowed not a single legal rule or procedural mechanism but a complex body of common-law jurisprudence and a sophisticated legal technology in the form of the shareholder rights plan that evolved over the course of two decades in tandem with market developments via an iterative process of strategic and adaptive responses. The takeover guidelines, by contrast, are the result of a rapid, top-down process of law reform. The consequences of this experiment grow even harder to discern when one considers that Delaware takeover jurisprudence, consisting of loosely defined, fact-intensive standards, is indeterminate even on home soil (Kamar 1998). If, as Hansmann and Kraakman (2001, 459) argue, Delaware law in the hands of the Delaware judiciary represents one of "the more extreme forms of unpredictable ex post decision making," application of those same open-textured standards by Japanese judges, operating with different professional training in a different social and economic climate, is likely to be all the more unpredictable. At a minimum, Japanese judges can be expected to demonstrate heightened concern for takeovers that pose a threat to stable employment, given the relatively illiquid labor market and tradition of judicial activism to protect workers against discharge. Delaware law may look quite different in Tokyo than it does in Wilmington.

As with any transplant, Japanese actors are adapting Delaware legal principles to suit their own interests, and the law is malleable enough to accommodate strategic use by managers and shareholders. This phenomenon is neither unusual nor necessarily negative, but it is noteworthy. The transplanted standards are being given different interpretations depending on the interests of the interpreter. Seeking to expand the market for the poison pill in the immediate wake of the *Livedoor* ruling, some Japanese lawyers promoted the view—certainly not dictated by Delaware law—that only preplanned defenses would withstand judicial scrutiny. Legal and financial advisors in the United States—arguably big winners in the evolution of Delaware corporate law (Macey and Miller 1987)—actively promoted the takeover guidelines as the optimal means of filling the void in Japanese law exposed by the recent hostile bids. In this regard, METI's role in spearheading the formulation of guidelines that led to Japan's embrace of Delaware is also noteworthy. Although METI's initiative is consistent with its involvement in other corporate governance reforms in recent years, METI may not be the most appropriate agency to formulate a coordinated response to hostile takeovers. It has no formal jurisdiction over the corporate or securities laws, and other governmental actors such as the Financial Supervisory Agency and the Securities Exchange Surveillance Commission (a rough analogue to the SEC) seem more appropriately situated to formulate a governmental response to this policy issue. But METI is close to the corporate sector, which obviously has a direct stake in the approved defenses to hostile bids. By responding rapidly with nonbinding guidelines crafted under its auspices, in contrast to a legislative response over which it may have had little control and in which it may have had no lasting role, METI deftly ensured that it would be at the center of future developments in this important area of economic policy. It is significant, however, that thus far the Japanese courts seem inclined to stake out a key role for *themselves* as arbiters of contests for control, not unlike the Delaware courts.

Evolving Functions of Law in Japanese Capitalism

The Livedoor case and its aftermath are symptomatic of a broad shift in the use of law to support market activity in Japan. Although Japan's economic success in the twentieth century rested in part on a legal system that successfully defined and enforced property rights (Ramseyer and Nakazato 1999), the demand for formal law throughout this period was relatively low.[19] Formal rules and institutions served principally to set the basic rules for coordination among key players (Milhaupt 1996) and as endgame norms (to borrow a term from Bernstein [1996]) in the event of a breakdown in relations. Protection was obtained, in the first instance, through membership in or affiliation with groups that enjoyed market power and influence with the regulatory authorities. Credibility in the system derived not primarily from legal authority but from the elite stature and central role of the bureaucracy in overseeing economic policies and markets. Regulators typically used informal means to signal policy shifts or to obtain compliance with regulatory goals. Legal change came about slowly, and seldom in response to the exigencies of the market. For example, in the words of one scholar, much of Japanese corporate law reform in the twentieth century was "policy pushed" rather than "demand driven" (Shishido 1999, 653). In short, although law was an important background element of the governance structure, many of law's functions were supplanted by informal substitutes based on relationships, and the law-making process itself was centralized and insulated from direct private participation.

But a host of factors tied in some way to the end of high growth, including the breakdown of stable corporate alliances, the erosion of bureaucratic
prestige, and the entrance of new players into markets, have increased the
demand for law to govern relationships among market players and helped
change the process of lawmaking. The recent evolution in the composition of shareholders and patterns of share ownership in Japan is perhaps
the most visible sign of change.[20] Shareholding by financial institutions
has declined from almost 43 percent of market capitalization in the early
1990s to less than 31 percent in 2006. Within this group, shareholding
by commercial banks has declined precipitously from almost 16 percent
in 1992 to less than 5 percent in 2006. Corporate share ownership has
declined from 29 percent to 21 percent during this same period. It is noteworthy that these declines in Japanese institutional share ownership have
been completely offset by increases in foreign ownership, which rose from
about 6 percent of market capitalization in 1992 to almost 30 percent
in 2006. Virtually all of these shares are held by foreign institutional investors, many of which are known for active engagement with the managers of their portfolio firms. Equally important, shareholding patterns
have changed, with significant declines in the cross-shareholding and stable "friendly" shareholding patterns that characterized postwar corporate
ownership structures in Japan. On a value basis, the cross-shareholding
ratio declined by more than 10 percent between the early 1990s and 2002.
The long-term shareholding ratio declined by almost 20 percent during this
period.

Actors now increasingly look to the formal legal system to define and
enforce property rights protections and to supply the rules for sophisticated
market activities. Informal methods of signaling and enforcing government
policy have been extensively criticized as nontransparent, inconsistent with
Japan's economic stature, and even corrosive of Japanese democracy.[21]
As an advisory council to the prime minister put it, recent reform of the
Japanese legal system has "sought to transform the excessive [ex ante] con-
trol/adjustment type society to an [ex post] review/remedy type of society
and, in promoting decentralization, to reform the bloated administrative
system and improve the quality of governing ability . . . of the political
branches" (Justice System Reform Council 2001, 8). As a result, the production of law in Japan has become comparatively more decentralized and
competitive. More actors are involved in lawmaking, and new rules are
crafted with a view toward expanding the options of market actors rather
than imposing mandatory requirements on them (see Gilson and Milhaupt
2005).

The Livedoor bid and its aftermath are emblematic of these shifting expectations concerning the role of law in the governance of the Japanese economy. In a major departure from typical past practices, the parties extensively used new legal technology (share purchase rights) and the courts to protect their interests. From this contested transaction, new corporate law (in the form of an important judicial ruling on defensive measures) was created to help dispel market uncertainty. Even the criminal law was invoked to protect the integrity of the stock market from misleading accounting and disclosure practices. Yet the episode also illustrates the complexities inherent in the shift toward more extensive legal governance. The bureaucrats did not completely cede authority to the legal system with regard to the key policy issue of how to respond to hostile takeovers. To the contrary, they mobilized quickly to gather the views of affected parties and formulate an *informal* (not legally binding) response that would coordinate expectations and market behavior in the form of takeover guidelines. Not coincidentally, this move also kept the bureaucrats at the center of the action. And as previously discussed, the signal sent by the use of criminal law enforcement in this case is highly ambiguous: Does it indicate heightened emphasis on market transparency and rule compliance, or does it indicate that market innovators will be punished?

The final point from the Livedoor episode and surrounding developments relates specifically to the role of *corporate* law in successful economies, the subject of much theorizing spawned by the law and finance literature. The implication widely drawn from this literature is that corporate law "matters"—and matters almost exclusively—for the protections it provides to minority shareholders. Yet given the ambiguities we have seen with regard to Delaware corporate law regarding this point, the Japanese case, particularly when examined alongside Delaware's experience in the 1980s, actually suggests that the coordination function of corporate law is important to successful economies in moments of institutional transition.

At key moments in the institutional transformation of the United States and Japan, the world's two largest economies, the corporate law became the focal point for a highly iterative process of market innovation and strategic legal response. The process involved an array of actors seeking to create or adapt to new rules in the pursuit of their respective interests. Although the precise manner in which market expectations were coordinated probably differed in the two systems, a similar pattern is evident: at pivotal moments in the process, market entrepreneurs such as the hostile bidder at the center of this institutional autopsy pushed the envelope of accepted conduct, forcing the legal system to respond anew, triggering yet another round of accommodating reactions. This process was repeated until all major actors internalized a relatively stable new set of expectations about how the world works, and a new system of corporate governance took shape that better fit the new market realities. This process came to rest in the United States, relatively speaking, with the Delaware Supreme Court's approval of the "just say no" defense and the acceptance by all relevant actors of the pill in its current form. In Japan, the process of internalizing a significant new set of judicial rulings, new legal technologies such as rights plans, and non-binding guidelines supplementing the formal corporate and securities laws has begun in earnest only recently. Yet already, market expectations about what constitutes a reasonable reaction to a hostile bid and the proper role of boards, shareholders, and other actors in erecting defensive measures have been affected. Japan will find its own equilibrium point in this process of shifting expectations as it fits unfamiliar takeover jurisprudence to the dictates of its own political economy.

Conclusion

Prompted by economic distress, Japan has undergone a remarkable period of institutional change in a short period of time. Far from the "lost decade," a moniker now associated with the 1990s, that period can more properly be thought of as a "sea change decade" for Japanese law and economic institutions. Whether and how Japan will absorb all of the new legal technology that has been introduced in the recent past, and what its institutions will look like as a result, are still open questions. But there can be little doubt that the Livedoor episode and surrounding developments marked a signal moment in Japan's institutional transformation to a more contested, law-structured economy.

Horie's prosecution constitutes an ambiguous footnote to this important episode. Does it signal fortified resolve on the part of regulators to create a more transparent and robust legal environment for Japanese capital markets? Or is it retribution for rocking the boat of traditional Japanese business ethics—a sign that changes in Japan are less far-reaching than they appear on the surface?

SIX

Law, Growth, and Reform in Korea: The SK Episode

Korea is one of the great economic success stories of the twentieth century. Yet its experience with law hardly fits the rule-of-law ideal promoted in the literature. Our institutional autopsy examines the recent proxy battle for control of the board of scandal-plagued SK Corporation by Sovereign Asset Management, a foreign institutional investor. The case provides an interesting vantage point from which to examine law's role in the Korean economic miracle and in the country's ongoing struggle to reorient its governance structure in the wake of the Asian financial crisis of the late 1990s.

The Players

Korea's largest oil refiner is SK Corporation (SK), which is also the flagship company in the SK Group, Korea's third-largest *chaebol* (conglomerate). The company serves as the de facto holding company for the group. Chey Tae-Won, chairman of the board of SK and a major protagonist in our story, is the nephew of the company's founder. The SK Group grew from a company founded in 1953 called Sunkyong Textiles. In 1980, Sunkyong (which eventually changed its name to SK) was the successful bidder in the privatization of the Korean Oil Corp., creating SK. In the 1980s and 1990s, Sunkyong had expanded into telecommunications, leading eventually to the creation of SK Telecom, one of Korea's premier publicly traded firms. Another key firm in the group is SK Global, a trading company. The insolvency of SK Global and its ensuing bailout constitute a major episode in the story.

In early April 2003, Sovereign Asset Management Limited (now called Sovereign Global) acquired 14.9 percent of SK's common stock. Sovereign is a Dubai-based private investment organization that serves as the investment vehicle for two wealthy brothers from New Zealand. Sovereign had previously made major portfolio investments in the steel, oil, and telecommunications industries in transition economies, including those of Russia and Brazil. For a hardcore capitalist enterprise, Sovereign presents a somewhat offbeat image. The firm's public relations literature, in mentioning its involvement with SK, is peppered with quotations from Shakespeare, Aldous Huxley, and Malcolm X.[1] Abiding by what it calls "the Law of the Farm" (you reap what you sow), Sovereign brands itself a "Responsible Investor, caring for and nurturing the market for the good of all." This requires that Sovereign sometimes "engage unethical managements and work to remove impediments to effective capital allocation." (Sovereign Asset Management 2005). As we will see, Sovereign's attempts to apply this philosophy to SK is the central dynamic in this institutional autopsy.

The Story

Sovereign's investment in SK coincided with the emergence of a major scandal in the SK Group brought on by the arrest in early 2003 of Chey Tae-Won and other SK executives on charges of accounting fraud, falsifying financial disclosures, and breach of fiduciary duty. The charges stemmed from several intragroup transactions dating from 1999 to 2002. The first involved improper share trading among member firms. Together with his family, Chey owns about 1 percent of the stock of SK. As an inheritance from his uncle, the founder of the SK Group, Chey also owns 44.5 percent of SK C&C, which in turn owns 11.17 percent of SK. Fair Trade Act limitations on investment in affiliated corporations threatened to restrict the ability of SK C&C to exercise its voting rights in SK. To find a way around the limitations, SK C&C exchanged shares in SK for overvalued privately held shares of Walker Hill, a hotel under Chey's control. Chey and several executives at SK C&C were convicted of breach of fiduciary duty in connection with the transfer. In the second episode, SK Securities and SK Global engaged in undisclosed derivatives transactions with JP Morgan designed to recoup large trading losses sustained by SK Securities. The transactions ultimately imposed losses of $88 million on SK affiliates. Chey and other executives were found guilty of breach of fiduciary duty in connection with these transactions. Finally, Chey and other executives were convicted of accounting fraud for misstating SK Global's 2001 earnings by 1.6 trillion won (about $1.4 billion). Chey received a three-year prison sentence. After serving seven months of the sentence, Chey was freed on bail and returned to the helm at SK.

After Chey was indicted for the accounting and share transfer scandals, the share price of most SK affiliates, including SK, plummeted. The latter's share price fell to an eighteen-year low. At the height of the turmoil in March and April 2003, Sovereign, through an affiliate called Crest Securities, acquired 14.9 percent of the shares of SK[2] and immediately began a campaign to remove Chey from the board and operate SK independent of the group's other firms. Sovereign explained its actions by arguing that "Korea's history of poor corporate governance is undermining its ability to attract the low-cost capital and investment necessary for long-term prosperity." Moreover, SK had "a unique opportunity to change investor perceptions of Korea and make the country's aspirations to join the club of first-world nations a reality."[3] Consistent with Sovereign's philosophy, it cast the campaign to oust Chey and chart an independent path for SK in historic terms: "The SK story is a landmark case for Korea. All of the challenges and opportunities that Korea faces in attracting investment and building a prosperous capital market are reflected in the SK story. If Korea is going to fulfill its vision of joining the club of first world nations . . . then it must build a reputation based on good corporate governance, shareholder rights, professional banking practices and free market principles. SK, having attracted considerable international attention, provides a good place to start. As goes SK, so goes Korea" (Sovereign Asset Management Limited 2003, 25).

Shortly after Sovereign became SK's largest shareholder, a controversial transaction took place that greatly exacerbated tensions between the foreign and the domestic investors. To calm the storm created by Chey's arrest, SK's directors issued a press release in March 2003 committing the firm to world-class corporate governance and promising not to provide unreasonable support to any companies that were related to SK Group, including SK Global. Despite this statement, in July 2003, SK and a group of Korean banks agreed to a multi-billion-dollar bailout of SK's deeply troubled and insolvent affiliate, SK Global. (Recall that accounting fraud at SK Global was one of the charges of which Chey had been convicted.) The creditor banks swapped debt for equity and rescheduled 4.2 trillion won (about $4 billion) of SK Global debt. The workout cost SK 1 trillion won (almost $1 billion). The agreement ignited a firestorm of controversy with Sovereign and an allied foreign institutional investor, Hermes Investment Management. Sovereign and Hermes demanded a halt to SK's support for ailing affiliates. Despite the demands, in December SK announced that it would lend 143 billion won (about $143 million) to another ailing affiliate, SK Shipping, which was embroiled in a political slush fund controversy. The stock of SK fell by 8 percent after the announcement.

In the face of the foreign shareholder insurgency, SK devised a plan to sell treasury shares carrying 10.4 percent of the voting power to the same group of banks that had arranged the rescue of SK Global.[4] The banks pledged to vote the shares to prevent a management change at SK's March 2004 shareholders' meeting. Sovereign sued to enjoin the plan, arguing that "[a]ny endeavor by the company to sell the shares in a closed manner which favours a preferred group of outside buyers to the exclusion of the existing shareholders would be a blatant breach of globally accepted standards of corporate governance" (Nam 2003, n.p.). The Seoul District Court, however, did not agree. The court allowed the share issuance to go forward, ruling that, "faced with Sovereign's possible takeover, the decision by SK's board, which was made to defend its management control, is legitimate."[5]

In January 2004 Sovereign launched a proxy contest in connection with the March 2004 shareholders' meeting, at which six directors were to be elected. Sovereign advanced a slate of five new independent, nonexecutive directors. In particular, Sovereign hoped to mobilize SK's other foreign shareholders, who collectively owned 42.3 percent of the outstanding shares (down from 46.9 percent as a result of the sale of treasury shares to the banks). Sovereign also sought various amendments to SK's articles of incorporation, including a prohibition (obviously aimed at Chey) against board service by anyone convicted of a serious crime, establishment of cumulative voting for directors, and the creation of a special board committee to approve related-party transactions.

In response, SK organized a plan of resistance to Sovereign's proxy contest. A variety of Korean firms, including Samsung Electronics and Korean Investment and Trust Management Company, purchased SK stock and pledged their support for Chey. A few days before the annual meeting, thirty-four of thirty-six domestic institutional shareholders in SK rejected the independent directors nominated by Sovereign. Perhaps fearing layoffs if the company ended up under foreign investors' control, SK's labor union sided with Chey. At the same time, SK made several concessions to foreign shareholders in the weeks leading up to the shareholders' meeting. It agreed to replace several officers who, despite having been convicted of breach of fiduciary duty in connection with the SK Global accounting scandal, had remained on SK's board. The company also agreed to increase the number of outside directors to seven from five. Meanwhile, Chey resigned from the board of SK Telecom, whose largest shareholder is SK. This may have constituted a small victory for Sovereign, but it was widely viewed as a gambit to undermine support for Sovereign's insurgency (Song 2004).

At the March 2004 shareholders' meeting, shareholders rejected Sovereign's nominees (who needed to obtain a majority of the vote), leaving Chey in control of the board.[6] Sovereign's shareholder proposals, which garnered majority support, were not adopted for failure to obtain the required two-thirds vote. Following the meeting, SK's board of directors refused to call an extraordinary shareholders meeting requested by Sovereign to obtain a vote ousting Chey from the board. Sovereign filed a suit challenging the decision, but in December 2004, the Seoul District Court rejected Sovereign's complaint. The court ruled that although Sovereign had the legal right to call an extraordinary meeting, because "continuous instability with respect to the management right might bring about the departure of investors and cause the investment value to decline," no extraordinary meeting should be held in order to ensure "management stability at least until the annual general shareholders meeting next year." In the course of its reasoning, the court implied that the exercise of minority shareholders' rights by corporate (as opposed to individual) shareholders deserves special scrutiny because "there is a high probability of sacrificing the interests of the corporation, whose stock it holds, for its own benefit."[7]

Sovereign continued its battle in the early part of 2005, running advertisements in local newspapers advocating a change in SK's management. In February SK's board rejected Sovereign's request to resubmit the agenda of the 2004 annual shareholders' meeting to the shareholders at the 2005 meeting. The board also highlighted the fact that there were now seven independent directors on the company's board as well as other corporate governance improvements. At the March 2005 shareholders' meeting, the first time Chey faced election since receiving his jail term, he received 55.3 percent of the vote.

In May the Seoul High Court affirmed the lower court's ruling denying Sovereign the opportunity to call an extraordinary meeting. The High Court ruled that Sovereign's request constituted an "abuse of right" because shareholders had already rejected Sovereign's agenda, and holding an extraordinary meeting so soon after the annual meeting could harm SK by creating a dispute over management control.[8] In June 2005 the Seoul High Court upheld Chey's conviction but suspended the sentence for five years. Chey was free to continue serving as SK's chairman. This ruling appeared to be the last straw for Sovereign. It declared SK's failure to reform "a national tragedy."[9] The following month, Sovereign sold its entire stake in SK. The struggle for control of the board of SK had come to an end.[10]

The SK Scandal in the Context of Korean Capitalism

Underlying the SK scandal is the problematic characteristic of Korean corporate ownership structures: a huge disparity between cash flow rights and voting rights. According to a study by the Korean Fair Trade Commission, as of 2005 there were thirty-eight business groups with more than 2 trillion won in assets each, which we will refer to for convenience as Article 9 groups.[11] Article 9 groups are subject to a prohibition on cross-shareholding and cross-debt guarantees. As of 2005, there were nine groups with more than 5 trillion won in assets, which we will refer to as Article 10 groups. These are prohibited from investing more than 25 percent of their assets in another Korean company, regardless of whether the other firm is an affiliate or lies outside the group. In Article 9 groups, owner families held an average of 4.94 percent of the outstanding shares but controlled the group via cross- and circular shareholding. In Article 10 groups, owner families held 4.64 percent of the outstanding shares. The average controlling shareholder in an Article 9 group held 9.13 percent of the cash flow rights but 40.33 percent of the voting rights. The average controlling shareholder in an Article 10 group held 6.49 percent of the cash flow rights and 41.73 percent of the voting rights. The study found that most groups with more than 6 trillion won in assets solidify control via circular equity linkages among affiliates. The SK Group provides an illustration. To take only one example, SK (publicly listed) held about 21 percent of the shares of SK Telecom (also publicly listed). The latter held 30 percent of the shares of SK C&C, a private company, which in turn held about 11 percent of the shares of SK. Figure 6.1 illustrates the tangled web of share ownership within the SK Group.

Among the Korean chaebol, at the time of this episode SK had the third-largest discrepancy between cash flow rights and voting rights. Controlling shareholders held 2.15 percent of cash flow rights and 34 percent of the voting rights. Chey Tae-Won owned only 0.6 percent of the shares of SK (about 1 percent if shares held by family members are included), yet he was able to effectively control the entire SK Group via circular and pyramidal share ownership structures. For example, together with his family, Chey owned 55 percent of the stock of SK C&C, which owned 11.17 percent of the stock of SK. And as noted above, control of SK constitutes de facto control over the entire group, because SK holds major stakes in the group's other publicly traded firms such as SK Telecom, SK Networks, and SKC. These firms, in turn, control many other affiliates, and—completing the ownership loop—hold significant stakes in SK or SK C&C.

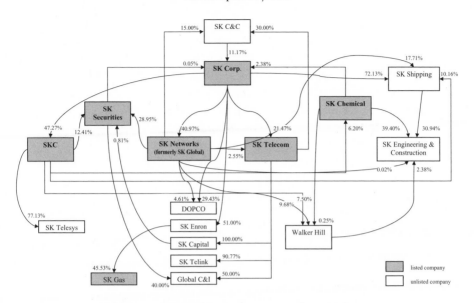

Figure 6.1. SK Group's ownership structure as of 1 November 2005
Source: Based on data disclosed in SK Corporation, Quarterly Report—Third
Quarter of 2005 (18 November). http:dart.fss.or.kr.
Note: Less significant subsidiaries without cross-shareholdings are excluded.
The SK Group is comprised of fifty-three affiliated companies.

As is now widely discussed in the literature, the separation of cash
flow and voting rights in this type of structure creates enormous potential
for exploitation of minority investors by controlling shareholders. Indeed,
the transactions leading to Chey's arrest and conviction, as well as the SK
Global bailout, are all textbook illustrations of "shareholder tunneling," the
label now attached to controlling shareholder exploitation (Johnson et al.
2000). This separation (together with the historically dominant position of
the founder and his heirs in Korean *chaebol*) facilitated manipulation of the
terms under which Chey swapped shares to avoid investment limitations,
allowed the balance sheet of SK Securities to be cleansed by imposing trading losses on other affiliates, and permitted SK's shareholders to shoulder
the cost of the SK Global workout, which prevented Chey from defaulting
on a personal guarantee. Similar problems at other *chaebol* gave rise to the
so called Korea Discount, a substantial market discount applied by minority investors to the shares of publicly traded firms. The Korean Discount
reflects the hazards inherent in minority ownership so vividly illustrated
by the SK episode.

Today, it is academically fashionable to view the *chaebol* simply as vehicles for the exploitation of minority shareholders. As we have noted,

scholars have extensively analyzed the shareholder tunneling problem. They emphasize the "private benefits of control" that account for the disparity in value between control shares and noncontrol shares in societies such as Korea with pyramidal share structures. And they argue that the persistence of corporate groups such as the *chaebol* is the result of weak investor protection laws. If investor protections are weak, the argument goes, controllers will not offer control blocks for sale because they fear exploitation themselves once they have become minority shareholders.[12]

Yet in order to better understand what the SK episode may tell us about law, capitalism, and the effects of globalization in Korea and to put the "*chaebol* problem" into context, we must turn the clock back four decades. The modern corporate governance literature's emphasis on agency costs overlooks a crucial point: as exemplified by the Korean case, corporate groups such as the *chaebol* provided a mechanism for rapid economic development in many countries throughout the twentieth century.

Although it is almost impossible to fathom today, in the early 1970s it was an open question whether the North Korean or the South Korean economy had more potential. In 1965, annual per capita income in South Korea was $100. By the mid-1990s, that figure reached $10,000 (Organization for Economic Cooperation and Development 2004, 23), and South Korea is now the world's eleventh-largest economy. The Korean model of development featured authoritarian political rule coupled with a small number of highly diversified business groups under the control of the founding entrepreneur. Government-directed capital allocations (called "policy loans") ensured a supply of capital to favored entrepreneurs and industries. The government's control over resource allocation provided the means to discipline large firms to pursue its development objectives and limited opportunistic behavior. Once this pattern of interaction got under way, the state and the *chaebol* became locked in a mutually interdependent relationship, for which continued growth was essential. The results for both the Korean economy and the *chaebol* were dramatic: by the early 1980s, per capita income had reached $2,000, and sales of South Korea's five largest groups accounted for 50 percent of GNP and employed almost half a million workers (Fields 1997).

Law and legal institutions, at least as conventionally understood, played a very small role in Korea's astonishing economic growth during this period. Beginning with Park Chung Hee, who ruled from 1961 until his assassination in 1979, a series of authoritarian rulers created an informal institutional structure to grow the economy. Park trained in a Japanese military academy during Japan's colonial occupation of Korea and looked to the Japanese postwar growth model as a template for Korea (Lee 2005). But to a greater extent than postwar Japan, Korea relied on alliances between powerful political leaders and a small number of *chaebol* entrepreneurs to bring the economy out of the devastation of war. The state provided subsidized credit from state-owned banks, lucrative licenses to engage in strategic industrial sectors, and labor repression to ensure industrial peace and low wages. The *chaebol* responded to market-oriented growth incentives provided by the state while simultaneously being protected from a variety of market risks that ordinarily attend expansion into new industrial sectors, such as insolvency, labor strife, and minority shareholder complaints (Lee 2005).

In the 1970s, in order to foster a capital market and a more open economy, the government pushed several of the largest *chaebol* to issue shares to the public. But legal structures for supporting minority shareholders were not developed in tandem with this policy, in part because strong investor protections would have worked at cross purposes with the drive to encourage *chaebol* founders to part with minority stakes.[13] Although capital market discipline in the form of shareholder pressure and takeovers was weak, Korean firms had to learn to compete in highly competitive international product markets, and the state disciplined the *chaebol* politically. In one instance, the government essentially launched a hostile takeover for a *chaebol* (the Kukje group) that had fallen into financial distress. The government dried up sources of credit for the group and eventually dismantled it, transferring assets to more politically favored business groups. The actions were justified by the government on the grounds that the group's management was ineffective and the assets could be more effectively utilized by others.[14]

To be sure, the legal environment was not irrelevant to the rise of the *chaebol*. For example, prohibitions against holding companies, intended to discourage close ties between financial institutions and industrial concerns, led to more complex schemes of corporate ownership among *chaebol* firms and the emergence of de facto holding companies such as SK.[15] Legal limitations on cross-shareholding arrangements had a similar effect, leading to complex webs of circular share ownership. Sometimes law was used to buttress political agendas. One example is the 1961 "Special Law for Dealing with Illicit Wealth Accumulation," which subjected businessmen to arrest and confiscation of their assets for engaging in corrupt activities under the prior political regime. The law, which was apparently never strictly enforced, was nonetheless used to bring the *chaebol* leaders into a more subservient position vis-à-vis the military regime and to provide the government with leverage to ensure private-sector investment in high-priority industries (see Lee [1997, 25]). In fact, selective enforcement of laws that are not widely enforced has been a common mechanism for disciplining the *chaebol* throughout the high-growth period. The tax laws are often used in this way. The absence of law was also relevant to the rise of the *chaebol*. In the absence of better investor protections and without access to private financial intermediaries, the *chaebol* were forced to deal extensively with the government, particularly for access to capital. This left them highly susceptible to government influence, but it also created a partnership between government and a small number of favored businessmen, who profited handsomely from government protection, licenses, and favors. In short, the *chaebol* can be viewed as a rational adaptation to the institutional environment in existence in Korea from the 1960s to 1990s (Milhaupt 1998).

Economic growth, in turn, provided legitimacy to the government and muted criticism of the *chaebol* owners' accumulation of wealth and power. As in present-day China, not only did rapid economic growth take place without much support from the formal legal system, but rapid growth itself contributed to a delay in the formation of a more robust legal system.[16] As in Japan, the success of the informal, relationship-based governance structures created little demand for development of a large, formal legal apparatus. Indeed, a more robust legal system would have been perceived as threatening to big business.

The corporate governance organs and enforcement mechanisms contemplated by the corporate law, which were not well attuned to corporate group structures, did not operate effectively in Korea. For example, boards of directors were essentially beholden to the founder of the *chaebol*. In many cases, board meetings of affiliated companies were not even held; minutes were drafted by a central planning office (Kim 2005). Similarly, an internal statutory auditor system designed to monitor directors' compliance with law (a transplantation of the German supervisory board filtered through Japan) did not operate effectively as a check on management. Loyalty to the founder was rewarded in a variety of ways, and the lack of an active market for managerial talent reinforced allegiance to the group. By contrast, directors and auditors felt little accountability toward shareholders. The corporate law itself may have contributed to this phenomenon. The threshold for exercise of shareholders' rights was high, making it virtually impossible for minority investors to challenge director conduct. Until 1997 there was no derivative litigation in Korea, so the duties of directors and auditors specified in the corporate law were entirely abstract,[17] so abstract that Korea had no market for director and officer liability insurance until recently (ibid.). Under these circumstances, political constraints served as important checks on the unbridled authority of controlling shareholders.

Korea began instituting macroeconomic reforms in the late 1980s. Fuelling the reform movement, President Kim Young Sam in 1993 endorsed a plan to enter the Organization for Economic Cooperation and Development (OECD), which Korea joined in 1996. But the reforms accomplished up to that point were not thorough or penetrating. Korea opened itself to global capital markets with an institutional structure still beset by structural problems: labor market rigidities, complex and opaque corporate governance structures, and highly leveraged firms that were reliant on subsidized credit.

The weak institutional structure underpinning Korea's *chaebol*-led economic success was exposed in the 1997 Asian financial crisis. Korea in many respects became the poster child for the emphasis of the so-called Washington Consensus on corporate and bankruptcy law reform, transparency, capital market development, and best practices in corporate governance.[18] The *chaebol*, whose relations with the government and the Korean public had always been stormy, suddenly faced their most serious challenge since President Park's attacks on them in the 1960s. Toleration of the *chaebol* as crucial, if problematic, engines of economic growth increasingly gave way to hostility toward the groups as black boxes of agency costs that perpetuate nontransparent business practices, poor corporate governance, and exploitation of minority shareholders. Today's negative academic perspective on business groups, as epitomized by the *chaebol*, is a direct result of the fallout from the Asian financial crisis.

In response, a host of legal reforms were enacted in Korea. These include an express codification of the fiduciary duty of corporate directors, imposition of liability on controlling shareholders who participate in the conduct of the business, enhanced enforcement efforts against *chaebol* insiders for improper intragroup transactions, and the rise, for the first time in Korean history, of shareholder derivative litigation against corporate directors (see Kim and Kim 2003). Other reforms imposed a requirement of outside directors for publicly traded firms, reduced the threshold for exercise of shareholders rights, and restricted intragroup transactions. The government also waged a concerted campaign to reduce debt levels and cross-guarantees in the large groups.

Alongside these legal reforms, shareholder activism, led by a number of nonprofit organizations concerned with corporate governance and anticorruption efforts, began to grow early in the twenty-first century (see

Milhaupt 2004). These organizations purchased publicly traded shares in *chaebol*-owned firms deemed to have problematic corporate governance in order to exercise the newly invigorated legal protections for minority investors. The first derivative suits in Korean history were brought and won by these organizations.

Partly in response to these reforms, the corporate sector has evolved substantially since the 1997 crisis. Seventeen of the top thirty *chaebol* entered bankruptcy or workout procedures. The surviving *chaebol* reduced their debt levels significantly. Debt-to-equity ratios fell from 500 percent at the time of the crisis to 116 percent in 2004 (Organization for Economic Cooperation and Development 2004, 105). Together with the increased commercial orientation of the financial sector, the Korean economy is much closer to a market-oriented model today than it was a decade ago. Law, in particular the concept of fiduciary duty, has begun to infuse the relations between managers and minority investors (Kim and Kim 2003).

The SK scandal, coming in the wake of these extensive reforms, called into question the extent to which Korean corporate governance practices and institutional structures had actually been improved. As the OECD commented, "[t]he financial health of the corporate sector has improved markedly since the crisis, while the legal framework for corporate governance and auditing has been upgraded. However, as the SK Global scandal demonstrated, there is still a lack of enforcement of the new framework and transparency is weak" (Organization for Economic Cooperation and Development 2004, 126).

The Response

The SK scandal had two seemingly contradictory effects on Korean institutional development. The scandal provided further momentum to the reform movement that began in the aftermath of the Asian financial crisis. Yet it simultaneously stirred a nationalist backlash and retrenchment that may have slowed efforts to deal with the *chaebol* problem. As we will see, however, these opposing trends are quite consistent with the pattern of legal reform in Korea since the beginning of the period of rapid economic growth.

Despite the reforms enacted after the Asian financial crisis, Chey was able to exploit group shareholding structures to his own benefit at the expense of outside investors, even a "minority" investor such as Sovereign that controlled the largest block of SK stock. The scandal added momentum to a series of reforms in Korea based on the Sarbanes-Oxley Act in the

United States: CEOs and CFOs of publicly traded companies are required to personally certify the accuracy of financial statements. Large corporations must have an audit committee of the board. At least one member of the audit committee must have professional accounting knowledge, and two-thirds of the committee must be made up of outside members. The outside auditor must be changed at least every six years to ensure its independence. Outside auditors are prohibited from providing nonaudit services if doing so is likely to create a conflict of interest, and outside directors must account for a majority of the board for listed companies of more than 2 trillion won. Class-action securities litigation was introduced in 2005 for large firms and became available for all stock exchange–listed firms in 2007.[19] Moreover, SK itself introduced a number of corporate governance reforms, including increasing the number of independent directors on its board and establishing a "transparent management committee" in an effort to strengthen the supervisory function of the board. Korean observers credit Sovereign's activism in part for motivating these reforms (for example, Lee 2005).

But the SK scandal also had precisely the opposite effect: motivating legal changes that undid some of the reforms enacted after the Asian financial crisis. The episode indicated to some observers (or at least was portrayed as indicating) that law and corporate governance reform can undermine the formula for Korea's economic success. Throughout the struggle for control of the SK board, editorials warned that although it is important to curb arbitrary *chaebol* expansion and enhance corporate transparency, reformers should not lose sight of the role of the *chaebol* in the national economy. The equity ceiling limitations in particular drew criticism as a form of "reverse discrimination" against Korean firms, exposing them to foreign takeover. The separation of voting rights and control rights that animates the *chaebol* structure ironically also makes the typical *chaebol* vulnerable to takeover by an outside investor. As Sovereign demonstrated, by acquiring a stake in a firm such as SK that serves as a de facto holding company for the group, it is at least theoretically possible to obtain control of the entire group with a relatively modest amount of capital. Korean editorials emphasized this point as soon as the news broke that SK shares had been purchased by Sovereign. For example, in April 2003 Korea's leading business daily argued that Korean companies are vulnerable to "attack" by foreign funds owing to the government's policy against *chaebol* expansion in the name of market-oriented reform (SK, woi "gieop sanyanggam" dwoina? 2003). This stance was consistent with the subsequent media portrayal of the episode, which emphasized that improving corporate governance and transparency is a questionable goal if it risks foreign takeover of Korean companies.[20]

Given this climate, it is not surprising that the struggle for control of the SK board resulted in the passage of rules that strengthen the legal defenses available to incumbent management, turning back earlier reforms designed to foster a market for corporate control. The Securities Exchange Act was amended to expand the disclosure obligations of 5 percent shareholders of public companies, effective in 2005. The original rule, modeled after Regulation 13D of the U.S. securities laws, had required the beneficial owner of more than 5 percent of the shares of a public company to disclose its identity and holdings. The amendment requires investors to disclose their investment intentions—in particular, whether they plan to "influence" management—and applies criminal sanctions for violations.[21] Implementing regulations define this rather vague term as "de facto influence on the company or its directors" including influence via the exercise of ordinary minority shareholders rights such as submitting shareholder proposals or requesting an extraordinary meeting.[22] In addition, tender offer regulations were amended to strengthen incumbent management's defenses against hostile bids. The amendment allows corporations to issue new shares even after a tender offer for the corporation's shares has been commenced.[23] Because the new shares will dilute the holdings of the bidder, the amendment can be viewed as validating a type of poison pill defense. The amendment was justified as a means of alleviating the excessive threat to management posed by hostile takeover attempts. Moreover, a graduated phaseout of the ceiling on equity investment in affiliates, the rule blamed for effecting reverse discrimination against the *chaebol*, was introduced for firms that meet specified criteria indicating improved corporate governance. Regulators also announced heightened supervision to prevent unfair practices by foreign capital investors.

So the SK saga ended ambiguously for Korea. The company itself appears to have responded to the discipline of the capital market—facilitated in part by recent legal reforms enhancing the rights of minority shareholders—by improving its corporate governance practices to some extent. The episode also seems to have lent momentum to further corporate law reforms in the style of Sarbanes-Oxley. Even if our analysis of the U.S. law is accurate in that the provisions per se do little to enhance investor protection, passage of the reforms in Korea signals continued governmental concern about governance practices at the *chaebol*. Yet the legal reforms of the takeover regime palpably strengthen the hand of incumbent management vis-à-vis investors and help defend the *chaebol* structure from outside attack.

Evaluation

The Korean case vividly illustrates a major theme of our book: that the relation between law and economic growth is much more dynamic and complex than the conventional wisdom suggests. Growth in Korea was not a result of the state's establishing legal property rights protections and then letting entrepreneurs and markets flourish. "Economically benevolent dictators" provided substitutes for legal institutions during the formative period of economic development (Gilson and Milhaupt 2008). Park and his successors provided credibility, coordination, a degree of property rights protection (at least with respect to potential competitors, if not always with respect to the state itself), and a political signal of the paramount goal of economic growth. These policies helped bridge the institutional gap between a desperately poor economy based on local reputation and relationships to a system capable of competing on a global scale. During this crucial transition, demand for the formation of legal institutions to support market activity was kept low, both by the structure of interactions between the state and the private sector (which internalized many of the functions typically performed by legal institutions in developed economies) and by straightforward political economy considerations: greater legal rights for investors and other corporate stakeholders could destabilize a system that was providing legitimacy to elite actors in society and growing the economy at a rapid rate.

The protective function of law developed much later, when the informal governance system became inconsistent with Korea's international economic aspirations and domestic political climate. Demand for law, most saliently investor protections in our example, grew only after the underpinnings of the high-growth bargain had been severely cracked by external forces (the Asian financial crisis), social transformations (the rise of civil society and greater political openness), and rising awareness of the economic cost of the status quo (the Korea Discount). Even now, investor protections remain somewhat underdeveloped. The judicial treatment of Sovereign's petition for an extraordinary meeting is one example. Although Sovereign plainly had a legal right to call such a meeting under the terms of the corporate code, the High Court used a separate legal doctrine—the abuse-of-right principle prevalent in civil-law jurisdictions—to refuse Sovereign's request in the interest of management stability.

This example raises a fundamental point about the protective function of law that highlights the political economy perspective: law protects, but in complex economies there are multiple and often conflicting interests vying for protection. Almost inevitably, producers of law make choices that affect these interests differently. Thus, the protective function of law has the potential to stymie economic growth and adaptation as well as promote it.

As the episode also illustrates, legal reform contains a deeply embedded irony. Legal processes can be used by challengers such as nonprofit good-governance organizations or foreign investors to confront entrenched players and practices. But by definition, legal processes are also available to incumbents, who can use the newly created legal mechanisms to defend the status quo, as the *chaebol* skillfully did to secure greater legal protection from hostile takeovers following Sovereign's insurgency. Apparently neutral rules that constitute "best practices" in the abstract (such as public disclosure requirements for large shareholders) can be used to handicap outsiders. Paradoxically, then, a move to more accessible and transparent legal processes can have the effect of locking the existing interest group structure in place.

Foreign observers have been critical of the backsliding on institutional reform suggested by the SK scandal and its aftermath. One knowledgeable observer sums up the sentiment: "Nearly a decade after the financial crisis, the Korean economy seemingly has not escaped the clutches of a model formulated two generations ago under very different circumstances."[24] Yet the seemingly contradictory responses to the SK episode have been recurring features of Korean institutional reform for the past several decades. Regimes subsequent to Park Chung Hee's "have all reneged on early promises of taming the *chaebol* and have pursued pro-growth strategies relying on the *chaebol* as the engines of that growth" (Fields 1997, 128). The reason for this pattern is evident in the SK episode: there is both a political economic logic and a legal logic in the continued power of the *chaebol* in the Korean system.

SEVEN

The China Aviation Oil Episode: Law and Development in China and Singapore

China is the latest and biggest of the economic miracles. Since its market opening in 1978, the Chinese economy has grown at an average annual rate of almost 10 percent, lifting perhaps hundreds of millions of people out of poverty. It accomplished this without a legal system that meets conventional notions of functionality and predictability. Surely the experience of China can tell us a great deal about the relation between law and economic development.

This institutional autopsy begins with the collapse of a company called China Aviation Oil (CAO), which was listed on the Singapore stock exchange (hereinafter SGX) but controlled by a mainland Chinese holding company with close ties to the state. The events of interest are not the problems that triggered the collapse of CAO but what these problems—and the parent company's response—reveal about the governance structure of Chinese state-controlled firms. The response included the sale of a substantial block of CAO shares owned by the parent company in an off-exchange placement to raise capital for a bailout of CAO—without accurately disclosing the financial status of CAO or the reasons for the share placement. Also heavily involved in the episode are Singaporean financial regulators and Temasek Holdings, a Singaporean state-owned investment company (hereinafter Temasek). Thus, the CAO case also provides an interesting perspective on the role of law in Singapore, one of the "Asian tigers." Singapore's model of law and growth, in turn, raises tantalizing suggestions for China as it continues to reform its legal and economic structures.

The Story

On 29 November 2004, CAO announced that it had suffered losses of US$550 million in oil derivatives trading and sought bankruptcy protection from its creditors in Singapore. Singapore's Securities Investor Association called the event a corporate governance disaster comparable to an earthquake registering 7 to 8 on the Richter scale and likened the incident to the collapse of Barings after the revelation of massive rogue trading losses, also incurred in derivatives trading in Singapore.[1]

The tale of massive derivative losses stemming from misguided trading strategies is a familiar one around the world. Less commonplace is the origin and ownership structure of CAO. The firm was formed in Singapore in 1993 as a joint venture between the China Aviation Oil Supply Corporation (CAOSC), the China Foreign Trade Transportation Corporation, and Singapore-based Neptune Orient Lines. In 1995 the company became a wholly owned subsidiary of CAOSC. In June 1997, the Chinese executive Chen Jiulin was appointed managing director and chief executive officer of CAO. He reinvigorated the firm, which had been dormant, and resumed its operations as an oil-trading company. The Singapore government granted CAO a preferential tax rate on income generated through oil trading in 1998, the first year in which it reported profits. In December 2001, CAO launched an initial public offering in which 25 percent of its shares were sold to the public, and the shares were listed on the main board of the SGX. The successful IPO brought the company gross proceeds of S$80.6 million (US$44.8 million). Company information disclosed at the time stated that the main business of CAO consisted of jet fuel procurement, international oil trading, and oil-related investment. In February 2002, CAO was ranked by the Singapore-based *Business Times* as the top company listed on the Singapore exchange in 2001.

Beginning in early 2003, the company began to diversify from oil trading into derivatives trading. This decision was apparently not shared with or approved by the company's board. PricewaterhouseCoopers (PwC), the auditing firm asked to investigate the matter on behalf of the SGX, concluded in its report that there was "no evidence" that CAO received formal approval from its board when it began options trading in March 2003 "without fully appreciating the risks associated with the instrument."[2] The lack of experience and expertise and the absence of effective oversight allowed CAO to fall prey to its initial success in derivatives trading. The first transaction, a bet on declining oil prices, occurred in the fall of 2003. After this trade proved to be profitable, CAO launched an aggressive and ultimately disastrous strategy of betting against the market, predicting that oil prices would continue to fall. But the price of oil reached a series of new highs. By the first quarter of 2004, the company faced losses of US$5.8 million, which breached CAO's internal trading loss limits. Rather than writing off the loss and correcting its strategy, CAO increased its bet on declining oil prices.

While the company was reporting record profits to investors for the second quarter of 2004 (48.6 percent year-on-year growth), it was piling up additional derivatives trading losses and had to respond to a series of margin calls by counterparties to the derivatives transactions. The losses continued throughout the fall but were suppressed in the company's financials. By October 2004, CAO's total position reached 52 million barrels at a time when oil prices reached a historic (nominal) level of US$55 per barrel.[3] Late in the month the counterparties to the derivative transactions began closing out their trades with CAO. Between October 29 and November 24 alone, margin calls amounted to US$247.5 million. On November 13, CAO released its third-quarter financials, which showed an unprecedented 15 percent decline in earnings. The company attributed the drop in part to losses in derivatives trading but did not disclose the amount of the losses. A few days later it publicly announced that it was ceasing speculative trading and would close out all positions by the end of the month. Trading losses subsequently reached US$381 million. On November 29, 2004 CAO filed for court protection from creditors.

Up to this point, the CAO episode is an all-too-familiar story of a company's rise and fall as a result of a poor business decision, greatly aggravated by ill-conceived attempts to recoup and then conceal the ensuing damage. One major aspect of the episode, however, distinguishes this from similar events: CAO's relationship to its parent company, CAOSC, a Chinese state-owned company affiliated with China's Civil Aviation Administration. After the initial public offering of CAO shares, CAOSC transferred the remaining 75 percent stake in CAO to China Aviation Oil Holding Company (CAOHC), established in the restructuring of China's aviation sector. Shares of CAOHC are held by state-owned enterprises in the aviation industry. According to CAO's 2003 annual report, its twenty largest shareholders included CAOHC, with 75 percent, and nineteen others (including Singapore subsidiaries of Citibank and HSBC), each holding an average of 0.82 percent, and none more than 1.78 percent, of the shares.[4] The high dispersion of the publicly traded shares left little doubt that CAOHC controlled CAO. How closely the parent monitored CAO's operations is not clear. What is apparent, however, is that CAOHC learned of CAO's financial difficulties before any of the other shareholders or prospective investors learned of them. In early October 2004, CEO Chen Jiulin turned to the parent company for assistance. According to Chen, he sought support for a possible rescue by British Petroleum or a cash infusion by the parent itself. But CAOHC rejected both proposals.

In order to rescue the company, CAOHC asked other investors to facilitate a bailout. This move is not uncommon in China but is sanctioned as insider trading and securities fraud in Singapore and many other developed market economies. The parent company decided to sell 15 percent of its stake in CAO through a block trade on the market, a strategy that did not require full disclosure of CAO's financial statements at the time of the placement.[5] The sale, which generated S$185 million (US$108 million) in proceeds, was conducted on 20 October at a 14 percent discount off the previously quoted market price. The proceeds went directly from the parent to CAO in the form of a loan to meet its trading partners' margin calls.

The placement was underwritten by Deutsche Bank. Some business reports voiced skepticism about the quality of Deutsche Bank's due diligence process, which may have been compromised by its eagerness to establish itself as a major player in Asian markets. But there is also evidence that the documents it reviewed were forged by Chen in a scheme to defraud Deutsche Bank.[6]

The sale was conducted a little more than a month before CAO filed for bankruptcy protection. The share placement triggered an investigation against CAOHC by the Singaporean authorities after CAO had filed for bankruptcy. On August 19, 2005, CAOHC admitted to civil liability for contravening section 218(2)(a) of Singapore's Securities and Futures Act (SFA)[7] and paid a civil penalty of S$8 million (US$4.4 million) to the financial regulatory authorities without court action. While accepting responsibility for violating Singaporean laws and regulations prohibiting insider trading, CAOHC submitted that the placement of CAO's shares in October 2004 "was not motivated by a desire to trade on inside information but to rescue CAO from its financial crisis." It also agreed to transfer to minority shareholders of CAO the shares in CAO that it was to receive under a debt-equity swap that was agreed to by CAO's commercial creditors.[8]

This was the first time a Chinese state-owned company had ever been penalized by Singaporean authorities. The official announcement of the civil penalty enforcement stated that CAOHC had placed CAO's shares on the market "while being in possession of material price sensitive information concerning the financial condition of CAO that was not generally available."[9] Apparently, CAOHC's stated motivation of rescuing CAO was recognized as a mitigating circumstance by the Monetary Authority of Singapore (MAS).

Key Players and Their Strategies

The massive trading losses that brought down CAO suggest major oversight and compliance problems within the firm. We analyze the source of these corporate governance problems below, but the aspect of the episode that is most revealing is what transpired after CAO's problems became apparent. Thus, we focus our analysis on the rescue attempt by CAOHC, the fallout from this rescue attempt, and the ensuing restructuring of CAO, CAOHC, and the Chinese aviation fuel industry. Three groups of players are at the core of our analysis: the primary protagonists, CAO and CAOHC and their respective leaders, Chen Jiulin and Jia Chiabing; the Singapore regulators and enforcement authorities; and, perhaps most important, the actors behind the scenes—the Chinese political authorities who oversaw CAOHC and Temasek, which emerged as CAO's savior.

CAO, CAOHC, and Their Leaders

Chen Jiulin, managing director and CEO of China Aviation Oil, was until the company's downfall a highly praised Chinese entrepreneur. He joined CAOSC, the company that served as co-founder of CAO, in 1993 as chief negotiator and project manager. In 1997 he was appointed managing director of CAO and was later promoted by the Work Committee of Enterprises of the Communist Party of China to vice president of CAOHC, which became CAO's parent company in 2002. The early success of CAO was largely attributed to Chen. The World Economic Forum voted him one of the "New Asian Leaders" in 2003, and the prestigious Singapore Institute of Management elected him as one of its new members in April 2004. As late as August 2004, newspapers hailed Chen as the man behind CAO's success.[10] According to these accounts, Chen's major assets were his entrepreneurial spirit and the management methods he brought to CAO.

The China Aviation Oil Holding Company was established in 2001 as part of China's effort to commercialize its aviation industry. Its shares were held by a variety of state-owned enterprises, including China Aviation Group, China Eastern Aviation Group, and China Southern Aviation Group. The chairman and president of CAOHC was Jia Changbin, who also served as chairman and nonexecutive director of the board of CAO. Jia spent the early part of his career in the Civil Aviation Administration of China, having been appointed to its Shanghai branch in 1973 and promoted to deputy director in 1984. In 1990 he became deputy general manager of CAOSC and in 2000 was brought to CAO. In 2002 he was appointed president of CAOHC.

Both companies were products of China's transition to a market economy. Neither firm was a state-owned enterprise as traditionally understood—an enterprise directly controlled by state bureaucrats. Rather, they were "corporatized" firms (that is, distinct legal entities that issued shares and were formally governed by a board of directors) with complex ownership structures and similar in form to corporations in developed market economies, but their shares were ultimately owned by the state. By turning state-owned enterprises into stock corporations, the government created the potential for future privatization and, at least on paper, new governance structures. One of the reasons for listing shares of state-owned enterprises on foreign exchanges was to expose management to new forms of discipline not possible if the ultimate owners of the firm consist exclusively of agents of the state (Clarke 2003).

Throughout the 1990s, companies in China were not permitted to freely list their shares on a domestic stock exchange, much less on a foreign exchange. Access to the capital market was limited to state-owned enterprises. These companies were vetted by local bureaucrats as well as national securities regulators before they were allowed to issue their shares to the public (Pistor and Xu 2005). In this respect CAO differs from the typical Chinese corporation in that it was established as an offshore joint venture with foreign partners. Its listing on the Singapore stock exchange came much later. Moreover, because the company was organized in Singapore, the exchange was domestic rather than foreign. Nonetheless, given the company's control by the Chinese holding company, listing ultimately had to be approved by CAOHC and state bureaucrats.

Given the close connection of their companies with the Chinese state bureaucracy, it is not surprising that the chief executives of the two companies were also products of China's hybrid system of state control and market elements. Jia, the older of the two, launched his career when China still had a centrally planned economy with little room for entrepreneurship and few legal mechanisms of governance. He seems to have ridden successfully on the waves of reform that swept the country, as suggested by his appointments to CAO and CAOHC, both creatures of the transition to a market economy. Still, it is worth noting that all of Jia's appointments— as well as his ultimate dismissal—were initiated by state bureaucrats, not private investors.[11]

Chen, though hailed as a proponent of China's new generation of entrepreneurial capitalists, also spent his career in companies that were directly or indirectly controlled by the state. Nevertheless, he appears to have been much more aggressive in pursuing new strategies and side-stepping the constraints imposed by state controls where possible. His posting in Singapore facilitated this agility, and postgraduate training at the National University of Singapore—which featured him on its Web site as a star alumnus—may have given him an appetite for freewheeling business strategies. His biography does not suggest that he ever operated in an environment where legal constraints were more important than bureaucratic controls or where shareholder concerns played a significant role in managerial decision making.

Singaporean Enforcement Authorities

In Singapore, the CAO case triggered enforcement actions by several organizations. First in line was the SGX, which had admitted the company to its main board in 2001 and was responsible for monitoring listed companies' compliance with listing and disclosure requirements. The Singapore Stock Exchange is a demutualized and integrated securities and derivatives exchange inaugurated in December 1999 following a merger between the Stock Exchange of Singapore and the Singapore International Monetary Exchange. Through SEL Holdings, Temasek indirectly holds almost 24 percent of SGX's shares and in 2004 controlled up to 20 percent of the companies listed on the exchange.[12]

The main goal of the SGX is to develop into a leading financial center in Asia. An important component of this strategy has been to attract listings by mainland Chinese firms. In 2000 there was only one listing from mainland China; there were five in 2001. By the end of 2004 there were thirty-three listings representing 7 percent of the combined market capitalization of the exchange.[13] Another thirty-four new listings from China were added in 2005.[14] Chinese firms were particularly attractive to investors in this period because they generated high rates of return, in contrast to many local firms in the aftermath of the Asian financial crisis.

There have been growing concerns about possible conflicts of interest posed by the exchange's aggressive recruitment of firms from mainland China while fulfilling its role of investor protection. The collapse of CAO, the poster child of successful Chinese listed firms, was a wake-up call. The exchange reacted swiftly, appointing PwC to conduct an investigation into CAO. The report produced in March 2004 was a blistering attack on CAO's top management, lack of transparency, and ineffective governance structures.[15]

Enforcement actions against CAO and its representatives were ultimately left to state regulators and criminal enforcement agents. As noted above, CAOHC entered into a settlement agreement with the Monetary Authority of Singapore, which serves as the country's central bank and main financial market supervisor. According to the revised Securities and Futures Act of Singapore, MAS has the authority to bring civil actions against natural as well as legal persons for alleged misconduct in financial markets.

At first, criminal enforcement agents moved only against Chen, who was arrested immediately after returning from China on December 6, 2004. In March 2006 he was sentenced to four years in prison.[16] To the surprise of most observers, however, criminal investigations were also initiated against other members of the CAO board, Jia Changbin, Gu Yanfei, and Li Yongji. They were required by a Singaporean judge to pay fines in the amount of US$247,000 (Jia) and US$92,600 (Gu and Li).[17]

According to press reports, it had been widely assumed that Chen would bear the brunt of Singaporean law enforcement efforts in the CAO scandal. Earlier episodes involving Chinese corporations that were listed on foreign exchanges and embroiled in corporate governance scandals suggested that implicated managers in the overseas offices would be replaced or punished but that high-level managers in mainland China would be shielded from law enforcement actions by foreign authorities. A case in point is the response to the fraud scandal that embroiled Bank of China's New York branch in 2004. The manager of the New York branch office received a twelve-year prison sentence for embezzlement and accepting bribes. Other local representatives of the bank in New York were indicted in a federal court in Manhattan.[18] No company officials at the Chinese parent company were implicated. This time, however, enforcement actions were taken against an important mainland corporate manager and party bureaucrat.[19]

The timing of the enforcement action was also notable. China Aviation Oil had tried to settle its debts with creditors since its collapse in December 2004. An earlier settlement proposed by the company in January 2005, which would have required the creditors to write off 58.5 percent of their debt, was rejected by creditors, some of which moved to sue CAO in various jurisdictions to recover on the debt. In late May a new proposal to write off 44.4 percent of the debt, with CAO to pay back $486 million over five years, gained the support of creditors. To finalize the deal, which was later approved by the High Court of Singapore,[20] CAO's board members traveled on June 8, 2005, to Singapore, where they were arrested at the airport. All of the directors were subsequently released on bail so that the agreement with creditors could be finalized, but the event solidified Singapore's reputation for tough law enforcement, including enforcement against powerful Chinese actors. Press reports suggest, however, that the highly publicized arrest of Jia in particular could not have proceeded without at least tacit approval from mainland China. As one reporter put it, the Chinese government allowed Singapore to "throw the books at them" in a willing sacrifice.[21]

This move seems to have served two interests. First, it allowed China to reinforce a warning to its own companies about risky investment strategies. In fact, the entire CAO debacle has been depicted by Chinese bureaucrats as a problem of excessive speculation, without much attention to the securities fraud and insider trading aspect of the scandal. Second, sacrificing Jia may have been the result of a compromise between the authorities in Singapore and China. As noted above, CAOHC escaped with what many considered to be a rather light fine, and the price may have been allowing the Singaporean police to take action against Jia directly. Moreover, subsequent reports that Temasek would rescue CAO by taking a 15 percent stake in the company suggest that China had a keen interest in ensuring that CAO would emerge from bankruptcy as a viable company.

By contrast, private enforcement actions initiated by investors did not play a role in the scandal in Singapore. The only private action against CAO and its affiliates was filed in the U.S. District Court for the Southern District of New York as a class-action suit, but it was ultimately dismissed for lack of jurisdiction.[22] Class-action suits are not recognized under Singapore law. Instead, MAS is authorized to initiate civil penalty actions and collect the penalties. This does not necessarily imply that investors go empty-handed. In fact, CAOHC's penalty decree provided that it would compensate minority shareholders of CAO in kind by turning over to them the shares that CAOHC was to acquire from CAO as part of the company's debt restructuring plan.

An alternative to US-style highly decentralized class-action suits may be found in lobbying efforts and potential legal actions by the Securities Investor Association of Singapore (SIAS). The association is a nonprofit organization established in June 1999 when more than one hundred seventy thousand retail investors in Singapore had their investments in Malaysian securities frozen by the Malaysian government in the aftermath of the East Asian financial crisis.[23] The emergence of the SIAS mirrors similar developments in other East Asian markets, where the fallout of the financial crisis triggered the formation of nonprofit investor protection organizations. In Korea, Taiwan, and even Japan the organizations have emerged as powerful agents of good corporate governance, launching lawsuits against selected companies and leveraging the combined force of an organization in systems where securities class-action or derivative suits are often unavailable (Milhaupt 2004).

In summarizing the enforcement actions that were taken against CAO, it seems fair to say that Singapore's regulators and criminal enforcement agents moved swiftly against individuals such as CAO's chief executive officer and representatives of its parent company. In the absence of a more viable system for private party enforcement, much depended on the effectiveness and political will of state regulators. The sequence of enforcement actions taken and the level of sanctions applied suggests that these actions were aimed at confirming Singapore's reputation for law enforcement while disturbing as little as possible the country's economic relations with mainland China. Given Singapore's dependence on Chinese markets, this is not surprising. But the episode highlights the limits of strategies aimed at outsourcing law enforcement, in this case by listing a Chinese company on a foreign stock exchange and thereby subjecting it to a more robust legal regime. This strategy has been the subject of a growing literature in recent years. The basic intuition of arguments pointing to the benefits of outsourcing law enforcement is that firms located in weak corporate governance environments, particularly firms in emerging markets and developing countries, may mitigate these problems by obtaining listing on a foreign stock exchange (Coffee 2002; Gilson 2000). In so doing, the theory goes, the firm bonds itself to the better disclosure regime and governance standards of the foreign country, simultaneously signaling to investors that its management has the capacity to abide by higher governance standards than those practiced in the home country.

Although there appears to be considerable empirical evidence in support of this theory (Reese and Weisbach 2001), the CAO case appears to be an inversion of the theoretical model: weak corporate governance practices of the home country are exported to the foreign listing environment. Rather than receiving additional protections, minority investors are (at least potentially) victimized by a distant parent company operating according to very different rules. In this case the parent company exploited a gap in the listing jurisdiction's law that allowed it to privately place shares without full disclosure in order to raise capital to cover its subsidiary's accumulated losses—all in the name of saving both the subsidiary and its Chinese parent from disgrace.

Perhaps the circumstances of the case are unique and unlikely to be repli-
cated in other markets where Chinese companies are listing their shares.
On the other hand, about seventy-eight Chinese companies are listed on
foreign exchanges around the world, including twenty on the New York
Stock Exchange as of 2007, and some estimate that Chinese IPOs will soon
become the second most important source of IPO investment banking fees
worldwide after the United States.[24] With so much at stake, the temptation
for foreign stock exchanges and underwriters to overlook uncomfortable
features of the Chinese corporate governance model may not be limited to
the CAO case. Indeed, author discussions with practitioners representing
Chinese companies indicate that the U.S. Securities and Exchange Commission and the New York Stock Exchange are concerned about losing Chinese
firms to other stock markets and as a result are granting exemptions from
various securities law requirements and listing standards.

Chinese Authorities and Temasek

The preceding discussion alludes to crucial behind-the-scenes players in
this episode: the Chinese political authorities and Temasek, which is closely
linked to Singaporean political authorities. Both sets of players were deeply
involved in managing the rescue of CAO, and their efforts are likely to
have influenced the law enforcement response. Not surprisingly, however,
little information is publicly available about the precise nature of their
involvement.

Although it remains a matter of speculation whether Chinese interests
had a direct influence on the outcome of Singaporean law enforcement
actions, the denouement of the crisis is highly suggestive of a strategy pursued by the Chinese authorities. Such a strategy would have entailed rescuing CAO, downplaying the crisis as a one-off event resulting from excessive
speculation, and avoiding the impression of a systemic governance failure
that would implicate a breakdown of the Chinese model of company transformation. To pursue this strategy, the Chinese government was willing to
play by Singapore's rules, at least to a point. This required sacrificing not
only the front-line protagonist Chen—a typical response to corporate governance scandals—but also the more politically connected Jia, while forcing CAOHC to take responsibility for violating Singapore's insider trading
rules.

Yet CAOHC's response to the insider charges, which in this context
can be equated with the response of the Chinese authorities, is highly suggestive of the difference between the norms operating in the Chinese model

and the legal rules of developed financial markets. In the Chinese model, where stability is more important than enforcement of individuals' rights, rescuing a company is the primary goal. Using a share transfer as part of a rescue scheme is not uncommon. Chinese state-owned or -affiliated entities are often asked to participate in rescues of individual firms (Chen 2003; Green and Ming 2004). More recently, foreign investors have agreed to bail out Chinese entities (primarily in the financial sector) as a means of gaining access to more lucrative investments in the Chinese market. A telling example is Goldman Sachs's bailout of Hainan Securities in 2004.[25] What the Chinese authorities overlooked in the CAO episode is that the purchasers of the CAO shares sold by CAOHC in October 2004 were not other state-controlled entities but private investors in foreign markets who were unconstrained by expectations of subordination to larger state interests.

There was one important exception, however: Temasek. Although organized as a private limited liability company, Temasek is owned by the state of Singapore and is typically referred to as the government's investment arm.[26] Created in 1974, it took over assets managed by the Ministry of Finance. Over the course of the past thirty years, Temasek has developed into a major holding company with investments in key industry sectors, including financial services (38 percent of total investments), telecommunications and media (23 percent), and transport and logistics (12 percent). Temasek has controlling stakes in a number of firms (including 100 percent of a leading telecommunications company and the largest broadcasting company in Singapore), but it often invests in combination with private investors. As of 2007, 38 percent of all investments of Temasek were located in Singapore, with 40 percent in the rest of Asia outside Japan. Temasek portrays itself as an active investor with concern for the long-term prospects of the companies in which it invests. The company expects to reduce its investments in Singapore to one-third of total holdings over the next eight to ten years, largely by expanding investments in other parts of Asia.

According to the company's reports, it is pursuing an aggressive strategy of expansion into China. In early July 2005 it announced that its wholly owned subsidiary, Asia Financial Holdings, had entered into a strategic partnership with China Construction Bank (CCB), a major state-owned bank that launched an initial public offering at the end of 2005. Asia Financial Holdings committed to investing $1 billion in the bank and purchasing "certain existing shares" from China SAFE Investment Ltd. subject to regulatory approvals.[27]

Temasek's governance structure reflects the philosophy of state-public partnership and close linkages among companies belonging to the Temasek Group. Numerous members of the board are chairmen of companies in which Temasek holds major stakes.[28] Others are senior government officials, including the permanent secretary of the Ministry of Finance and a member of the Council of Presidential Advisors. Temasek is not only wholly owned by the Ministry of Finance; it also enjoys family ties with Singapore's "founding father," Lee Kuan Yew. The current executive director and CEO of Temasek, Ho Ching, is married to the prime minister, Lee Hsien Loong. Loong happens to be the son of Lee Kuan Yew.[29]

When CAOHC sold 15 percent of its shares in CAO in October 2004, Temasek and several of its affiliates purchased a 2 percent stake.[30] Although the investment was relatively small, it was the largest single purchase of shares in the placement, and the fact that Temasek purchased shares was viewed by market participants as a sign that CAO was still a good investment. As a stock broker linked to a local firm put it, "Small investors often look to government-linked corporations such as Temasek for what stock to buy. . . . They seem to think that they have better information sources than the market would."[31] Whether it had better information or not, like other shareholders Temasek had to write off its investment when the firm's stock collapsed only a month later.

But this did not end Temasek's involvement in CAO. Only one week after CAOHC settled with the MAS, Temasek announced its willingness to acquire a 15 percent stake in CAO. Press reports about the pending deal suggested that the investment would fit Temasek's China expansion strategy, referring to the company's recent commitment to invest in China Construction Bank.[32] A slightly broader reading of events is that Temasek was serving as a proxy for Singapore's long-term interest in promoting business ties with China. Temasek had participated indirectly in the establishment of CAO in 1993. After having sold the initial stake back to the Chinese parent in 1995, Temasek participated in the share placement in October 2004. There were rumors that Temasek might inject millions of dollars in an attempt to get CAO out of bankruptcy when the first credit restructuring plan was floated in January 2004.[33] It is also suggestive of the cooperative climate between China and Singapore that none of the bank creditors controlled by Temasek filed suit against CAO or the parent company to recover their loans. They stand in contrast to other international banks, which initiated legal action against CAO (although they ultimately settled their claims).[34] This would be puzzling if Temasek were simply viewed as

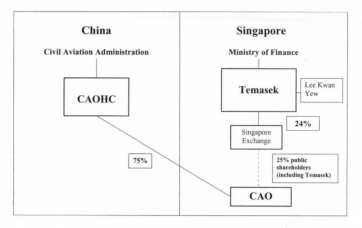

Figure 7.1. CAO's ties with China and Singapore

a burned investor. It is far less surprising considering Singapore's broader interests in promoting closer links with mainland China (see figure 7.1). Consistent with this strategy, Temasek emerged as a guardian angel for CAO. Seen in this light, Temasek's role is not fundamentally different from the role many parent companies in China (also with state backing) have assumed with regard to their "offspring."

China's Model of Corporate Governance

Until 1978, China had a socialist economy relying primarily on central planning and government control over the means of production. Reforms introduced in the following decade were centered on the agricultural sector as well as the rationalization of the state sector, along with some opening for entrepreneurial activities, particularly in coastal areas and in the vicinity of large urban centers. In the ensuing decades the economy gradually grew out of the plan (Naughton 1996). The relative share of the exclusively state-owned enterprises (SOEs) in the economy declined, while new entrants, including hybrid structures co-owned by state entities and nonstate actors, accounted for the bulk of economic growth (Qian 2000; Walder and Oi 1999). An important step in the reform of the SOEs was the "corporatization" of state-owned enterprises—their legal repackaging and the listing of some firms on domestic or foreign stock exchanges to raise capital (Lichtenstein 1993). According to standard theory, the formation of separate legal entities with shares held by outside owners facilitates several efficiency-enhancing measures. Professional managers pursuing business rather than political objectives could be recruited to run the enterprises. Investors could supervise management through a board of directors. Finally, the public listing of firms would not only bring capital into the firm but also would expose management to the discipline of the capital markets.

In practice, China developed a distinctive model of governance for publicly traded firms in the 1990s. Most of the nearly fourteen hundred companies currently listed on the Shanghai and Shenzhen stock exchanges are still controlled by the state. On average, less than 40 percent of the shares of these "public" companies are publicly traded. Typically, 60 percent or more of the shares are held by the state or by state-controlled enterprises and agents. Until 2006, these shares were not tradable except among state-controlled enterprises.[35] Though technically most shares are now tradable, shares held by the state and its affiliates are not widely traded. Thus, in contrast to the privatization campaigns in Russia and Eastern Europe in the early 1990s, China's motive for establishing stock exchanges and listing firms was not to move assets from state control into private hands.[36] Instead, the goal was to create an alternative to enterprises' exclusive reliance on debt finance provided mainly by China's state-owned banks. Equity finance from a large number of investors would provide such an alternative, as well as perhaps a measure of outside managerial expertise, while allowing the state to retain control over the listed assets. As a sweetener for investors, the listed firms' prospects were often greatly enhanced by the fact that they held monopolies in key sectors of the economy (Pistor and Xu 2005).

The major challenge that Beijing faced with this approach was the design of a governance structure for listed firms. Thus far, that structure can be best described as an "administrative model" performing mainly coordinating functions. Bureaucrats thought to have superior information and monitoring capacities with respect to a given firm played a lead role in selecting which firms to list. There is historical precedent in China for this type of official bureaucratic supervision and sponsorship of enterprise as a substitute for a legal regime (Goetzmann and Koll 2003).[37] The model appears to have worked reasonably well at the listing stage, but it has been much less effective for continuous monitoring of companies thereafter. The explanation is straightforward: local and regional bureaucrats have strong incentives to bring firms to the capital market. If the IPO is successful, the firm raises new capital and thus relieves the local budget of the burden of funding its investments. Additional incentives result from the fact that the local bureaucrats' own career prospects are closely tied to their region's performance (Huang 1996), including the performance of firms from that region on the stock market.[38] Because the central government controls access to the stock market, local bureaucrats have strong incentives to invest enough in the selection process ex ante to avoid failure of the firm, which would reduce future access by other companies from the same region. A potential downside of using regional competition in the selection process, however, is that once a company has been listed, the same incentive structure induces local and regional bureaucrats to cover up negative information that might reveal failure and necessitate a costly rescue. Moreover, the state-owned companies and their representatives who serve as shareholder-monitors often do not have the capacity to closely oversee the actions taken by the listed company. This is evident in the CAO case, in which the younger, more aggressive, and financially minded—if ultimately misguided—management team outran the monitoring capacities of bureaucrats at the parent company.

Formal Law as a Governance Device for Chinese Companies

There is little doubt that China's growth has been supported by nonlegal substitutes, some of which have deep historical roots. Some researchers have gone as far as to suggest that formal law has played virtually no role in the nonstate sector, which has been largely responsible for the rapid growth and development of the past two to three decades. Allen et al. (2005), for example, use the shareholder and creditor rights indicators compiled by La Porta et al. to assess China's formal legal system and suggest that formal law is weak at best. They also document the fact that China's state-owned sector, for which much of the transitional legislation has been adopted (including the company law of 1994, revised in 2006, and the securities law of 1999) contributes only a small share to economic growth and investment. The major source of growth is the nonstate sector, which includes hybrid structures such as Township and Village Enterprises that are often co-owned by public and private agents. This sector has flourished largely beyond the reach of formal laws promulgated by the central government.

Still, it may not be quite accurate to conclude from this analysis that formal law in China has been irrelevant. The indicators devised by La Porta and colleagues may not be the appropriate benchmarks to use. One reason is that a focus on laws and regulations enacted by the central government misses regional and local rules and regulations. The special economic zones, for example, were authorized to develop a set of rules and regulations aimed at promoting investment as well as exports. The scope of autonomous regulation at this level typically included tax incentives, joint venture regulations, land use rights, and the governance of imports and exports (Sonoko 1983). Outside these zones, regions were free to enact their own law, at least in areas where lawmaking was not preempted by central government legislation. Regional company laws, securities regulations, and bankruptcy rules typically preceded centrally enacted laws, which were often criticized for imposing greater controls and higher costs on economic agents (Pistor and Wellons 1999). Another reason why using the indicators of La Porta et al. as benchmarks might mislead is that it assumes that law is used for similar purposes in different settings. There is little doubt that in terms of sheer volume formal law has expanded rapidly in China in the past thirty years. It is therefore important to analyze the various functions to which formal law was put to use by different actors.

We begin with the supply side. Formal law has developed into an important tool for the central government to use in managing the state-owned sector. The 1994 Company Law's primary purpose was to create a framework for the reorganization of state-owned enterprises into corporate entities (Fang 1995). Previously, state-owned enterprises functioned as legal entities that could act in their own name, but their governance and control structures within the state apparatus were ill defined. By transforming these enterprises into corporations, the government could streamline relations within the state-owned sector. Shares of the corporation were allocated to particular government agencies or organizations controlled by the agencies. These public shareholders were vested with the right to hire and fire management and to take critical decisions, such as triggering a bankruptcy proceeding. In 2006 a revised company law entered into force.[39] It is much more focused on the internal governance structure of firms and the protection of minority shareholder rights, and thus it is more like Western models than the 1994 version.

Another example of using formal law in an attempt to improve the state's control over the state-owned sector is the 1987 Bankruptcy Law.[40] As with the 1994 Company Law, it targeted state-owned enterprises, not the nonstate sector, even though subsequent changes in the civil procedure law expanded its application (Li 1999). It would be difficult to directly link the enactment of these and other laws to economic growth in China. But they were not entirely irrelevant, either. Thousands of companies were incorporated after the 1994 law was enacted, and more than thirteen hundred state-controlled entities were listed on China's two official stock exchanges by the end of 2004. Between 1998 and 2001 these companies raised more US$61 billion (Pistor and Xu 2005). Between 1989 and 1997 the number of state-owned enterprises that entered bankruptcy proceedings increased from eighty-nine to more than five thousand per year (Li 1999). Like the Company Law, the Bankruptcy Law was revised recently and for the first time explicitly targets private companies, not only state-owned enterprises.[41]

Although the central government has increasingly used formal law as a governance device for the state-owned sector, it has shied away from giving law primacy over other governance mechanisms. The rules set forth in the 1994 Company Law stipulating the conditions under which a company could issue shares to the public and seek listing on a stock exchange were complemented shortly afterward by a set of regulations promulgated by the State Council and the China Securities Regulatory Commission (CSRC), much to the dismay of legal observers in China who viewed this as weakening the commitment to the rule of law (Fang 1995; Gao 1996). The governance structure that emerged on the basis of these rules and regulations was more administrative than legal. Its foundation was the quota system, which was used to allocate scarce resources including energy, credit, and now access to equity finance among China's regions.

Given the lack of reliable company-specific information and the absence of a well-developed legal system for stock markets, this may have ultimately been a sensible strategy, at least for the early days of China's stock market development. The fact that it reinforced state control over listed companies at a time when they were seeking capital from nonstate investors is unlikely to have been an oversight. From the perspective of investors, this was not necessarily a negative consequence. In light of the pervasive influence that state agents continued to have in these companies, the quasi insurance of the implicit bailout guarantee that regional governments made when bringing their companies to the market gave investors some measure of protection against abuse. In short, the legal system was highly centralized and coordinated. Little thought was given to the development of legal protections for investor interests.

Once enacted, however, law often takes on a life of its own as different agents begin to explore how it might advance their own interests. Shareholders and investors who were defrauded began to take the law into their own hands. The first series of investor lawsuits was filed in the summer of 2001 by law firms in Beijing. This clearly came as a surprise to government officials. The first response was to deny investors access to the courts. The Supreme People's Court issued guidelines stating that in light of the legal and regulatory uncertainties surrounding these cases, China's civil courts were not in a position to hear investor lawsuits at that point in time (Chen 2003).[42] Only a few months later, however, in January 2002, the court reversed this position in part. The new guidelines of the Supreme People's Court allowed lower courts to hear securities actions for false or misleading statements—not other types of securities fraud—but only if the firm had already been administratively sanctioned by the CSRC or the Ministry of Finance or if company officials had been found criminally liable. The motive for this apparent change in position seems clear: the incompetence argument was untenable over the long term. If the government wanted to retain control over the litigation and the companies against which suits could be brought, it had to devise a better strategy. This was achieved by giving these three bodies a de facto veto right.[43] In fact, even after the Supreme People's Court issued a set of detailed guidelines for investor suits, litigation was brought against only about 20 percent of the companies eligible to be sued between 2001 and 2006 (Liebman and Milhaupt 2008). In the absence of a clear mandate for class actions, the costs of litigation are substantial, although some bundling of cases by investors against the same company is possible (Chen 2003). Where lawsuits have been filed, the courts have sometimes used the strict causation requirements set forth in the guidelines to deny plaintiffs recovery. Many cases appear to have been settled or complaints have been withdrawn. Without information about the settlement details it is difficult to assess whether settlement in the shadow of the law, which is also common in the United States, is of greater benefit to plaintiffs or defendants.

As this example suggests, China has been willing, within limits, to experiment with legal reforms and to decentralize law making and enforcement. Some of these experiments may have a Trojan horse effect unanticipated by the lawmakers.[44] The pattern (legal change designed to improve state economic governance leads to a loss of control over the legal mechanisms) can be found elsewhere in China. For example, in 1989 China enacted the Administrative Litigation Law, allowing individuals and nongovernmental organizations for the first time to sue government agencies for violation of existing laws and regulations (Potter 1994). The law was not intended to fundamentally alter the relation between state agents and citizens or to be a commitment to a rights-based system subjecting government actions to strict legal scrutiny. Its major function was to reform the state bureaucracy and bring corruption under control. The government hoped to instrumentalize administrative litigation for its own purposes. This move, however, also had unintended consequences. Since the Administrative Litigation Law was promulgated in 1989, People's Courts of first instance have heard more than one million cases brought by aggrieved citizens, with plaintiffs winning about 30 percent of the cases (Conk 2005).

Of course, not all judgments are successfully enforced against government officials. Nonetheless, the possibility of bringing legal action against state officials has advanced the notion that there are individual rights that may be upheld against intrusion by the state (Pils 2005). Another example is media control. By empowering the media in China to uncover and report on abuse of investors rights, the Chinese government has unleashed the powers of the so-called fourth branch of government. Once again, the motive was to create a check against abuse, but the actions taken by some of the media have created serious challenges to government control over news and information (Liebman 2005).

Closer inspection reveals that the very function of law in China today is far from settled. The lawmakers view law primarily as a means to control and coordinate the economy and society. Law's control function is exercised by either vesting government agencies with legal (in addition to bureaucratic and political) rights of control or at times by allocating some rights of control to individuals (litigants in administrative procedures or the media) as a check on the vast bureaucratic machinery that rules the country. But lawyers have used the possibilities provided by the decentralized approach to legal governance (however modest) and have begun to explore the possibility of invoking the protective function of law.

This ambiguity is heightened by the signaling function of law. In China, as elsewhere, legal reform has a tendency to take on a life of its own because the signals received by law's consumers are not necessarily limited to the ones intended by state actors. Through two decades of steady legal reform in the economic sector, China's leadership has signaled that the country is moving (unevenly and imperfectly, to be sure) in the direction of market-oriented institutions and legal governance. Although the leadership has clearly determined that legal governance in the economic sphere is "safer" and more manageable than reforms in the political and social arenas, it is proving difficult for those in power to rein in all of the connotations any move toward the "rule of law" entails, which, at least according to Western standards, would include using the law to control governmental actions. Plainly, the protective function of law is still a work in progress in China; developments to date have not fundamentally altered the predominant role of law as an instrument of state control and state coordination. But it is not accurate to claim, as many have, that law has played no role in China's economic growth. The law has provided important information about the direction of future reforms, raised societal expectations about the protective capacity of law, and laid a modest platform for individual initiative and experimentation (what we call contestability)—sometimes even directed against state actors.

Interlude: Law and Growth in Singapore

The CAO case provides insights not only into China's legal and market development but also that of Singapore. The case is particularly interesting because of the interface between China's unabashedly centralized administrative governance model and the Singaporean system of financial market governance, which seeks to emulate protective features of more highly developed market economies. Singapore is widely depicted in the corporate governance literature and surveys as an example of an emerging common-law country with strong investor protections and effective financial regulation.[45] Yet the actual governance structure employed in Singapore's economy is more complicated than this depiction would suggest. Singapore does have an "English origin" common-law system that has been hailed for having investor rights that are superior to those of civil-law systems (La Porta et al. 1998). But the ability of individual investors to enforce their rights in court is in fact severely constrained. Law enforcement rests firmly in the hands of regulators and criminal law enforcement agents, not civil courts or private plaintiffs. Moreover, the good reputation of the Singapore legal system in perception indices notwithstanding, the CAO episode suggests that Singapore relies heavily on centralized administrative mechanisms other than law. Though formally governed by Singapore's bankruptcy and corporate law regime, the final outcome of the CAO crisis depended on the intervention and support of one Singaporean governmental entity—Temasek—in consultation with other such entities—MAS and SGX. Indeed, with the exception of the important criminal prosecution of the executives involved, resolution of the financial crisis at CAO rested on a negotiated solution among governmental entities and affiliates from Singapore and China. Put differently, investor protection was achieved not principally by enforcement of corporate and securities laws but through political mechanisms.

To the extent that law was invoked in the CAO case, it was used to punish individuals such as Chen and Jia. The outcome of the case has puzzled some observers who expressed surprise that a parent company based on the mainland was implicated at all. At the same time, most commentators suggested that the punishment of both CAOHC and the individuals involved was rather mild.[46] These contradictory impressions reflect the dilemma that Singaporean regulators and law enforcers faced in this case. Given its aspiration to become a leading financial market, Singapore had little choice but to adhere to the dominant Western model of financial market regulation. For the Singaporean authorities, it was therefore crucial to demonstrate that insider trading rules were taken seriously and would be enforced against any violator. Indeed, in sentencing Jia and other CAO officials for insider trading, the judge explicitly remarked that the case was about "a larger issue, and the broader public interest in good corporate governance."[47] At the same time, Singapore could hardly afford to offend Chinese authorities. The future of the SGX depends on its ability to attract a constant flow of firms from mainland China. Moreover, key players in the Singapore market, foremost among them Temasek, have a keen interest in investing in Chinese markets. It is impossible to imagine that enforcement agents in Singapore were not conscious of Temasek's involvement in CAO or the strong national interest in maintaining good relations with China when taking enforcement actions in this case.

The Role of Law in China's Economic Success:
A View from Singapore

China's 10 percent annual growth for more than two decades is remarkable. For most observers it is even more remarkable given that China lacks a well-developed legal system. Not surprisingly, some observers predict that China will eventually either converge on the dominant Western model or experience considerable setbacks in economic development (Dam 2006).

Our institutional autopsy of the CAO case, however, suggests that this may be a false choice. In particular, our analysis of Singaporean capitalism demonstrates that there are viable alternatives to the ideal-type market economy, in which law has a primarily protective function for individual rights holders. Singapore has successfully marketed itself as a leading capitalist system in East Asia and received high scores on indices of institutional quality. Yet Singapore's commitment to the protective function of law is highly state-centered and state-administered.[48] Personal relationships and coordination of state- and private-sector interests are key components of the economic governance structure. Indeed, the very efficiency of the legal system appears to derive from the highly state-coordinated nature of enforcement. The CAO case was resolved within ten months, from the date CAO filed for bankruptcy in November 2004 to the Temasek-orchestrated capital injection in August 2005. Within this time frame, CAO settled with other creditors, CAOHC was fined for insider trading, and a criminal action was brought against Chen, Jia. and other board members of CAO (although it took an additional seven months to reach sentencing). This quick resolution demonstrates the advantage of close coordination among economic players and government agents in resolving a case so as to maximize common interests.

Such an approach does not come without costs, however. Viewed from a Western rights-based perspective, the system exposed individual shareholders to the risk that their financial interests might be sacrificed for whatever Temasek and its partners in government and business might deem to be the greater social good. In the end, the minority shareholders were compensated in kind (by CAOHC's transferring to them the shares it had received in the debt-equity swap), but the deal was brokered by state regulators. Minority shareholders cannot easily recover damages in their own right in Singapore.

Singapore's model of market coordination and limited private enforcement in conjunction with its more authoritarian political system is likely to be much more appealing to officials in Beijing than a decentralized rights protection regime based on the U.S. model. Indeed, China's legal and political reform strategy appears to reflect key features of the Singaporean model or that of other countries in East Asia that were traditionally characterized by strong government coordination such as South Korea (Wade 2003; Amsden 1989). Legal reforms are injected where necessary to advance the project of economic growth and development, particularly in order to bolster the confidence of foreign investors and to hold in check the untrammeled authority of state agents. Individual rights protections are used only sparingly as a governance device, and they tend to be paired with veto powers exercised by the state or its agents. Recent history has shown that this model can produce dramatic economic growth and the perception of governance by the rule of law.[49]

A critical question, of course, is whether a country of 1.3 billion people can emulate the governance structure of a city-state. As a tiny country without substantial resources, Singapore must remain economically competitive. It has little alternative but to foster and market its role as a leading financial center. Market forces may therefore place enough pressure on firms and government agents to ensure that coordination strategies enhance rather than reduce the competitiveness of Singaporean entities, whether private or (partly) government-owned. And finally, the small size of the country facilitates the operation of informal governance mechanisms, including reputation effects and mutual monitoring, thus restraining abuse of dominant positions.[50] In this sense, Singapore is not unlike the state of Delaware.[51] Roe (2005) argues that Delaware's governmental actors are keenly attentive to the competitive implications of changes to its corporate law, because the state has no alternative but to retain its leading position in this field. Economic actors can thus be confident that other interests reflected in the political process will not be allowed to undermine the quality of its corporate law over time.

By virtue of its size, China is in a very different position. The country does not have to vie for foreign investors because they have proved willing to pay substantial "admission fees" to gain access to its huge potential market.[52] In other words, in many respects China is a price setter, not a price taker, and by implication is less subject to external market pressures than Singapore. Nonetheless, China's leadership is acutely aware of the fact that its future depends on delivering sustained economic growth. It is therefore in the Communist Party's interest to ensure continuous growth and build a reputation for clean and neutral enforcement rather than intervening in ways that might undermine the country's prospects for growth. At times these considerations have caused officials to tolerate or even encourage governance mechanisms that—like a Trojan horse—may ultimately turn against the current leadership's hold on power. This need not imply that China must turn to an elaborate rights-based governance regime built around an independent judiciary. As the example of other countries examined in this book suggests, few countries have decentralized and "judicified" governance and enforcement to the extent of the United States. Instead, many successful systems place greater confidence in state regulators and prosecutors. Thus, although formal legal governance may play an increasingly important role in China, administrative coordination of state- and private-sector interests is likely to remain the dominant feature of Chinese law, even in a capitalist China.

EIGHT

"Renationalizing" Yukos: Law and Control over Natural Resources in the Russian Economy

Unlike the countries involved in the five cases we have analyzed thus far, Russia is hardly a success story.[1] It has struggled greatly to achieve economic and social stability in the post-Soviet era, and it has passed an impressive number of laws. In practice, however, Russia's legal system deviates substantially from the systems that served as models for legal transplantation. Moreover, Russia's political system, though in name a democracy, displays strong features of autocracy. Precisely for that reason, and because it illustrates so well the extreme example of legal centralization, we believe it makes for an excellent comparison with the preceding case studies.

The Yukos episode is at the heart of the prolonged battle for control of Russia's vast natural resources in the post-Soviet era. In Soviet times these resources were owned and controlled by the state. After the collapse of the Soviet Union, the natural gas companies were consolidated into a single state-owned monopoly, Gazprom. There was significant consolidation in the oil industry as well, with several independent entities emerging from the reorganization of the state-owned oil sector.[2] Yukos, for example, was created in 1993 by a presidential decree that consolidated two former state-owned oil companies.[3] Russia launched an aggressive mass privatization program at the end of 1992, but at first companies in the oil and gas sectors were not included. Officially, they remained under state control. With the weakening of state control in Russia during Boris Yeltsin's presidency (1991–1999),[4] however, actual exercise of control rights was often usurped by other actors. Different factions, including the former "red managers," state bureaucrats, and the emerging "new Russians," often with close ties to insiders in the state bureaucracies, attempted to gain control over assets by placing loyal management within the companies or striking deals with the government.

In 1995–1996 a number of companies in the natural resources sector, including Yukos, were slated for privatization as part of the so-called loans-for-shares program (Lieberman, Nestor, and Desai 1997). This episode is the prelude to the reversal of fortune for the new private owners of Yukos, foremost among them Mikhail Khodorkovsky, the former president and largest shareholder of the company, which forms the core of this institutional autopsy. After becoming the richest man in post-Soviet Russia, Khodorkovsky was sentenced to a nine-year jail term in a Siberian correction camp for tax evasion and other crimes.[5] The company he ran and in which he held a 6 percent stake in 2003 was liquidated, and the remaining assets were auctioned off in the spring of 2007.[6]

The rise and fall of Yukos and Khodorkovsky mirror the battle for control over Russia's most valuable resources and the political power such control confers on their owners. This battle has overshadowed the development of law as well as the development of Russia's post-Soviet economy. As we argue below in greater detail, in this battle, law has figured primarily as an instrument for acquiring control rights and fending off competitors, not as a means of establishing effective governance and incentive structures for economic activity. Although the identity of those who succeeded in obtaining control—first the oligarchs, now the state bureaucrats—has changed, the means to ensure control and the role law has played in this battle remain the same.

The Story

By 2003, Yukos AO had established itself as the most successful Russian oil company.[7] The company's stock, which had fallen to US$1.30 per share during Russia's 1998 financial crisis, was trading at US$10 (Yousef-Martinek, Knight-Bagehot, and Rabimoc 2003). As the first oil company in Russia, in 2000 Yukos had begun to pay dividends to its shareholders and reported its financial accounts using American accounting standards (U.S. GAAP). Its market value reached US$30 billion, and foreign investors hailed the company as the best-governed and most transparent Russian firm. In June 2003 the company announced plans to merge with Sibneft, another Russian oil company, which along with Yukos, had been privatized in 1995–1996. Moreover, Yukos entered into talks with two American oil companies, ExxonMobil and Chevron-Texaco, about the possibility of their taking a strategic stake in the company (Goldman 2004).

In July 2003, Platon Lebedev, a Yukos shareholder and board member, was arrested. Lebedev was also the chairman of Group Menatep, the financial holding company also controlled by Mikhail Khodorkovsky, which had substantial stakes in the Yukos group. The initial accusation focused on illegal acquisition of shares in a fertilizer company in 1994 (Goriaev and Sonin 2005). Subsequently, Lebedev was charged with embezzling state assets and tax evasion. Shortly after his arrest, authorities raided the headquarters of Yukos AO and secured records, allegedly to buttress the investigation against Lebedev.

Three months later, Khodorkovsky was arrested at gunpoint while his private jet was being refueled in Siberia. According to some reports, he was en route to a safe haven outside the country.[8] While the investigations against Khodorkovsky and Lebedev continued, the Russian tax authorities also charged Yukos with tax evasion. Initially, the amount of allegedly unpaid taxes was stated to be US$7 billion, but by the fall of 2004, an additional US$10 billion had been added to the tax bill. Some commentators suggested that the additional claims were trumped up in order to ensure that the state could auction off Yuganskneftegaz, Yukos's main production unit and the most valuable part of the group, with an estimated value of US$17 to $24 billion (Goldman 2004).[9] To secure the tax claims, Russian authorities froze the 44 percent stake that Group Menatep held in Yukos; subsequently they seized Yuganskneftegaz. On December 19, 2004, Yuganskneftegaz was sold off by the government to recover the outstanding tax claims. The company was acquired by a little-known firm called Baikal Finans for US$9.35 billion. No competing bids were made. In February 2005, Baikal Finans sold Yuganskneftegaz to Rosneft, a major state-owned oil company. In May 2005, Khodorkovsky and Lebedev were found guilty of six criminal charges, including tax evasion, and sentenced to nine years in prison. Yukos was liquidated in the fall of 2006.[10]

Key Players and Their Strategies

Mikhail Khodorkovsky is the most prominent actor in the Yukos affair.[11] He emerged as one of the Russian oligarchs, a label given to the most powerful of the new Russian businessmen who made their fortunes during the early years of transition. The oligarchs ultimately secured control over banks, media, and natural resources. Khodorkovsky, born in 1963, was not yet thirty years old when the Soviet Union collapsed. An engineer by training, he graduated from the prestigious Mendeleev Institute in Moscow. In the late 1980s he took advantage of legislation passed during the period of *perestroika* launched by former Soviet president Mikhail Gorbachev to establish a cooperative called the Center for the Scientific-Technical Creativity of Young People, abbreviated as "Menatep." The center engaged in trading of computers from abroad, currency exchange, software development, and construction. Not only were the early ventures tolerated by the Soviet regime, but the Communist Party actively used Khodorkovsky's venture for its own business operations and thus protected and promoted him (Freeland 2000). Menatep was transformed into a bank prior to the collapse of the Soviet Union. In 1990 Khodorkovsky, then twenty-seven years old, was appointed economic advisor to Ivan Silaev, prime minister of the Russian Federation.

The close connection that Khodorkovsky established with the government allowed him to take advantage of the collapsing central planning system when Russia plunged into radical market reforms under the leadership of Yegor Gaidar in 1991–1992. Most important, he was able to position Menatep Bank as a critical intermediary, providing bridge financing to companies, municipalities, and regional governments. High rates of inflation during Russia's transition period fueled the lucrative business. Menatep also took advantage of the privatization of Russia's vast state-owned enterprise sector. Although the bank was not active in the voucher auctions of the mass privatization scheme,[12] it did successfully participate in many subsequent tenders in which remaining stakes of 20 percent were sold to private investors. In the process, Menatep Bank built a large industrial financial group with investments in an eclectic assortment of industry sectors (Freeland 2000).

The largest and most important acquisition by Menatep was Yukos, which was privatized as part of the loans-for-shares program, a scheme conceived by a group of new Russian bankers led by Vladimir Potanin. Under the scheme, a consortium of ten banks proposed to make a sizeable loan to the Russian government, taking collateral in the form of large stakes in Russia's natural resource companies. The collateral stakes were auctioned under the auspices of the State Privatization Committee (Goskomimushchestvo, or GKI), organized by the same banks that formed the consortium. Foreigners were explicitly barred from participating, at least directly, and bidders not belonging to the consortium were excluded, mostly on technical or fabricated grounds (Black, Kraakman, and Tarassova 2000).

The influence of the members of the consortium over the design of the program did not stop at the basic structure of the scheme but affected the details of the auction procedures. Keeping foreigners out of the bidding process was crucial to the insiders, because major foreign oil companies could have easily outbid the Russian banks. Freeland reports that Khodorkovsky's confidant Konstantin Kagalovsky, who had served in the Russian government and held a position as Russia's representative at the IMF, explained to her how he accomplished this task: "The key, he said, was to ensure that the law banning foreign participation was intentionally vague. It would thus be open to multiple interpretations. If the foreign firms did decide to try to find a legal loophole and make a bid for Yukos through Russian partners, Kagalovsky would warn them that Menatep would take them to court. With a law so open to interpretation, and the home court advantage, Menatep would stand a strong chance of winning" (Freeland 2000, 184).

Foreign companies stayed out of the contest for Yukos.[13] As a result of the intentionally ambiguous auction procedures and the deep involvement of the bidders in the conduct of the auctions, the companies were sold at just above the reservation price. Typically the only two bidders were members of the consortium that had previously agreed on how to divide the spoils. As a result, Khodorkovsky—through another company set up for the purpose of the auction—acquired a 45 percent stake in Yukos for US$159 million, only US$9 million above the reservation price.

The terms of such loans required the Russian government to pay only modest interest rates during the first several months. The loans were to expire in September 1996, at which time the government was required either to repay the entire amount and take back the shares or sell the shares. In the latter event, the banks were allowed to take 30 percent of the difference between the sale price and the amount lent. Moreover, they had the right to organize the auctions that would transfer the shares to private ownership. Confronted with dwindling budget resources and facing a potential victory of the Communists in the presidential elections in 1996, the government agreed to the "Faustian bargain" (Freeland 2000, 169). Chrystia Freeland argues that the audacious plan was put into effect "for one central reason: . . . Loans-for-shares bought Yeltsin the political, financial, and strategic support of the future oligarchs in the upcoming presidential elections" (170). The oligarchs presented themselves to Prime Minister Chernomyrdin's government as white knights who would save Russia from two dangers: the Communist threat embodied in the presidential contender Zyganov, on one hand, and insolvency, on the other. The US$1.8 billion in loans extended by the oligarchs certainly helped the Russian government meet its short-term financial obligations. Anatoly B. Chubais, the father of Russia's mass privatization program and a member of the team that initiated radical economic reforms in 1992, justified the loans-for-shares deal by suggesting that it brought "real money" to the Russian budget

(Desai 2005), whereas the mass privatization program had given assets away for free.

Legal constraints played no role in the design or implementation of this program. The transfer of critical assets to a handful of self-selected businessmen was backed by presidential decree.[14] Although there was substantial haggling about the details of the arrangement, a bargain among the interested parties eventually was struck. Parliament and the public at large were excluded. The amounts that were raised in the loans-for-shares program were far below world market prices for similar assets, calling into question whether Russia benefited financially from the plan. Indeed, the short-term bailout did not put government finances on a healthy footing. Only two years after the government's failure to repay the loans triggered the sale of the shares held as security, the Russian government defaulted on its other payment obligations (Nesvetailova 2004).

This crisis also exposed the short-lived role of the oligarchs as white knights. The government's general default saddled the oligarch-controlled banks with huge losses. Menatep alone had invested more than 300 trillion rubles in Russian treasury bonds. Khodorkovsky for his part sought to salvage whatever he could. He arranged for Menatep's good assets to be transferred to a new bank, Menatep–St. Petersburg, while he dissolved the old bank. To disguise the transaction he allegedly arranged for a truck carrying Menatep's documents to be driven off a bridge into the Dybna River (Black, Kraakman, and Tarassova 2000). Yukos also suffered greatly from the government default. Yukos had borrowed heavily from Western banks, using its shares and guarantees as collateral. As a result, 30 percent of the company's shares were seized by foreign banks in the aftermath of the ruble's collapse. But for the most part foreign investors dumped these shares, seeing little chance of a recovery in their value. This allowed Khodorkovsky to repurchase many of the shares and regain control. In the aftermath of the 1998 financial crisis, he created a new control structure for the most valuable assets of the Yukos group by tunneling them to subsidiaries under his control (that is, by stealing them from minority shareholders of Yukos). He ensured that the shareholders' meetings at Yukos's three major subsidiaries adopted resolutions causing each to issue new shares to offshore companies controlled by him (Black, Kraakman, and Tarassova 2000). For the most part, payment was in the form of promissory notes issued by other Yukos subsidiaries. Moreover, each of the subsidiaries "contracted" to sell its output to these offshore companies at the comically below-market price of US$1.30 per barrel.[15] Khodorkovsky dealt with noncompliant shareholders by mobilizing the Russian courts, which invoked the antimonopoly law to prevent voting by minority share-holders who tried to organize themselves against the deal.

Less than two years after having effectively expropriated the funds of minority shareholders of Yukos, however, the company nevertheless became the darling of foreign investors. The nonprofit organization Corporate Governance in Russia reported in the summer of 2000 that the Yukos board had pledged allegiance to international principles of good corporate governance.[16] The company charter was brought into full compliance with Russia's corporate law. The risk of diluting existing shareholders was eliminated by canceling all authorized but unissued stock. Future share issuances would now require explicit shareholder approval. Moreover, a new board that included representatives of the international finance and oil industries was elected at the annual meeting. It vowed to govern the company according to principles of Russian law and the OECD's new code on corporate governance and to disclose financials that were audited according to GAAP in all future years.

The timing of this reversal in the company's basic attitude toward corporate governance coincides with critical political and economic events in Russia. Yeltsin's second and final term as president was to come to an end in March 2000. It was not known who would succeed him or what economic policies might be pursued by his successor.[17] Khodorkovsky seemed to have realized that it was time to diversify, move away from the Kremlin, and seek allies in the form of international investors in order to fend off any possible attacks by future leaders. In fact, he not only improved corporate governance at Yukos but he also emulated Western business magnates by turning himself into a philanthropist, donating substantial amounts to foreign nongovernmental organizations such as the Carnegie Endowment and the Library of Congress.[18] The turnaround was also fueled by changes in the world market price for crude oil. Oil prices jumped from US$10 per barrel in early 1999 to US$28 per barrel in early 2000 (Yousef-Martinek, Knight-Bagehot, and Rabimoc 2003). These changes in the business environment made the prospect of additional profits from more efficient operations highly attractive—even if they had to be shared with the company's minority shareholders.

In March 2000, Vladimir Putin was elected president of the Russian Federation. His election campaign was supported by the young reformers, as well as the oligarchs who hoped that Yeltsin's hand-picked successor would also support their interests. In contrast to Yeltsin in 1996, Putin did not owe his political ascendance primarily to the oligarchs. Indeed, Putin sought to free himself from excessive influence from that quarter by recentralizing state control and using the reclaimed state powers to build his political and economic base (Hashim 2005). He dealt with the oligarchs by announcing new ground rules. They would be allowed to retain the assets they had accumulated in the shady privatization deals of the 1990s on the condition that they stay out of politics (Goldman 2004). In a series of radio interviews, Putin compared the oligarchs to shoe sellers and bakers, indicating their new lowly status as simple peddlers of products.

Putin nonetheless began to use the tax regime to cut the oligarchs and their empires back down to size. The first target was Media-Most, the media company owned by oligarch Vladimir Gusinski. The company was raided as early as May 2000 on charges of tax evasion and nonpayment of $380 million in loans that had been guaranteed by Gazprom. After Gusinski spent a few days in jail, he relinquished control over his company and was allowed to flee into exile. He now lives in Israel. His former archrival Boris Berezhovsky, who had been a close friend of the Yeltsin family and had made his fortune in television, aviation, and oil (he acquired the oil giant Sidanko in the loans-for-shares deals), sought asylum in the United Kingdom after selling Sidanko to his business partner and relinquishing his 49 percent stake in the television station ORT (Hashim 2005). Khodorkovsky dared to remain in the country and declined to pay his way out by relinquishing his wealth. When he finally attempted to leave, it was too late, and he began serving a sentence in a Siberian correction camp.

To examine the fall of the oligarchs and the attack against Yukos after the company had been transformed into a shareholder-friendly international corporation, we now turn to Vladimir Putin, the other major player in the case. This is not to suggest that personal rivalry between the two men was the main factor behind the harsh measures taken against Khodorkovsky. Although several observers speculated that Putin attacked him because he announced that he might run for president in 2008,[19] Putin did not really have to fear a rival who was loathed by the public at large. Indeed, after Khodorkovsky was imprisoned, Putin's approval ratings increased from 70 to 80 percent (Goldman 2004). It is more likely that Putin "eliminated" Khodorkovsky because his business strategies, including his courting of foreign investors without consulting the Kremlin, posed the greatest challenge to the realization of Putin's strategy for Russia: rebuilding the country as a world power on the basis of the country's natural resources and the state's direct or indirect control over them.

Vladimir Putin was nominated by Yeltsin in August 1999 to be the fifth prime minister in less than seventeen months.[20] When Yeltsin announced his surprise resignation on New Year's Eve, 1999, a few months prior to the scheduled presidential elections, Putin automatically became acting president.[21] Before becoming prime minister, Putin served two years as head of the FSB, Russia's new intelligence service. Prior to that, he had worked in the St. Petersburg mayor's office. Until 1990 he worked in the foreign intelligence directorate of the KGB. In this capacity, he served several years in Dresden (the former German Democratic Republic), where he acquired fluency in German, a skill he later used to forge ties with Gerhard Schroeder of Germany. Politically, Putin was an unknown figure until late 1999, when the strong showing of his party in the elections to the Duma came as a surprise to many.

To the majority of Russian voters, Putin has been an extraordinarily successful president. Voters reelected him in 2004 with 71.4 percent of the vote. His most widely perceived successes were establishing control over the state bureaucracy, creating at least a semblance of law and order, ensuring regular payment of pensions and wages, and regaining an important place for Russia in world politics. Yeltsin had been able to secure a seat for Russia in the G-7, thereby transforming it into the G-8; Putin's ambition was to re-create a powerful state with global ambitions whose participation in world politics was not left to the good will of the West, but was a reflection of Russia's true stature. The strategy he chose to accomplish this goal was to use Russia's wealth in natural resources (Twining 2006). In his dissertation, written in 1997, Putin estimates that this wealth will contribute up to 50 percent of GDP and 70 percent of export revenues throughout the first half of the twenty-first century (Balzer 2005). Putin clearly envisioned a strong role for the state in managing Russia's natural resource wealth: "The basic strategic tasks for the natural resource bloc involve achieving the transition to a rational combination of administrative and economic methods of government relations" (quoted in Balzer 2005, n.p.).

In fact, Putin's ideas were not very different from Khodorkovsky's. The latter had envisioned building new oil pipelines—"one to the Arctic port of Murmansk (as a base for exports to the United States), another through Siberia (toward Asian markets)" (Goldman 2004, 88). Putin began putting his plans into action by building new gas pipelines that for the first time linked Russian gas deposits directly to Italy and Turkey and constructing a new gas pipeline through the Baltic Sea that would link western Europe directly to Russia without crossing former satellite states such as Ukraine and Poland (Twining 2006). The initial focus on gas for expanding Russia's economic and political influence can be explained by the fact that Gazprom, the monopoly that controls Russia's gas resources, had remained largely under state control.[22] The major difference between Khodorkovsky's scheme and Putin's plan was whether control of the natural resources that formed the basis for the great expansion of Russian influence would be wielded by private individuals or the Kremlin.

The Role of Law in the Battle over Yukos

The battle over Yukos illustrates the ways law has been used to gain control by different parties in the post-Soviet era. The loans-for-shares program was put in place by presidential decree.[23] The implementing rules and regulations for the program were designed to ensure a predetermined outcome. The rules were left sufficiently vague to deter foreign investors and to give bureaucrats in the privatization agency enough discretion to prevent competing bids. Law was thus used to disguise an insider deal between the government and the oligarchs.

Law played a similar role in the demise of Yukos. Yuganskneftegaz was auctioned off because its liabilities—tax arrears amounting to billions of dollars—far exceeded its assets. That is the ordinary function of bankruptcy law. Yet the basis for the claims by the tax authorities is highly dubious. The Russian government had originally claimed that the company owed US$3.4 billion in tax arrears. In preparation for the seizure and sale of Yuganskneftegaz, the government employed an international auditor, Dresdner Kleinwort Wasserstein, which valued the company at US$14.7 to $17.3 billion. The government first announced that the auditor had valued the company at US$10.4 billion, apparently the worst-case valuation among several that the auditor had provided.[24] On November 19, 2004, Russia's Federal Property Fund announced that a 76.79 percent stake in Yuganskneftegaz would be auctioned off on December 19 with an opening price of US$8.6 billion—roughly 65 percent of the value of the upper bound of the auditor's evaluation. On the same day, Yukos received another tax bill of US$5.95 billion for the year 2003. On November 23, the tax bill for 2002 was increased by another US$2.53 billion. By December 8, 2004, the total tax claims against Yukos reached US$26.3 billion, which, according to advocates of Yukos and Khodorkovsky, exceeded Russia's planned spending in 2005 for defense and education.[25] On December 26, three days before the auction, Yukos announced that the total tax bill for the years 2000–2003 amounted to US$27.5 billion. The company claimed that the bills for 2001 and 2002 exceeded company revenue for those years.[26]

Yukos was not the only company pursued by the tax authorities in recent years. Between 1998 and 2002, more than 50 percent of all bankruptcy cases each year were brought by the state, including the tax authorities, the federal agency for bankruptcy, and other state agents with the power to file bankruptcy charges against a nonperforming debtor (Pistor 2008). The aggressive enforcement practices of the tax authorities after Putin came to power has raised concerns about possible excesses (Amsterdam and Peroff 2007).

Meanwhile, the transfer of Yuganskneftegaz back to the state proceeded smoothly, and according to Putin, "in strict accordance with the law."[27] Managers of Yukos made one final attempt to alter the firm's fate by filing for bankruptcy protection in U.S. bankruptcy court in Houston, Texas. The court held that it had jurisdiction over the case because Yukos had a presence in Houston, and it issued a preliminary injunction against Gazprom, which had announced its intention to bid, as well as Gazprom's lenders.[28] The ruling was later reversed, however, on the ground that the Houston court did not have personal jurisdiction over Yukos.[29] The intervention of a U.S. court in the fall of 2004, however, caused the international banks, led by Deutsche Bank, to withdraw their offer to finance the Gazprom bid for fear of legal repercussions in the United States.[30] As a result, Gazprom had no choice but to refrain from bidding. Not surprisingly, the Russian government remained unperturbed and launched "Plan B" to secure control over Yuganskneftegaz. The auction went forward as scheduled and was won by Baikal Finans Group (Baikal), a company whose listed address is the same as that of a cell phone store in Tver. Baikal acquired a 76.79 percent stake in Yuganskneftegaz for US$9.35 billion.[31]

Many observers immediately suspected that Baikal had acted as a straw company for either Gazprom or another state-affiliated enterprise that had received the Kremlin's backing.[32] It thus came as little surprise when Rosneft, the state-owned oil giant, acquired Yuganskneftegaz from Baikal only a few weeks later for precisely the amount Baikal had paid. A consortium of Russian banks—allegedly with the support of the Kremlin—had secured financing for this transaction.[33] Yukos unsuccessfully sought to prevent the initial public offering of Rosneft in June 2006 on the London Stock Exchange. Yukos management called on the British Financial Services Authority to halt the IPO, "claiming that the listing would be tantamount to abetting the sale of stolen property,"[34] but again to no avail.

Shortly afterwards, Yukos's creditors—foremost among them the Russian tax authorities—declared the company insolvent and agreed to liquidated it. The company was sold off in a series of auctions in the spring of 2007. The first of these auctions was won by Rosneft. The only other bidder was TNK-BP, the Russian co-venture of British Petroleum and its partner

TNK. The auction was a mirror image of the loans-for-shares auctions held ten years earlier. Within ten minutes of the start of the auction, TNK-BP pulled out, explaining that the US$90 million increase over the start price of US$7.5 billion exceeded the amount it was willing pay. This paved the way for Rosneft—the company that had already secured Yugaskneftegaz—to acquire the assets.[35]

With the completion of the liquidation auctions, the Yukos episode effectively came to a close. The "renationalization" of Yukos's major asset and the subsequent liquidation of the parent company mirror the transaction in which it had passed from state to private control ten years earlier. In both cases, there was little doubt as to who would control the company at the end of the day. Laws, regulations, and auction procedures served the purpose of creating the appearance of due process but were never intended to actually implement fair, transparent, and competitive procedures. The participants in the loans-for-shares deals openly admitted that the assets were divvied up prior to the auction (Freeland 2000). The Kremlin was not quite as forthcoming, but there is little doubt that the purpose of the tax claims against Yukos was to return the company's assets to state control. Law was used as an instrument in the hands of the powerful to secure control over key assets in the economy—a role of law with a long tradition in Russia.

The Role of Law in Post-Soviet Russia

When the Soviet Union collapsed, the political leaders of the newly independent Russia put economic reforms at the top of their agenda. Political reforms were deferred; legal reforms were made on an ad hoc basis to advance economic policies. Existing legal rules, though formally still binding law, had little legitimacy because they dated from the Soviet era. Certainly, the young reformers felt fairly unconstrained by Soviet-era law and sidestepped or ignored it when it ran counter to their ambitions (Sachs and Pistor 1997). New policy initiatives were introduced not by legislation but by presidential decree. That allowed the president and his reform team to produce law while ignoring the political process, because legislation would have required consultation and consensus-building. They feared that the legislative process would slow the pace of economic reform and close the window of opportunity to push through their projects. In other words, the end justified the means.

The instrumentalization of law to advance political ends has been a constant in Russia's political history. Karl Marx's notion that law is but an instrument in the hands of the ruling class was probably more fully realized in Russia than in the countries he actually had in mind when he wrote it. Russia never created a formal framework for market-based transactions before the 1917 revolution. Attempts to introduce codes modeled on continental European systems, including a civil code and corporate law, had only reached the drafting stages at the time of the Russian revolution. Instead, corporations were individually licensed by the state bureaucracy (Owen 1991) until their ability to engage in private transactions outside state plans was curtailed with the advent of socialism.

The Soviet Union was a totalitarian regime, but on paper it was not lawless. A substantial body of laws and regulations was enacted, amended, and fine-tuned over the years. Their purpose was not to lay the ground rules for independent economic activity and provide governance structures that could be used by a diverse set of agents but to facilitate the centrally planned economy (Butler 1988).

This changed only in the late 1980s with the legal reforms introduced during the period of *perestroika*, which granted some autonomy to firms and allowed the creation of new firms outside the state-owned sector. As noted, Khodorkovsky used these laws to establish Menatep as a cooperative that later became his financial holding company. Few of these legal instruments, however, were enacted with a radical transformation of economic relations in mind. The 1990 government decree concerning joint stock companies, for example, provided only a skeleton of a company law, stripped of the accumulated experience other countries had incorporated into either statutory or case law (Pistor 1995). Nonetheless, this decree was used as the basis for the incorporation and rapid privatization of thousands of state-owned enterprises (Pistor 1997). Rather than embarking on comprehensive legal reforms in an uncertain political landscape, the reform team relied almost exclusively on the decree power of the president, thereby minimizing the contestability of law. The 1990 government decree concerning corporate law was supplemented by a model charter for companies slated for privatization, which was adopted by presidential decree. The first few privatization programs were adopted by presidential decree, even though Russia's privatization law, adopted in 1990 (prior to the coup), required such a program to be adopted by the legislature (then still the Supreme Soviet).

Originally, the power of the president to issue decrees rested on the extraordinary powers of the Supreme Soviet. They vested with the president in the fall of 1991 for a period of twelve months until November 1992 (Sachs and Pistor 1997). When these powers expired, Yeltsin showed little inclination to yield his control over the economy, and a battle erupted between the president and the Supreme Soviet. The former president of Russia's first Constitutional Court actively participated in this debate, siding on formal legal grounds with the Supreme Soviet in a battle that grew more hostile by the day. By the spring of 1993 the two sides found themselves in a stalemate. Yeltsin tried to break the impasse by launching a referendum to secure support for his reforms. But the referendum could not possibly resolve the underlying constitutional question: Who controlled major policy choices in the country, the president or Parliament? When Yeltsin tried to dissolve the Parliament because it did not support reform policies aimed at reining in the looming hyperinflation, a group of parliamentarians openly called for insurrection. The president sent in the troops and called for new elections. In these elections, voters were also asked to approve a new constitution by referendum.

It is not surprising that the constitution created a strong presidency with extensive decree powers (Chandler 2001). Although decrees may not contradict the constitution or existing Russian federal laws, the president still has tremendous discretion in lawmaking. Any conflict between preexisting legislation or the constitution and a presidential decree must be brought to the attention of the Constitutional Court, which has the sole power to resolve the conflict.[36] Although Russia had no shortage of regulations and decrees issued at the federal, regional, or local level, many of which contradicted each other in a fashion that some commentators described as a "war of laws" (Barber 1994), there were relatively few laws in place to create a functioning market economy. The first book of the Civil Code was enacted only in 1995. The first company law came into force in 1996—two years *after* the completion of the mass privatization program.[37] The first securities law was also enacted in 1996; it confirmed the creation of a federal securities regulatory commission (KZB), which had already been established by presidential decree in the fall of 1994.

Yeltsin's central involvement in the adoption of reform strategies before and after the enactment of the 1994 constitution gave the reformers and their international backers the much-desired flexibility to bypass the political process in their economic reform agenda. This strategy did not come without costs, however. First, it granted whoever had access to the president enormous influence on the design of policies without much public debate or input. Second, the lack of contestation of any of the major reforms weakened Russia's prospects for democratization and added to the cynicism so prevalent in postcommunist Russia. Political parties remained weak because final authority rested in the hands of a president who preferred not to engage in party politics and a reform team that also viewed politics with disdain. Third, it undermined the prospects for building the rule of law in Russia. Everyday experience reinforced citizens' perception that law was a tool for the government and well-connected insiders to achieve their ends, not a means for citizens to constrain the use or abuse of state power. As Sergei Rogov, the director of Moscow's Institute of U.S. and Canadian Studies, put it, "We adopted a constitution toward the end of 1993 which gave enormous authority to the executive without appropriate checks and balances. The legislative branch is weak and is dominated by the executive authority. The judiciary is not independent. . . . Yeltsin abandoned the notion of checks and balances, and created a democracy for the bureaucracy and operated by the bureaucracy" (quoted in Desai 2005, 101). This form of government and extreme centralization of law may have been created by Yeltsin, but it was perfected by his successor, Vladimir Putin.

Putin immediately centralized control over the country by weakening the governors of Russia's regions.[38] He brought into positions of power many of the state security service personnel he knew from his days at the KGB and the FSB. These *siloviki* control the military and law enforcement agencies, including the procuracy, the Ministry of Justice, and the tax service. They gained the president's support to expand their influence at the expense of other portfolios, such as social and economic affairs (Goldman 2004). It is telling that since Putin became president, the Duma has not rejected a single bill submitted by the president or members of his close circle (Hashim 2005).

Law and Capitalism in Russia Today

The Yukos episode is inextricably linked with the battle for control over Russia's natural resources. One might argue that such a battle was neither surprising nor exceptional. Cross-country empirical evidence suggests that resource-rich countries are often afflicted by the "resource curse": rather than boosting economic growth and prosperity, an abundance of natural resources is correlated with high levels of corruption and huge disparities in income between the ruling elites, who capture the resources, and the general population, which scarcely participates in the windfall (Sachs and Warner 1995). Others have suggested that natural resources contribute to civil strife and war because competing factions use armed force to gain control over such resources (Ross 2004). In this light, there is perhaps a glimmer of hope in the Yukos story, because the capture of natural resources was at least disguised as regular government enforcement action and did not deteriorate into armed conflict.

That the Yukos episode involves a company in Russia's natural resource sector raises a methodological concern for our study, however. Is Yukos too unique a case to allow generalizations about Russia's model of capitalism and the role of law in that system? To address this concern, we first consider Yukos in the context of the natural resource sector. We then ask whether other sectors in the economy function according to different rules.

In the natural resources sector, Yukos might be an outlier in the particular way in which the company's most valuable assets were returned to state control. Leaving aside the process, however, Yukos squarely falls into a trend of expanding state control over Russia's natural resource sector. Another oil giant that has again come under state control is Sidanko, a company that was also privatized in the loans-for-shares program and acquired by Boris Berezovsky. When he was forced into exile in 2003, Berezovsky sold his stake to his business partner, Roman Abramovich, for US$1.3 billion. In September 2005, Gazprom acquired the company from Abramovich for US$13.1 billion. Commentators argued that the deeper reasons for the deal were more political than economic. This transaction, coming less than a year after Rosneft acquired Yuganskneftegaz, ensured that the Kremlin had regained control over at least 30 percent of the country's crude oil production.[39]

Gazprom has also felt the expansion of state control. The company never participated in the loans-for-shares program, but it had gradually sold more than 50 percent of its shares to investors. In 2005, however, Rosneftegaz purchased a 10.7 percent stake in Gazprom,[40] increasing the controlling stake of the state (or state entities) from 40 percent to a little more than 50 percent. Gazprom's 2005 financial statements commented that the transaction "resulted in higher governmental control over the company, which is strategically important for the national economy."[41] The deal not only placed Gazprom firmly under state control but also consolidated Russia's gas and oil sectors. Rosneftegaz happens to be the core shareholder of Rosneft, the company that acquired Yuganskneftegaz after Gazprom was forced out of the transaction by the intervention of the Houston bankruptcy court. The consolidation was completed with Rosneft acquiring core Yukos assets in the liquidation sale conducted in March 2007.[42]

The consolidation of state ownership of Russia's natural resources suggests that the government itself is skeptical of law's ability to protect its interests. Just as private investors either avoid buying shares in or consolidate rights of control over firms when legal protections are weak, the government is opting for control rather than legal protection. In a highly influential survey on corporate governance, Shleifer and Vishny (1997) suggested that the relatively wide dispersion of ownership in corporations across countries is a function of the quality of investor protections provided by law. In an environment with good legal protections, they argue, investors can afford to take minority stakes and diversify their holdings. By contrast, where investor protection is weak, ownership tends to be highly concentrated, because hands-on control is required to safeguard investments.

These predictions have been borne out in transition economies, including Russia's, which have all witnessed a substantial consolidation of ownership (Berglöf and Pajuste 2003; Berglöf and Bolton 2002). More interesting is how little trust the government itself has in legal protection. Were this not the case, the government would have had few reasons to increase its direct holdings in Gazprom to more than 50 percent and to further consolidate control over the oil sector. Not surprisingly, direct ownership of stakes by the government is reinforced by close political ties of management.[43]

The role of law in all of these transactions (not only in the Yukos case) has been purely instrumental. Law, regulations, and contracts were used to provide a patina of legitimacy and to signal (superficial) lawfulness. But law was not used to constrain those in power, to create and protect rights, or to provide outsiders with access to economic and political markets. Even if Yukos is not an outlier in the natural resource sector, one might still hesitate to generalize from the natural resource sector to other parts of the economy. It is at least conceivable that law plays a more substantial protective function in less politicized sectors of the economy. Goriaev and Sonin (2005) have tested whether the political risk that afflicted Yukos was firm-specific or whether it affected other companies as well. Comparing the effect of enforcement events on the share price of Yukos with that of twenty-five other large companies that were actively traded during the relevant time period,[44] they find that enforcement actions taken against Yukos as well as Khodorkovsky and Lebedev had repercussions far beyond that one firm. Still, the most significant effects were found in companies that had also been privatized in the loans-for-shares deals of the 1990s.

Any attempt to differentiate the natural resource sector from the rest of the Russian economy assumes that they can be separated. In a recent study of ownership concentration in Russia, Guriev et al. (2004) find that most of the largest Russian firms belong to business groups with strong links to the natural resource sector. This suggests that whatever happens in that sector might at least indirectly affect other sectors of the economy as well.

It therefore makes little sense to try to insulate the natural resource sector from the rest of the economy and assume that law might play a completely different role in other sectors. The fact that Russian business is so highly integrated with the natural resources sector indicates that direct control paired with personal relations—not law—is the major governance mechanism in Russia today. Putin has effectively copied this business strategy, which had emerged in the 1990s in response to the uncertainties created by the radical reforms.

Russia Compared to Other Emerging Markets

In a recent paper, Shleifer and Treisman (2005) advance the proposition that Russia is a "normal country":

> Russia's remaining defects are typical of countries at that level of economic development. Both in 1990 and in 2003, Russia was a middle-income country, with GDP per capita around $8,000 at purchasing power parity according to the UN International Comparison Project, a level comparable to that of Argentina in 1991 and Mexico in 1999. Countries in this income range have democracies that are rough around the edges, if they are democratic at all. Their governments suffer from corruption, and their press is almost never entirely free. Most have high income inequality, concentrated corporate ownership and turbulent macroeconomic performance. In all these regards, Russia is quite normal. (152)

As we have suggested previously,[45] although economic diagnosis of this type may be accurate at a high level of generality, it is not very helpful in understanding institutions or comparing them across countries. That middle-income countries generally suffer from bad governance does not reveal how institutional mechanisms operate in these countries and whether they are indeed similar. It offers no hint about the role law and legal institutions might play in stemming corruption and other abuses of power, nor does it provide a basis for any policy conclusions. Using the microlevel tools that we have developed in this book, we suggest that there are some similarities but also important differences between Russia and other emerging markets in the way they currently use law and in the prospect that meaningful legal governance will develop in the future.

Starting with the similarities, the most apparent parallel to the Yukos episode in our sample is the China Aviation Oil case (see chapter 7). The facts of the two cases differ in important ways, of course. In Russia, the state used the law to regain control over valuable assets. In China, the state used control rights to bail out a subsidiary whose management had misbehaved. In both cases, however, the primary concern of the government was to maintain control over the company and its resources. Investor interests were of little or no concern. The management of CAOHC, the holding company of the troubled firm, sold the shares of its subsidiary at a time when it knew (or at least should have known) that the company was approaching insolvency. The tax authorities in Russia and the politicians behind them knew or at least should have known that they were severely damaging the interests of Yukos's shareholders when they enforced highly inflated tax claims against the firm. In both countries the laws were instrumentalized to reallocate valuable assets to the state. The two cases offer similar insights into how a state intent on maintaining control over economic assets perceives capital markets and corporate governance. Markets are used to raise capital for business strategies that have the state's interests at their core; investor interests are an afterthought, if they are considered at all.

As similar as the governance structures of the state-controlled sectors might be in China and Russia, a crucial difference between the two countries remains: China's growth has been fueled not by the state sector, which has been declining since 1980, but by township and village enterprises and other ventures that emerged in the so-called nonstate sectors (Allen 2005). These sectors are not part of the system of state control that we have observed in the CAO case. In Russia, by contrast, the natural resource sector dominates the economy[46] and is intertwined with other business groups and industrial sectors. Although all of these groups do not have direct equity links to the state, the degree of vertical and horizontal integration of Russian firms, including firms in the natural resource sector, as evidenced by Guriev et al. (2004), suggests that the tentacles of state control reach much further in Russia than in China. Another important difference between the two countries is that the Chinese government has been much more willing to experiment with legal governance structures and to encourage legal innovation and experimentation at the regional level. This has created an environment where legal governance has become more contestable as state authorities have competed for optimizing governance structures. In Russia, by contrast, local experimentation has been suppressed by Putin. Lawmaking and law enforcement are controlled by the center with little room for private input, use, or challenge.

From a comparative perspective, our analysis of the SK case is also of interest. Despite some interesting parallels between Korea in the 1970s and

1980s and Russia today—autocratic government, a weak protective function of law, and the important role of business groups in the economy—there are critical differences as well. The Korean state was not a shareholder in the *chaebol* conglomerates and has never held significant stakes in nonfinancial companies. Instead, the Korean government controlled the major banks, which allowed it to channel resources to favored sectors. Even after the banks were privatized in the early 1980s, more than 60 percent of loans were "policy credits" to sectors or *chaebols* favored by the state (Patrick and Park 1994; Amsden and Euh 1993). Whereas in Russia, control over companies in the natural resource sector is the fulcrum for exerting control over the entire economy, in Korea, industrial policy was conducted via control over the financial sector. Financial resources were made available to multiple sectors, ensuring that the economy was diversified. The ultimate check on this strategy was the international product market, because Korea's growth was heavily export-dependent. At present, there is less of a check on the Russian strategy because it is concentrated on natural resources at the expense of manufacturing.

In both countries formal law has become more important as a governance device in recent years, but to further quite different ends. In Korea, today law is often invoked by groups outside the political and business elites that have traditionally dominated the economy. An example is the growth of nonprofit organizations specializing in enforcing minority shareholder rights against prominent *chaebol*-affiliated companies (Milhaupt 2004). To be sure, as the SK case has shown, legal claims by minority shareholders do not always succeed. Nonetheless, the use of law as a means of enforcing investor rights indicates that law is perceived to have important protective functions for the less powerful.

In Russia, by contrast, law continues to be invoked almost exclusively by those in power to further self-defined state interests. During the Yeltsin era, law was at times used to protect private interests during a brief period in which the private sector was ascendant (Hellman, Jones, and Kaufmann 2003). In the Putin era, however, law has been primarily used to strengthen the grip of the state on society and the economy.

Conclusion

The relation between law and capitalism in Russia has taken a different path than the rolling relation between economic change and legal change that we suggested in our analytical framework. Russia today represents extreme centralization of the legal system for purposes of coordinating the economy and, in particular, controlling the natural resource sector. Lawmaking and law enforcement have been principally supply-driven, with little input or feedback from entrepreneurs, civil society, or other actors directly affected by the law. Changes in the contents of the law can be attributed primarily to changes in political power.[47]

PART III

Implications and Extensions

NINE

Understanding Legal Systems

In Part II we conducted institutional autopsies of governance crises that have taken place around the world. Each of these studies allowed us to examine the dynamic interplay among law, markets, and the political economy within a particular system. Now we expand the analysis across systems, both to gauge how well the prevailing analytical approaches discussed in chapter 1 help us understand the phenomena witnessed in the six countries (not very well, we conclude) and to show that the alternative framework for thinking about how real-world legal systems operate we outlined in chapter 2 proves more helpful in understanding how law actually relates to markets. In addition, we show how our approach advances understanding of what globalization means for legal governance of economic activity.

The Institutional Autopsies and the Prevailing Approach

Recall Max Weber's famous assertion that a rational legal system is the foundation for the development of capitalism. This seems to have been interpreted by modern-day Weberians in the economics profession and the international lending organizations to mean that law's exclusive role in a well-functioning capitalist system is to provide protection, particularly through detailed statutory rules governing investors' and other property rights, complemented by an institutional infrastructure to enforce those rights in a neutral fashion.[1] It is a small step from here to the conclusion that these attributes are or should be shared by all legal systems in successful market-oriented economies.

The institutional autopsies we have conducted in this book, however, have demonstrated that broad classifications of legal systems reveal relatively little about the internal operation of legal systems, specifically changing patterns of demand for and supply of legal governance. Our analysis suggests that the dominant classification scheme based on legal "families" is inadequate as an analytical framework. First, note that the classification scheme seriously understates differences among countries said to belong to the same legal family. The German legal system was the model for the Japanese and Korean legal systems. All three countries retain some basic similarities in the structure of their legal system—most notably in the basic code structure and organization of the judiciary—but as we have seen, the legal systems and the economic structures of these countries have deviated substantially over the course of the past fifty years, particularly in the extent to which they have embraced features of the U.S. legal system. The most recent example is Japan's departure from the German or European model in the design of its takeover regime in favor of Delaware judicial doctrine.

Second, note that the canonical classification has no explanatory power over the question why some legal systems belonging to the same family deviate from the supposed key characteristics of that family over time. Take the case of Japan again. At the mid-point of the twentieth century, its legal system bore the strong imprint of the German civil law system. By the beginning of the twenty-first century, it had become much more similar to the U.S. legal system in key areas of economic regulation, though the German system largely resisted such a move during the same time period. Japan's gravitation toward the U.S. system in practice did *not* occur immediately after U.S. principles of shareholders' rights and citizen participation in the legal system were introduced into Japan after World War II but decades later, when the socioeconomic underpinnings of its postwar governance system were cracking. In our view, this timing is critical, because it highlights the importance of the demand for law and the relevance of factors external to law. This dynamic interaction between economic and legal change goes completely unnoticed in a scheme that focuses on historical models and classification into legal families. Recall that one of the best explanations offered in the law and finance literature for the supposed superiority of the common law is that England created the jury trial in the twelfth century (Glaeser and Shleifer 2002)—a rather strong endorsement of the notion that systems are path-dependent! Yet our studies have shown substantial legal change over relatively short periods of time. Thus, for legal systems, explaining change is at least as important as explaining stasis. We devote chapter 10 to this topic.

Third, the countries analyzed in this book defy the notion that market-supportive law must have a uniform set of characteristics, particularly the protective attributes of the common-law systems identified as being of great significance in the law and finance literature and World Bank reform agenda. Despite the formal classification of Germany, Japan, Korea, and China as civil-law countries, which, the empirical studies suggest, economically underperform in comparison to common-law systems, the growth experience of each of these countries had been called an "economic miracle" at some point in latter half of the twentieth century. Moreover, in the economic heyday of each, none of these legal systems as they related to economic governance was centered on property rights protections and private enforcement actions in the courts. This historical experience is supportive of the data we presented in chapter 1 suggesting that growth episodes vary over time and across countries and legal systems in ways that cannot easily be traced to a particular set of institutions or legal attributes.[2]

Finally, in none of the cases we examined were we able to trace the crisis, breakdown, or controversy in corporate governance to a specific "defect" in the law that could be remedied simply by adopting "better," more protective rules and enforcement institutions. Instead, the problems typically stemmed from deep-seated conflicts over the allocation of control and decision-making rights in society and from often equally deep-seated controversy about the very role that law should play in the country's economic governance structure. Conversely, we often saw that importation of new legal rules patterned after law in more advanced economies (typically the United States) had ambiguous, unintended, or delayed consequences for economic activity.

These findings defy attempts to fix governance problems according to the simple algorithm of importing legal rules from more advanced economies to plug holes in the legal systems of less advanced economies. More generally, they defy attempts to associate a particular type of legal system with higher economic growth or other attractive economic outcomes such as larger capital markets. Instead, as we urged in chapter 2, they call for a reconceptualization of the different ways in which legal systems are actually organized in support of markets and a new set of analytical tools with which to examine the challenges different types of legal systems face in supporting markets, which are changing constantly. We now turn to that task by returning to our analytical framework with evidence from the institutional autopsies.

The Organization of Legal Systems

An important organizational dimension of legal systems is their relative degree of centralization or decentralization. The degree of centralization is determined by the number as well as the identity of social actors who participate in the production and enforcement of law. In principle, the more actors a system has, the more decentralized it is. Focusing on numbers of actors alone, however, may be misleading, because the size of all modern states makes direct individual participation in the production of law too costly. Thus, not surprisingly, representative forms of governance (organized interests) exist in every system we have analyzed. Even in the United States, which we describe as having the most decentralized legal system, active participation in the production and enforcement of law occurs via organized interests. But the nature of these organizations differs markedly from those observed in postwar Japan, Germany, and Korea. In the latter three countries, at least in the heyday of their postwar period of high growth, interest groups tended to be large, few in number, relatively stable, and possessed of cohesive policy agendas. These attributes endowed the organizations with considerable bargaining power vis-à-vis governmental actors and made them relatively accountable to their members. For example, unions and employer associations have influenced the production of law in Germany for decades, leading it to be described as corporatist in the literature about comparative capitalist systems. In Japan and Korea, business interests were well represented in the production of law, mostly by way of informal means of consultation among the business elite (acting on behalf of individual firms and, more important, through trade or industry associations), politicians, and bureaucrats. Moreover, as we discussed in chapter 2, the law-making process in all three countries partly insulated policy makers from direct lobbying by interest groups and relied instead on "committees of experts" or consultative bodies made up of interest group representatives, academics, and government officials.

The situation in the United States is different. Organized interest groups form an integral part of the political and social fabric, with lobbyists for virtually every policy issue that could conceivably be pursued by lawmakers and regulators in Washington. But the identity of these lobbying groups and their agendas are more fluid than those in Germany, Japan, or Korea. In the United States, from the perspective of stability and influence on lawmaking, the closest equivalent to German labor unions and employer associations is the organized bar. Yet the legal profession in the United States does not represent a common set of economic interests—other than those of legal professionals themselves—but rather promotes the ability of plaintiffs, whose interests vary from case to case, to join their claims and pursue legal remedies for a host of alleged rights infringements. The long-term impact of this group on specific policy outcomes is far less apparent than is the case in the other countries. Rather, the legal profession plays a critical role in maintaining and advancing the basic structure of the U.S. governance system, namely, its decentralized nature and the prevalence of the protective function of law.

The actual changes experienced by legal systems around the world are better explained by leaving behind schematic classifications and historical origins and analyzing the interplay of existing governance structures and changes in the demand side of law at critical junctures in a country's history. Using the organization of a legal system as a critical parameter for predicting specific outcomes, we suggest that a legal regime that protects individual investors' interests will be produced in response to growing demand, provided that the system is sufficiently decentralized at that point to foster contestation of governance structures.

In the United States, for example, we observe the emergence of minority shareholder protection rules at the state and federal levels in the first two decades of the twentieth century (Pistor et al. 2002), a time when the ownership structure of firms was shifting from a concentrated to a highly dispersed form (Berle and Means 1932). The demand for better protection of minority investors' rights triggered a series of legislative interventions at the state level, as well as federal intervention after the stock market crash of 1929 (Mahoney 2001b). The demise of concentrated ownership and the diminished reputation of major financial institutions as a result of the crisis in the late 1920s undermined the banks' bargaining power and facilitated this change (Roe 1990). In the United Kingdom—the mother country of the common law—changes in the ownership structure of firms occurred later and never to the same extent as in the United States. Not surprisingly, legal change lagged behind as well, and important aspects of corporate governance continue to deviate from the U.S. model (Black and Coffee 1994). The interests of relatively large owners and major players in the marketplace prevented decentralization of corporate governance to the extent witnessed in the United States. Instead, coordination among these powerful private players has played a critical role in corporate governance in the United Kingdom. A major example is the U.K. Takeover Panel, a self-governing organization that manages disputes in a highly coordinative fashion.

This dichotomy between centralized and decentralized systems is agnostic with regard to state structure. The classification does not depend on whether a country has a federal or a unitary system of government. Nor does it matter whether the relevant players are state or private actors. It thereby departs from other usages of the centralization-decentralization terminology that is common in the social sciences (Lieberman 2005).[3] The reason for this departure is that, in practice, the degree of centralization of a legal system does not correlate neatly with state structure. The United States, Germany, and Russia are all federal systems, but the allocation of law-making and law enforcement functions between the federation and its constituent parts (states, *Länder*, and *oblasts*, respectively) differs considerably among them. In the United States, jurisdiction over key areas of law, including corporate law, lies with the states, whereas they lie within the jurisdiction of the federation in Germany and Russia. More strikingly, in the United States, corporate law is made concurrently by many different actors at all levels of governmental structure. This includes the state legislatures but also state courts, state regulators, the Congress, federal regulators, and the federal courts. By contrast, in Germany and Russia lawmaking concerning virtually all matters related to the corporation is centralized at the federal level, and central government regulators play a dominant role in law enforcement. To the extent that courts play a role in enforcing corporate law at all—and that role is quite limited in Germany and Russia (Pistor and Xu 2003)—they are part of a unified judicial system.[4]

Furthermore, as the comparison between China and Russia suggests, a de jure unitary state can de facto be more decentralized than a federal state. China is formally a unitary state; Russia is a federal state. Yet China is substantially more decentralized in its governance structures than is Russia (Qian, Roland, and Xu 2006). This is in part a product of the Cultural Revolution, which undermined the central state bureaucracy and positioned local and regional governments as key actors at the outset of economic reforms. This devolution of de facto powers has been reinforced by a reform strategy that encouraged local experimentation and used competition among bureaucrats as a tool of governance (Huang 1996; Qian 2003; Pistor and Xu 2005). The Chinese experience also illustrates that even within a system where governance is controlled by state agents there can be substantial decentralization. It is therefore not always appropriate to associate higher levels of state control with greater centralization. Conversely, Yeltsin's Russia provided powerful evidence of state capture by private interest groups (Hellman, Jones, and Kaufmann 2003), contrary to the notion that private control of economic assets is necessarily associated with decentralized forms of control.

Different theories exist as to *why* some countries have a more or less centralized economic, political, or legal system. Gerschenkron (1962) famously attributed the organization of economic systems to the relative positioning of a country in the quest for economic development. Early developers such as England were comparatively decentralized, whereas late developers had to make greater efforts to mobilize capital, giving rise to coordinated or even state-managed efforts toward capital accumulation. Djankov et al. (2003) attribute the organization of political systems to the challenges a state faces at some critical constituting moment. This moment defines and limits the potential scope for subsequent change. Damaška (1986) attributes the organization of legal systems to the political history of a country—witness the legacy of liberalism in England and feudalism in Continental Europe. Similarly, Glaeser and Shleifer (2002) trace the origins of legal systems to the political economy of England and France in the Middle Ages.

We do not attempt to offer yet another theory as to why some systems are more centralized than others. We simply note that throughout the world there appears to be a strong (but not perfect) affinity in the organization of the political, economic, and legal systems in a given country. Moreover, most commentators agree that the organization of the polity is an important predictor of the organization of a country's legal and economic systems.

Where we depart from existing theories is in the conclusion that typically follows from this analysis: that once these features are in place, the system follows a highly path-dependent process of institutional change. Instead, we argue that under certain circumstances the system as such—not only elements within systems—can and does change quite significantly. A critical variable for change in the organization and function of the *legal system* suggested by our institutional autopsies is a challenge (an economic or political crisis or entry of a new market actor) that undermines the position of the relevant social elites that govern each of the six systems we have analyzed—although the identity of these elites and their position within each system differs.[5]

In the United States, the indictment of Arthur Anderson and questions raised about the ability of other intermediaries such as lawyers, auditors, and boards of directors to adequately monitor the highly decentralized legal system provided the political opportunity for a legislative shift toward a more centralized legal system—at least as it relates to corporate governance—that relies more on mandatory regulation and less on the judgments and initiative of private intermediaries. In Germany, the changing composition of top management in flagship companies and their refocusing on international rather than domestic markets, paired with the weakening of labor unions, left the maintenance of the traditional postwar system to the criminal justice system. In Japan, the change in the ownership structure of firms, itself a result of the prolonged recession in the 1990s, made the governance system vulnerable to new entrants who challenged the viability and legitimacy of the prevailing rules of market conduct. A similar process has occurred in Korea, although in that case the newcomer was a foreign investor. In the CAO case, a scandal threatened the existing order, although the collaborative efforts of Singaporean regulators and Chinese officials in control of CAO's parent company ensured that any serious challenge to the Chinese governance system was diffused. Finally, Putin's ascension to power and his relative independence from the oligarchs who had dominated the Yeltsin era stripped away the protections that had been available to Khodorkovsky.

The Functions of Law

On the functional dimension, we have characterized legal systems as either primarily protective or coordinative, with signaling and credibility enhancement serving auxiliary functions. The protection of individual property rights and contractual claims is often described as the core function of law in a market economy. In fact, the nature of the rights or entitlements that are protected in a market-oriented economy is determined by political compromises and depends on the balance of power among those who supply and demand law in a given country. The Yukos case illustrates the plastic nature of property rights protection. In this episode, the legal protection of creditors' rights turned into state control over private assets because the tax authorities were the firm's largest creditors. The case suggests that rules ostensibly designed for the protection of a particular stakeholder may be secondary in importance to access to judicial review by an independent and impartial judiciary. This in turn is a function of the willingness of the political rulers to subject themselves to legal constraints (Landes and Posner 1975; Ramseyer 1994). In fact, empirical data suggest that the de facto independence of the judiciary is a product of the competitiveness of the legal system (Stephenson 2003).

A legal system reveals itself as protective or coordinative in part in the design of substantive rules that allocate rights. Substantive rules or standards may announce a particular allocation of rights. Examples include the right of landowners to protect their property against intruders, the right of shareholders to elect a company's directors, the right of a tort victim to claim compensation, and so forth. But a clear allocation of rights ex ante that takes full account of all future claims is simply impossible.[6] Competing claims may arise over the right to emit noise or pollutants, the right of nonowners to trespass on property (Coase 1960), or the ability of a large blockholder in a corporation to exercise its property rights without consideration for minority investors (Bebchuk 1999). Put differently, most substantive entitlements in any legal system are inherently mixed (Calabresi and Melamed 1972). A clear allocation of rights and entitlements ex ante is therefore difficult, if not impossible. A more important indicator of whether a legal system is protective or coordinative is how it purports to resolve competing interests. Some systems opt for litigation among competing claimants, each of them maintaining that they have an exclusive right. The function of the court then is to allocate this right to one of the parties. In practice, claimants often settle prior to a final ruling, not least in order to avoid the steep costs of prolonged litigation (Hughes and Snyder 1999). In this context, the allocation of legal rights serves as a coordinating device around which parties negotiate a settlement. Nonetheless, the availability of litigation provides an important "shadow of the law" for this kind of coordination.

Contrast this with systems that openly discourage formal mechanisms of dispute resolution and instead encourage or force competing claimants into less formal means of bargaining and coordination. An important example is Japan, where the number of lawyers admitted to bar in a given year is subject to state regulation. The quota has been increased, but the fact remains that government intervention affects the options available for dispute settlement. This is not to say that law plays no role in resolving disputes. In several areas special administrative agencies have been established to resolve social problems, including damages inflicted by malfunctioning consumer products, dangerous pollutants, and the like (Upham 1987). These agencies encourage mediation and bargaining instead of adversarial individualized dispute settlement. Another often-cited example of law's coordinative function is the German model of codetermination. By requiring that 50 percent of a company's board members be elected by employees, not shareholders, the law ensures that the interests of employees will be represented at the board level and not only on the shop floor. Their presence on the board gives employees critical information that they can use to challenge the implementation of policies to which they have not consented, though the decisive vote is typically held by the shareholder side.

Finally, recent legal developments in China suggest that lawmakers favor a coordinative role for law and enforcement institutions rather than a protective one. Recall that in investor disputes courts may grant civil damages only after the securities regulator (the CSRC) or the criminal justice system has affirmed a violation of the law. Note the important gatekeeper function retained by the state over efforts to protect individual interests, ensuring that, at least in broad terms, the state coordinates responses to firm-level disputes. The Singaporean model of centralized law enforcement similarly places higher value on state-structured problem resolution than on the interests of affected individuals.

In the legal systems we have examined in this book, we detect a close affinity between coordination and centralization, on one hand, and protection and decentralization, on the other. The reason seems fairly straightforward: the difficulty of collective action make it costly if not impossible to coordinate atomized individual interests (Olson 1971). Effective coordination over long periods therefore requires a stable set of organized interest groups that can effectively act on behalf of others. To the extent that such groups dominate the production and enforcement of law, the legal system becomes more centralized. At the same time, since the groups exist largely to protect the interests of their members and by definition maintain close (often informal) connections with the state, legal governance in concentrated legal systems tends to reinforce coordination and to resist the centripetal pull of creation and enforcement of individual rights. Conversely, in societies organized around a plethora of constantly shifting interest groups, none of which enjoys stable and intimate access to the law-making and enforcement processes, the legal system is comparatively decentralized. In such a system, the protection of individual entitlements tends to be the central function. Thus, in our view, a more helpful way of understanding differences across legal systems around the world is seeing how they vary along two dimensions: centralized-decentralized and coordinative-protective.

We hasten to underscore several points. First, virtually all legal systems are blends of the two dimensions. Second, the polar ends of the functional dimension are mixed rather than pure: coordination often entails a degree of protection; protection often requires a degree of coordination. Third, the labels we have chosen are not intended to carry normative significance. No polar end of the spectrum represents an ideal type legal system. Indeed, the major thrust of the analysis thus far has been to reject the notion that one type of legal system is inherently superior to another.

Typology of Legal Governance around the World

In this chapter we reproduce the matrix we introduced in chapter 2 (figure 2.1). We have now situated the seven countries discussed in this book in

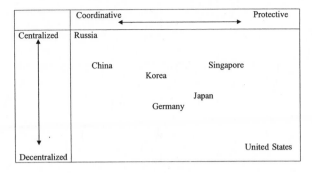

Figure 9.1. Legal systems matrix, completed

the space between the two axes (see figure 9.1). The matrix obviously serves only illustrative purposes, and the precise position of each country could be debated. The important point for our purposes is the relative position of individual countries vis-à-vis the others.

Based on our analysis of the institutional autopsies, we have located Russia and the United States at opposite corners of the matrix. Russia has the most centralized and least protective of the legal systems we analyzed; the United States has the most decentralized and protective. In Russia the state continues to play a major role not only in the design of law but in the use of law as a means to control the economy and society. In many instances this goes far beyond coordination as defined above and may be more aptly described as state ordering through law. Under Putin the state has regained a near-monopoly over law and limits the extent to which law can be used autonomously. A highly centralized structure allows only few agents outside the president's inner circle access to the law-making and law enforcement processes. Private parties therefore have few incentives to use the legal system except to use it against the state when this is the only line of defense available, however ineffective it might be in specific cases (Pistor 1996). Demand for law by private parties is therefore low. Consistent with these general characteristics, disputes against the state today far outnumber those filed against private parties.[7] These features make Russia's the least contested and contestable governance system among the seven countries we have analyzed. That is, parties outside the president's inner orbit have virtually no capacity to adapt the legal system to their needs or to participate in the process of legal governance. Instead, they use the legal system as a last resort to protect themselves against intrusions by the state.

The Yukos affair illustrates an attempt by an individual (albeit a rich and powerful one) to use the protective function of law to challenge a state that had monopolized legal governance. We argue that Putin understood the nature of this challenge. He was keenly aware that granting full private autonomy and the protection of the law to oligarchs such as Khodorkovsky would weaken his ability to exert full control over Russia's economic and political systems. Nonetheless, the state's response to the challenge posed by Khodorkovsky was not unconstrained. The constraints, however, were external; they were not internal legal or political restraints on the exercise of government power. Instead, the Russian government's actions against Yukos had to be consistent with the objective of raising capital on international markets in order to realize the economic and political potential of Russia's rich resource endowment. They were therefore disguised as (pure) law enforcement actions. In fact, Putin emphasized repeatedly that the tax authorities and courts were in full compliance with the letter of the law. For now, this strategy has succeeded. Khodorkovsky is in jail, and Rosneft acquired Yuganskneftegaz in 2005 and the remainder of Yukos's most valuable assets in 2007.

The legal system of the United States presents a striking contrast. Private law enforcement is critical to many areas of economic governance and the "private attorney general" plays a key role in expanding the reach of law and increasing demand for the enforcement of private entitlements. Kagan (2001) argues that "the United States has by far the world's largest cadre of special 'cause lawyers' seeking to influence public policy and institutional practices by means of innovative litigation. In no other country are lawyers so entrepreneurial in seeking out new kinds of business, so eager to challenge authority, or so quick to propose new liability-expanding legal theories" (8–9). Even when the legislature creates an important new body of law (such as the securities laws) and a powerful central regulator (the Securities and Exchange Commission) is charged with its enforcement, in practice enforcement is often dominated by private attorneys and their clients. Under pressure from the private bar, which greatly expanded its powers after World War II (Witt 2007),[8] courts increasingly recognized private rights of action, which allowed private investors to sue issuers and underwriters and their agents for violations of the securities laws. As a result, the class-action securities suit has become the most powerful weapon for enforcing compliance and may now be serving as a substitute enforcement mechanism for some state law rules that are no longer meaningfully enforced in state courts (Thompson and Sale 2003; Coffee 2007).

Contrast this with the approach that courts in other countries have taken in similar situations. German and Japanese courts have denied a private right of action under the securities laws in the absence of explicit instructions from the legislature.[9] In both countries, judicial deference not only to the legislature but also to the existing governmental enforcement apparatus appears to explain the result. By contrast, virtually every important public policy issue in the United States—economic or otherwise—is susceptible to legal challenge and often to multiple and even conflicting enforcement actions at different levels of the system, many of which provide alternative means of private participation in the law-making and enforcement processes.

The passage and aftermath of the Sarbanes-Oxley Act (SOX), discussed in chapter 3, is a prime illustration of the highly decentralized and contested legal system in the United States. The Enron crisis demonstrated that a governance structure that relies on multiple agents can, under certain market conditions (in this case a stock market bubble and misaligned incentive structures), succumb to the agency costs that are inherent in a system of decentralized monitors. A blizzard of legal responses followed the collapse of Enron. Numerous lawsuits were brought by attorneys on behalf of investors and pension plan beneficiaries in different states. Creditors filed claims in the bankruptcy court whose protection Enron had sought after it failed to find a white knight. They also initiated litigation against individuals for failure to disclose what they knew about Enron's problems. Prosecutors brought criminal charges against key players. The Securities and Exchange Commission and state attorneys general launched investigations against financial intermediaries that might have aided and abetted Enron in its fraudulent dealings. And of course, Congress enacted SOX.

The legislation sought to improve legal governance by establishing uniform central standards for governing publicly traded corporations and by establishing a new independent but state-monitored body that would monitor the auditing profession (the Public Company Accounting Oversight Board). The law can therefore be described as an attempt to centralize legal governance on the lawmaking side as well as on the regulatory or law enforcement side. On the regulatory side the act has arguably succeeded. The oversight board shifts regulation of the auditing industry from a self-governing, or decentralized, model toward a centralized one. The board has been actively establishing new standards, conducts regular inspections, and has launched a number of enforcement actions. With regard to firm governance, however, the result is far less clear. Firms regulated by the act have spent millions of dollars to bring their governance structure into compliance—the major beneficiaries being accounting firms, law firms, and consultants. This has taken place amid complaints about compliance costs and warnings that these costs undermine the competitiveness of the U.S. capital markets.[10] As a result, a government working group was formed to study the question of exempting small firms from SOX's more costly requirements, and private-sector groups, at times with the endorsement of the Bush administration, sought to roll back some features of the law.[11]

The fact that shortly after SOX was enacted, concerted efforts at partial repeal were made (even as some vehemently argued that it did not effect meaningful change in the first place) demonstrates how powerful the centripetal forces in this system are and how strongly attempts at centralization are resisted. The most surprising aspect of SOX was perhaps that the law was enacted at all. Earlier attempts to address the costs of a highly decentralized legal governance structure did not fare very well. Consider the 1995 Private Securities Litigation Reform Act, which was supposed to address widely conflicting requirements for securities class-action suits based on fraudulent conduct.[12] The goal was to unify as well as raise standing requirements in order to filter out strike suits—those brought by law firms based on little evidence of malfeasance but in the hope of extorting a quick settlement from a firm that wishes to avoid prolonged litigation. What Congress in fact produced was a statute with a multiple personality disorder (Grundfest and Pritchard 2002) that failed to clarify the relevant procedural standards, as suggested by the different interpretations that emerged after the act was passed,[13] and that failed to effect any long-term reduction in the amount of securities litigation in the United States.

In sum, legal governance is probably more crucial to the U.S. economic system than to that of any other country in the world. In the United States, legal governance takes the form of decentralized contestation of individual rights and interests. This has many virtues, including allowing the governance system to respond flexibly to new challenges. The same attributes, however, have many costs. The most important of these are not lawyers' fees, the focus of so much public criticism. Rather, effective coordinated intervention is difficult, even when serious systemic weaknesses may call for such intervention. Moreover, passage of major legal reforms alone does not guarantee that they will be sustained or implemented as intended, given the tremendous pressures of decentralization, competition for enforcement authority, and incessant contestation of rules. The costs of such a system and its potential incompatibility with legal and economic systems organized around quite different principles are routinely overlooked by scholars and policy makers fixated on a single vision of "good law" for economic growth.

The other five legal systems examined in this book in detail are situated at various points between these two extremes. We included Singapore in this matrix because the institutional autopsy of the CAO case involved an analysis of the Chinese and Singaporean legal systems. It is somewhat of an outlier because it defies the notion that protection and decentralization necessarily go together. Singapore (a common-law country) displays important features of protective law but uses state agents in enforcement practices that are closely coordinated. Although we do not have a case from the United Kingdom in our sample, we would suggest that it would fall somewhere between Singapore and the United States on the vertical axis of figure 9.1.

China shares with Russia a socialist legacy and an institutional inclination to manage economic and social affairs from the center. For example, we showed that the CAO crisis was resolved by coordination among powerful state actors and their agents in China and Singapore. Still, important decision-making power over economic and social affairs in China has devolved to the provinces and municipalities to some extent. Many reforms, including legal reforms introduced during the past three decades, originated at the provincial level and subsequently spread nationwide (Lubman 1995). The unifying force in this competitive administration continues to be the Communist Party. It exerts control today primarily by controlling the appointment and promotion of cadres and thus the careers of key bureaucrats across the country (Huang 1996). In the past, law tended to complement and support coordination by the state or was used largely for signaling purposes. Although the trends thus far are clearly reversible, law seems to be claiming some autonomous space in China. Private attorneys have brought suits to protect peasants against land seizure by the state (Pils 2005) and to protect shareholders victimized by fraud at the publicly traded SOEs in which they had invested (Chen 2003). These actions seek to assert a more protective function of law. Not infrequently, the attempts to create a more protective role for law have been rebuked or severely limited—as was the case, for example, with investor lawsuits as discussed in the institutional autopsy of the CAO scandal. Nonetheless, the institutional compromise that was eventually reached in China, which allows investors to bring legal action for misrepresentation if a state actor (the CSRC, Ministry of Finance, or prosecutors) has verified a violation, suggests that the state was unwilling or unable to completely suppress this bottom-up process of rights enforcement. It remains to be seen whether in the long run contestability can take hold in China.

Our institutional autopsy of the CAO case is consistent with this analysis. At first reading the case suggests that law can contest and even trump state interests, at least when legal governance is invoked by foreign regulators. The firm went into bankruptcy, and enforcement actions were initiated against its management. The very fact that its Chinese parent company allowed these actions to take place without attempting another bailout of its subsidiary was a wake-up call to investors, who had relied on implicit state insurance. More important, the parent company itself was sanctioned for insider trading. This was a novelty for a Chinese state-owned company, and it is an open question whether sanctions would have been applied had the incident occurred in mainland China. The legal interventions by the Singaporean authorities signaled that law enforcement could be a means of contesting the control of Chinese state-owned enterprises over subsidiaries listed abroad. In the end, however, law did not fundamentally challenge the prevailing mode of governance. Instead, law enforcement actions were tailored to accommodate the crisis resolution negotiated by the major parties: CAOHC, on one hand, and Temasek on the other. The tailoring of the legal intervention to support the coordinated resolution of the crisis was made possible by the Singapore legal system—highly centralized in its own right— which discourages private enforcement and places state agents at the center of legal governance. The CAO episode did not challenge this governance system and triggered no further institutional reforms in Singapore; rather, it reinforced the existing organizational structure. The speed with which the crisis was resolved and confidence in the market reestablished silenced any doubts about the efficacy of Singapore's coordinative governance structure.

Germany, Korea, and Japan all are located toward the center of our matrix. This reflects the postwar role of major organized interest groups in the production and enforcement of law in these countries, though the nature of these interest groups varies considerably. Moreover, their composition and influence have changed quite considerably in recent years, as has the role of litigation as an alternative means of legal governance. In the postwar period, all three countries placed considerable constraints on access to decentralized judicial lawmaking and law enforcement. In Japan and Korea, for example, the size of the legal profession has been closely regulated by strict quotas on the number of candidates that can pass the bar examination in a given year. Although the number of new lawyers has been increased in recent years as a result of demand-side pressures see (Milhaupt and West [2004]), the fact remains that the state (and sectors of the legal profession itself) assiduously seek to control the size of the profession. Moreover, institutional barriers to litigation in these two countries, such as high filing fees in Japan and high thresholds for the exercise of shareholders' rights in Korea, discouraged resort to legal governance.[14] Only when such barriers were abolished in Japan did the number of shareholder suits, for example, increase (West 2001). Similarly, in Korea, it took the Asian financial crisis to prompt lowering of the thresholds for exercise of shareholders' rights, after which derivative suits began to be filed for the first time in Korea's history. Partly in response to the difficult enforcement environment, many of the first such suits were brought by nonprofit shareholder interest groups rather than individual shareholders (Milhaupt 2004).

In Germany, litigation is common and widely used in principle (Ietswaart 1990). In the corporate context, however, litigation has been restricted purposefully to ensure that stakeholders bargain for mutually agreeable outcomes within the governance structures provided by law. Originally, shareholders could not litigate directly but had to force the supervisory board into action. Subsequent change empowered shareholders who represented a substantial part of the outstanding stock (at first 10 percent, later 5 percent and now 1 percent) to bring legal action should the supervisory board fail to take action. Thus, in the postwar period, all three countries shunned overt endorsement of the protective function of law in corporate governance, instead encouraging key stakeholders to coordinate their actions by raising the cost of access to courts and other formal mechanisms of governance.

All three, however, are increasingly incorporating more protective features into their legal systems. Several factors have contributed to this change. First, the power of organized interests has declined over time. Dwindling membership in labor unions has undercut their power in Germany, and the long recession in Japan and the financial crisis in Korea weakened organized interests that were central to the coordinative systems that emerged in the postwar era, in particular, banks, corporate groups, and bureaucrats in key economic ministries. Meanwhile, globalization has undermined the established bargaining systems in important ways. It created new market entrants who are not part of the established system, as well as new business opportunities for incumbents. It also provided means of exit from the domestic institutions for many of the most competitive firms (in the form of foreign capital and product markets, for example). These changes diminished the attractiveness and continued viability of the established bargaining system. The ensuing governance vacuum had to be filled in some way. In each of the three countries, to different degrees, the "something" was law—specifically, legal rights premised on a more decentralized and aggressive enforcement infrastructure.

The crises we examined in these three countries challenged the mode of legal governance, in particular by triggering debates about the proper role of law in the country's governance structure. Though not framed in the terms we have used, fundamentally the debate in Japan and Korea involved the questions of how much legal access and protection should be granted to newcomers and whether they were using the legal tools at hand properly. All three countries had already introduced reforms that strengthened the protective function of law. Unlike the investors in the CAO case, for example, the foreign investor in Korea (Sovereign) could bring its own legal action in court and did not have to rely on the judgment or benevolence of a regulator to seek a remedy. But Sovereign lost each of the legal battles it fought. The court appeared to interpret Sovereign's actions as a hostile takeover attempt and granted SK's management the right to defend itself. In its ruling, the court focused on the specific case before it and gave a formalistic legal interpretation to the questions presented. To an outside observer, it may appear that the court was biased in favor of SK's management. But it can easily be imagined that from the perspective of an honest judge trained in the Korean system,[15] the sudden attempt by an unknown foreign investor to oust the management of a major *chaebol* amounted to a threat not only to the firm's stability but to the foundations of Korea's system of governance.

This outcome notwithstanding, the fact that an investor mounted a sustained challenge to *chaebol* management using mechanisms prescribed by law, including a proxy battle and litigation, marks an important change in the governance of large Korean firms.[16] In the past, control over the *chaebol* by the founding families and their descendants was essentially uncontested, except perhaps by the government itself. It took an outsider to mount such an open challenge to the modus operandi. That Sovereign lost may therefore be less relevant in the long term than the impact its actions had on the corporate governance environment in Korea.[17] The availability of legal recourse, which was facilitated by the legal reforms of the late 1990s, together with the entry of new (foreign) players into a system that had relied primarily on coordination and informal governance among insiders has increased the contestability of governance.

Unlike the episode in Korea, the Mannesmann trial did not involve a direct confrontation between foreigners as the new entrants and insiders as the incumbents. Rather, it was a conflict among critical stakeholders of the traditional German governance system, some of whom defected as a result of globalization. Greater exposure of German firms to foreign markets, and in particular their participation in mergers and acquisition as both targets and acquirers, has been accompanied by the introduction of different norms and practices that have challenged both informal norms and formal law. In the Mannesmann case, law was mobilized to defend rather than attack the existing governance system. Backed by public opinion, the prosecutor acted as the major defender of the system, and this position was endorsed by the courts. But important legal changes were introduced even as the case unfolded, and they paint a very different picture of the German legal system. Stakeholders who expected to gain from globalization and changes in Germany's governance structures, including corporations with an international profile as well as investors, played a critical role in supporting these changes. Legal reforms that were implemented before the retrial of Esser, Ackermann, and the other defendants was terminated in the fall of 2006 included important changes in corporate, capital market, and civil procedure laws. The combined impact of these changes is to strengthen the protective function of law. Shareholders and their legal advocates are the greatest beneficiaries. In the past, labor unions or banks might have blocked such change, but their relative bargaining power and stake in the traditional German governance system has changed. Labor unions have lost membership and public support. Banks have reduced their holdings in German corporations and turned to international capital markets instead.

The Mannesmann trial was not a catalyst for these changes. Rather, it generated controversy because a battle over the direction of Germany's governance systems was already under way. The final outcome of this contest is still uncertain. Although shareholder rights have been strengthened on paper, they still need to be tested in the courts. As in Korea and elsewhere, German judges have their own perceptions and value systems, which influence their interpretation of the law. And as previously noted, although decentralized law enforcement has become more feasible, cases remain scarce. Moreover, as evidenced in the Mannesmann case, the criminal justice system can be used to counter the forces of individualized contestation of law and uphold the social norms on which Germany's model of a market economy has rested.

As in Germany, the events that gave rise to the Livedoor case in Japan were triggered most directly not by changes in the law but by changes in the economic landscape. The ownership structures of Japanese firms underwent considerable change over the course of the 1990s. They became less concentrated and more heterogeneous as more foreign investors bought shares in Japanese firms. New entrants, including domestic players such as Livedoor, discovered that they could use the law to protect their interests. Unlike incumbents, they did not shy away from turning to law instead of relying on bargaining within established networks. Incumbents who had relied on social norms that discouraged the use of legal contestation even when formally available were caught in a bind. They could either lobby for constraints on the protective function of law or they could respond in kind by mobilizing law for their own ends.

The arrest and successful prosecution of Horie also suggests that law is not only a weapon for new entrants; it can be used to defend the old system, as it has in Germany and in Korea. Nonetheless, the Livedoor episode seems to have enhanced the role of formal law as a governance device. Since the conclusion of the Livedoor litigation, several other hostile takeover attempts have generated litigation and important court rulings. A return to the kind of informal governance that dominated Japan's business relations until the early 1990s (see Milhaupt 1996) would now be too risky in the face of possible legal attacks. Changes in the demand for law have thus triggered legal responses in a system where a rolling relation between legal and economic change is now well established. These developments have propelled the Japanese governance system much further toward a decentralized and protective function of law than did the formal legal changes that were introduced by the U.S. occupation after World War II.

Globalization and Changing Demand for Legal Governance

In four of the cases we have analyzed—Mannesmann, Livedoor, SK, and CAO—exposure of a governance regime designed for domestic markets to international markets and practices was a prominent catalyst for change. This raises the question of whether the process of globalization enhances not only legal governance in general but the protective function of law in particular. Recall that the key finding of the law and finance research is that common-law systems are associated with larger capital markets. Thus, perhaps it is primarily the increasing importance of global capital markets that is driving the transition of many legal systems toward U.S.-style legal protections.

That outsiders are drawn to law as a tool to advance their interests is not surprising. Outsiders lack access to the networks of exchange and information on which insiders rely (Landa 1981; Kali 1999). Protective features of a legal system have the advantage of being accessible by anyone, particularly when complemented by open access and decentralized enforcement regimes. By contrast, coordinative governance systems, particularly when supported by legal systems that limit access to legal remedies and place many enforcement decisions in the hands of state actors, advantage insiders rather than outsiders. Increasing participation of outsiders in governance systems around the globe might therefore put pressure on legal systems to embrace the protective function of law. In fact, emerging markets are often advised to change their laws in this fashion as a way to attract foreign capital flows (World Bank 2001). A natural conjecture is that systems of governance will converge in countries that participate in world markets.

We discuss the patterns of legal change and the likelihood of legal convergence in chapter 10. However, two points seem critical in assessing the implications of legal and governance change that we have analyzed in the present chapter. The first is that broad access to legal protection is likely to change the dynamics of governance in ways that are difficult to predict. Law can be mobilized for a variety of purposes and used to protect different interests. The actual use of law therefore has an inherently political dimension, regardless of how objectively neutral the law appears on its face. It is often assumed that shifting the resolution of conflicts from bargaining among stakeholders (or under the supervision of political actors) to courts will neutralize the political nature of disputes. In fact, it simply shifts the means of the contestation from new entrants demanding that incumbents grant them access on one hand, to an institution (the judiciary) that itself is embedded in the norms, practices, and beliefs of a given country, on the other.[18] In the SK and Mannesmann cases, courts performed the role of guardians of the basic social norms.[19] These norms tend to change at a much slower rate than formal law or markets.

The second point is that a new entrant (foreign or domestic) will take social norms into account when deciding whether to mount a legal attack on the prevailing governance system. Recall that in the SK case other foreign investors could have sided with Sovereign and brought about a change in management at the shareholder meeting in March 2004. They chose not to, because such a move would have entailed substantial costs for them in light of the prevailing normative system and power relations in the country. Similarly, Vodafone could have completed a hostile takeover of Mannesmann but chose to pursue a friendly merger though it was the economically more costly option, most likely because the company did not want to alienate the German domestic market, which after all was their intended target. The demand for legal governance, and in particular for a highly protective law, is determined not only by the availability of legal remedies and enforcement mechanisms (the supply of formal law) but also by the expected costs the exercise of legal rights may entail. Cost includes not only the actual expense of invoking the legal system's protection but also the social or political cost of having deviated from the "accepted" institutional path. This cost-benefit calculus appears to propel an interesting dynamic in the process of legal change as a result of globalization. Often it seems that foreign players are adept at getting new formal legal changes adopted. Perhaps this is because their outside status gives them leverage to push for legislative change that domestic actors lack. But foreign players are often treated with considerable skepticism when they actually seek to *use* legal mechanisms for their own ends.

On the other hand, as the German and Japanese cases demonstrate, when players within the system make use of new legal tools or governance practices, they can be potent forces for challenging prevailing assumptions about how the world should operate, because their actions cannot be written off as the work of an outsider. Collective expectations form the very essence of institutions (Aoki 2001). Thus, the uncoordinated but cumulative efforts of foreign and domestic actors appear to make a powerful combination for inducing institutional change in an increasingly globalized world. Sill, the Singaporean example similarly suggests that as long as a governance regime is sufficiently responsive to the interests of foreign investors, the way it accomplishes this goal is far less relevant. Singapore has strong incentives to be responsive to investor interests in a way that more directly satisfies the demand for legal governance. It is a small country that faces stiff competition in its ambition to establish itself as an international marketplace in Southeast Asia. In fact, using a coordinative system plays to the advantages of a small countries governed by well-connected insiders. It has also allowed the country to be responsive to rather divergent interests—those of small investors from all over the world and those of China as the major supplier of firms to be listed on the Singaporean stock exchange. China seems to be poised to follow this example rather than converge on a U.S.-style decentralized and rights-focused legal system. The implicit (and sometimes explicit) claim that in order to achieve sustained economic success countries must endorse a court-centered system of decentralized and protective legal governance thus appears to be unfounded. In particular, informal and coordinative forms of governance have proved to be highly successful and long-lived, as the Japanese, German, and Korean examples demonstrate.

Conclusion

Our analytical framework has allowed us to examine legal systems as they operate in the real world. Some general lessons can be learned from the comparative analysis of different legal systems based on our work thus far. The first is that legal systems can be classified according to two important dimensions: their organization and the major functions they perform. This classification has an affinity with the traditional distinction between civil-law and common-law systems, but our analytical framework is better suited to account for change over time within and across systems. Second, each system has its own costs and benefits and its own system-inherent vulnerabilities, which may trigger a crisis and, in the extreme case, collapse of the system. A decentralized system is prone to waste of resources that results from multiple contestations of identical issues at different levels. It may be captured by interest groups that benefit from contestation as such without respect to the social gains or losses derived from it. Most fundamentally, as the struggle to reach equilibrium in U.S. corporate governance after the Enron scandal has illustrated, some serious governance problems require coordination, not a blizzard of individuated and competing enforcement efforts. Conversely, coordinative systems may lend greater stability to a system and be less wasteful. What makes for stability in some contexts, however, may amount to petrification in others. Moreover, a coordinative system relies not only on formal processes that can be changed fairly easily but also on the capacity of important interest groups to organize themselves and engage in bargaining and monitoring with other interest groups. When changes in the broader environment undercut these groups, the overall system is weakened. This can result in greater decentralization and formal legal empowerment. It might also result in a greater centralization of governance in the hands of the state.

TEN

Legal Change

We began the description of our analytical framework by noting that the prevailing view of law's relation to markets is overly static, largely failing to account for the possibility that legal systems change. In fact, the institutional autopsies and chapter 9 have exposed legal change as an important feature common to all the systems we have studied.[1] We devote this chapter to an exploration of several important questions related to legal change, legal transplants, and legal harmonization and convergence. We begin with the simple observation that all countries constantly change some subset of the rules that form part of their legal systems via legislative change, regulatory change, or case law. The critical question thus is not whether countries change their laws but whether a country's legal *system* changes over time, and if so, what triggers such systemic changes. How do they affect the overall characteristics of legal systems, namely, their organization and function?

How Do Legal Systems Change? The Evolutionary Approach and Its Weaknesses

The question is deceptively simple: How do legal systems change? As noted at the outset of this book, some models of law and markets do not contemplate the possibility that legal systems change by means other than colonization or military occupation. Where the possibility of legal change is contemplated in the literature, the answer, often implicit, is that legal change is an evolutionary process. Robert Clark (1981) has stated the outlines of a theory about the evolution of legal systems more explicitly and cogently than most commentators, so we summarize his argument. Discussing the United States, Clark argues that the history of capitalist

enterprise can be divided into four stages and that the legal system responded by employing regulatory strategies appropriate to each stage. The
first, the entrepreneurial (or "robber baron") stage, was assisted by laws that
permitted the rise of the corporate form. The enactment of broadly enabling
state corporation laws was the hallmark of this stage. The second stage witnessed the rise of the professional business manager, which required the
legal system to develop stable relationships between these managers and
public investors through the creation of accountability mechanisms such
as disclosure requirements and conflict-of-interest rules. The federal securities laws and fiduciary relationships delineated in the corporate laws are
the major legal manifestations of this stage.

In the third stage, financial intermediaries and institutional investors
emerged as professional investment managers, splitting ownership into
capital supply and investment. The legal system responded to this development with a welter of regulations designed to ensure the soundness
of financial intermediaries, insulating public suppliers of capital from the
insolvency of the intermediaries. In the fourth stage, the savings function was professionalized as workers delegated the authority to invest in
particular financial claims to plan sponsors and other professionals. The
legal correlate is the rise of financial consumer protection legislation such
as ERISA, which regulates the terms of participation and benefits of the
savers. Clark (1981) argues that in each new stage, the prior legal response
is not abandoned; rather, a new regulatory strategy is added to the existing
framework. Clark explicitly views this process in evolutionary terms: "[I]f
we focus on the mechanisms of change, the way in which the institutions
of each stage emerged seems roughly analogous to the evolution of species
by natural selection" (569). But he argues that unlike the random mutation
of genes, new institutional forms are preferentially selected for their efficiency advantages by the cumulative decisions of rationally self-interested
capitalists.

It is a small step from this scheme to a universal theory of legal change
in capitalist systems. Through a process akin to natural selection, advanced
legal systems everywhere arrive at a comparable menu of strategies to address the common functional needs of market actors. Indeed, scholars of
comparative corporate law have already articulated such a theory. Kraakman et al. (2004) claim that "the exigencies of commercial activity and
organization present practical problems that have a rough similarity in
developed market economies throughout the world, that corporate law
everywhere must necessarily address these problems, and that the forces
of logic, competition, interest group pressure, imitation, and compatibility

tend to lead different jurisdictions to choose roughly similar solutions to these problems" (4).

This universal evolutionary theory of legal change in capitalist systems has also been used to explain the phenomenon of legal transplants and predict the future direction of legal change. Mattei (1994), Ogus (1999), and others have suggested that legal borrowing reflects a drive toward efficiency. Competition among the producers of law in a "market for legal culture" influences legal evolution and determines which rules are transplanted from abroad. These commentators claim that ultimately, the lowest-cost legal doctrine is widely adopted to prevent migration of firms and markets to more favorable jurisdictions. Commentators who predict convergence of governance regimes rest their arguments on similar assumptions about legal change. The most ardent convergence theorists in comparative corporate law, for example, claim that widespread ideological agreement on shareholder wealth maximization as the most efficient way to organize capital in an economy will bring about similar rules of corporate law *and practice* around the world (Hansmann and Kraakman 2001).

At the stratospheric level of abstraction at which it is typically presented, the evolutionary theory almost certainly captures important features of the process of legal change in market-oriented societies. As markets change and mature, they throw off new and increasingly complex governance questions, some of which are answered by the legal system. One of the motivations in fashioning a legal response is efficiency, the desire to implement the most effective resolution of the problem at the lowest cost. Over time, societies with market-oriented economies face roughly similar governance issues and settle on a relatively standard menu of solutions to common problems of economic growth and development. So it is true, for example, as Kraakman et al. (2004) point out, that the corporate laws of all developed economies are broadly similar. No doubt comparative analysis of the antitrust laws, securities laws, intellectual property laws, and other laws of developed economies would reveal similar patterns of basic resemblance. Market economies are governed, more or less, by a similar constellation of laws and regulations that arise from the key requirements of any capitalist system: raising capital, allocating property rights, fostering the growth of financial intermediaries, policing predatory market conduct, facilitating the exit of failing firms from the market, and so on. We do not observe any developed market economies that are governed by, say, religious law, committees of elders, or a reign of terror. Nor do we see developing economies creating legal systems that deviate drastically from the basic constellation of laws and regulations found in developed economies. In that sense, the convergence claim is accurate, and predictions of further legal convergence are probably quite safe.

The problem with the evolutionary approach to understanding legal change is that once one moves beyond simple abstractions, it does not tell us very much.[2] For example, it is true that a basic function of corporate law everywhere is to respond to agency problems. In no developed economy is all the capital required to finance firms provided solely by the entrepreneurs who run them from day to day, so agency problems are unavoidable, and it is the corporate law's task to respond. But as our institutional autopsies have illustrated (in rather dramatic fashion, we hope), the *location and severity* of agency problems in firms, as well as what might be called the *institutional inclination* to use law (corporate or otherwise) to address these problems, differ widely from system to system.

To take only one example, four of the countries examined in this book—the United States, Japan, Korea, and China—now all use independent directors in an attempt to address agency problems at the firm level. The corporate *laws* of different countries have converged on use of the independent director as a solution to an agency problem. But this fact reveals nothing about how these changes have affected the legal *system*, in particular, the diverse paths by which they arrived at this institution, the different ways in which "independence" is understood in the various countries, and the widely divergent agency problems in each country that the institution attempts to mitigate. These problems range from absentee political oversight of publicly traded Chinese firms with close governmental ties, to controlling shareholder exploitation of minority shareholders in the Korean *chaebol*, to potentially excessive managerial identification with employee interests in Japan, to the problems of highly dispersed share ownership and an ineffectual shareholder franchise in the United States. There is reason to doubt the efficacy of the independent director in the United States, the country where it originated (Bhagat 2002), although one can tell a convincing story about how independent directors complement other features of the U.S. corporate governance system as they have developed over the past fifty years (Gordon 2007). There is some evidence that independent directors may actually mitigate the controlling minority shareholder problem in the Korean context (Black 2006). Available evidence suggests that independent directors as currently utilized in Japan (Gilson and Milhaupt 2005) and China (Clarke 2006) are not very effective in addressing the respective agency problems afflicting these systems. Thus, sweeping the trend toward independent directors under the adjoining rugs of evolution and convergence guts the comparative analysis of this development by hiding its most important features.

Worse yet, the evolutionary approach can mislead theorists and policy-makers. There are many problems with viewing legal change principally in terms of an evolutionary drive toward efficiency. Some of these problems have been identified by Roe (1996), who points out that legal change is affected by chaos, path-dependence, and punctuated evolution, which can result in the formation of institutions that deviate from the survival-of-the-fittest paradigm. (We believe that path-dependence as a brake on legal change may be overstated in the literature. We elaborate on this below.) At this point we wish to emphasize several other problems with this approach, focusing our analysis again on the *process* of lawmaking.

In doing so, we again depart from the endowment theories of law and legal systems. Legal systems do appear to have distinctive characteristics that color both the types of problems they face and the way in which they respond to them, a point we emphasized in chapter 9. Those traits, however, probably have little to do with the formal legal rules themselves, as the conventional taxonomists and the economists assume. Rather, they stem from the proclivities of the people who operate the legal system, the producers of law. Hadfield (2006), for example, argues that differences in "legal human capital" fostered by distinctive incentive structures for judges and lawyers in various legal systems produce the observable differences in the civil- and common-law systems. In the United States, the power of the bar as an interest group (or cartel, if you prefer Posner [1995]) has contributed enormously to the complex, decentralized, "judicialized" system of lawmaking we identified as a hallmark of the U.S. legal system.[3]

Countries with more highly centralized lawmaking traditions resist de-volution of authority in this way, in part for social reasons (fear of a "litigation explosion"), but also because it represents a major threat to the small group of players with control over the law-making process. Centralized legal systems reduce pressure for decentralization by limiting the supply of lawyers and resisting introduction of mechanisms such as class-action litigation and contingency fees for attorneys. The basic point is that in any system, whether centralized or decentralized, the producers of law will tend to favor certain interests. In the market for law and legal services these interests can cause substantial deviation from the competitive model. It is plausible that decentralized law-making processes that emphasize the protective function of law complement dispersed share ownership patterns in the economy, whereas centralized and coordinative legal systems complement more concentrated corporate ownership patterns. But if true (and our case studies lend some support to this proposition), it suggests the existence of more than one evolutionary path for legal change. In fact, as we further argue below, legal evolution does not necessarily follow a predetermined path (decentralized or centralized) for all time. Rather, changes introduced into a legal system may alter the process of future change.

Demand-side analysis similarly fails to support the view that legal change is an evolutionary path toward a single set of efficient legal structures. It is not simply that economic incumbents can block the passage of rules that would be more efficient for the economy as a whole. Certainly we have seen that phenomenon at work in our institutional autopsies (for example, the lack of investor protections in Korea during the heyday of the growth pact between the *chaebol* founders and authoritarian political rulers). We have seen as well the related phenomenon of crises creating political opportunities for the passage of law that would not have been possible in equilibrium owing to resistance from economic incumbents (for example, the Asian financial crisis and legal reform in Korea and the Enron scandal and SOX).

A less well noted but equally pernicious problem for the development of efficient law is one we alluded to several times in the institutional autopsies: sometimes economic incumbents use newly enacted "efficient" law in ways that increase social costs. In Russia, for example, the state is essentially using the new bankruptcy law to nationalize assets. In Korea, *chaebol* leaders use legal arguments in the courts (in addition to more traditional political connections and so on) to fend off challenges to their business empires. This paradox of law reform, which afflicts all societies to some extent, results from the basic pattern of development we noted at the outset of this book: legal change often generates adaptive responses by different actors, including state and private agents. Ex ante, it is impossible to create a legal rule that will only generate "efficient" behavioral responses, and in particular, a rule adopted across a range of economies facing very different governance challenges and a range of legal systems that differ in degree of centralization and function of law.

Overattachment to the simplified evolutionary model of legal change may also taint law reform efforts. It may prompt international organizations and collective bodies such as the European Union to pursue misplaced legal transplants and legal harmonization projects. If legal systems are believed to develop in stages correlated with economic development, and if the legal rules found in successful economies are (at least subconsciously) deemed to be effective precisely because they are in place in developed markets, a natural impulse is to encourage countries to skip over some stages of legal development by enacting law found in the type of markets to which they aspire. The transition economies of central and eastern

Europe have copied extensively from other jurisdictions to catch up with the West and to comply with entry requirements for the European Union. Empirical evidence, however, suggests that these reforms have had, at best, mixed results. Analyzing the relation between legal change in the area of investor rights protection and financial market development in twenty-four transition economies, Pistor et al. (2000) find that neither the level of legal protection nor legal change over time has had much impact on financial market development in the region. In fact, few of the laws that were introduced in the new member states of the European Union from this region addressed the specific governance problems they faced (Pistor 2004).[4]

A separate example of possibly misplaced legal reform efforts can be found in the IMF's response to the Asian financial crisis. The IMF required that Korea adopt the minority shareholder rights found in U.S. corporate law as a means of improving corporate governance. Yet as we have indicated, the nature of the agency problem affecting shareholders in U.S. and Korean firms differs dramatically. The continuing struggle to resolve the *chaebol* problem and the halting nature of corporate governance reform in post-crisis Korea at least suggests that U.S.-style legal protections, though helpful in certain respects, did not reach the core of the problem. Finally, note that the European Union pursues legal harmonization for countries at—and aspiring to be at—similar stages of economic development in order to eliminate barriers to growth. For reasons we explore below, however, harmonization policies may be ineffectual or harmful to the development of effective legal institutions for market activity.

How Do Legal Systems Change?
A Demand-Adaptation Approach

If the evolutionary approach to legal change is accurate only in broad strokes and misleading in many respects, what is needed to clarify the picture? Inherent in the analytical framework with which we began this book is a powerful view of legal change centered on demand for governance. This demand-adaptation perspective generates very different predictions about legal change than does an efficiency-oriented evolutionary approach. First, it suggests that the supply of new legal rules alone is unlikely to change the legal system. This is because legal systems, which include enforcement institutions and the legal professionals who intermediate between the legal rules and the market actors on whom law operates, must be distinguished from law, that is, formal legal rules enacted by legislatures or regulations promulgated by bureaucrats.[5] Second, changes in the demand for legal governance may affect the overall governance structure of a system absent formal legal change, because new constituencies may make use of existing yet dormant rules. Third, the most powerful determinants of change in the organization and function of the legal system are changes in the major constituencies (social or political elites) that affect the demand for law as a device for governance. Our six institutional autopsies illustrate the critical importance of the identity, interests, and relative power of those supporting a particular system of governance (whether legal or informal) for the potentially system-altering power of formal legal change.

The United States and Russia are examples of relatively stable systems that either have reverted or are in the process of reverting to the previous governance equilibrium following a crisis or economic shock—even a shock accompanied by major legal reforms, as in the case of the United States. As previously discussed, SOX sought to centralize lawmaking and law enforcement in response to the series of corporate governance scandals epitomized by the Enron debacle. But neither the crisis nor the legal actions taken in response to it altered the major protagonists in the U.S. system of highly decentralized legal governance: the organized bar and the multiplicity of federal and state law enforcement authorities. Not surprisingly, once the crisis subsided, centrifugal forces quickly began to undermine the attempt to centralize or simplify governance in the interests of investor protection.

In Russia the law reforms of the 1990s did not fundamentally alter the highly centralized nature of the political system and the de facto control that the Kremlin exerts over powerful economic agents. Laws that in other legal systems may be primarily used to enforce private investors' rights such as bankruptcy laws were used to reestablish central control over Russia's natural resources sector. Attempts by members of the new business elite that had emerged under Yeltsin to neutralize the Kremlin under different leadership by seeking foreign investments and playing by international rules concerning best (legal) practices were perceived by Putin as a threat, not as a natural or desirable result of the legal reforms of the post-Soviet era. In response, he used the newly created legal apparatus to reallocate control over assets from disloyal members of the elite to loyal ones, thereby entrenching centralized political control over the economy as well as the legal system.

By contrast, in Germany, Japan, and Korea we observe systems that are in disequilibrium because the constituencies supporting the previous governance regime have been weakened and new groups from inside and outside the country are competing not only for resources but also for the appropriate form of (legal) governance. Globalization has led to a diffusion of governance practices from abroad into these countries and a greater outward orientation of domestic players on whose loyalty the old system had depended. The ensuing vacuum created opportunities for new entrants to challenge the governance structure. Legal change was not strictly necessary for these changes to occur; new players could push the boundaries using the old rules. Notice that in the cases of Germany and Japan, existing criminal law was used in an attempt to stabilize the system in the face of the new actors. At first glance, the mobilization of the criminal justice system to protect these fairly centralized and coordinative systems suggests greater centralization. Other legal changes adopted in both systems, however, could be used to counter these tendencies and lead to a greater decentralization of legal governance and a more protective (as opposed to coordinative) legal system. In Japan, this trend is already evident in the increasing amount of shareholder and takeover litigation. In Germany, the effect of legal change that vests greater procedural powers with individual shareholders still remains to be seen. As in Germany and Japan, new entrants in Korea have challenged the preexisting governance structure. Formal legal change introduced after the East Asian crisis has potentially rooted these changes more deeply than has been the case in either Japan or Germany. Yet the real impact of legal reforms in all three countries may depend in large part on the courts, whose stature in the governance structure of all three countries has been elevated. Their understanding and interpretation of the law will be critical in determining whether the evolution toward decentralization continues or whether the systems will be stabilized in their current intermediate state.

China may be best described as moving toward a decentralized governance structure as a result of changes introduced or tolerated by the ruling elite. Changes are permitted in an attempt to adapt governance structures to ensure the continuation of both economic growth and political control. Decentralized mechanisms of legal accountability (protection), such as shareholder suits, are tolerated because they may improve governance, but they are nonetheless viewed with suspicion because they could ultimately pose a challenge to centralized political control. Not surprisingly, access to the courts for this purpose was made contingent on a central regulator's first establishing a violation of the law. In other words, protective law enforcement is made contingent on coordination by agencies directly linked to centralized political control. As long as this persists, there will be inherent limits on the extent to which the Chinese legal system embraces decentralization.

In sum, formal legal change is not necessarily system-altering, even in times of crisis. This implies that economic change alone is typically not a good predictor of change in a legal *system*, at least unless the signal sent by formal legal change is powerful enough to provoke novel market or governance activities. Typically more is needed: a change in demand for legal governance by local constituencies generally brought on by a change in the composition of the constituencies. Demand is the motivation for legal change and the ongoing deconstruction and reconstruction of legal governance in the context of a changing market economy. We believe that the notion of contestability, a term we introduced in chapter 2, is useful in understanding the mechanisms by which law rolls with market change, and the degree of contestability is an important explanatory variable in differences in the rate and form of legal change around the world.[6]

Contestation

As we use the term, contestation is the process by which existing governance structures can be challenged and adapted to a changing socioeconomic environment in response to demand. Contestation may take the form of widespread political participation in the production and enforcement of law, but it is not limited to political contestation in a democratic system. Avenues for demand for alternative governance mechanisms to be expressed in the legal system may include access to courts or bureaucrats, politicians, or even business elites who operate as gatekeepers for centralized governance structures.

What determines the contestability of a given legal system? Our institutional autopsies suggest that contestability is a byproduct of a country's relative location along the two dimensions of legal systems that we outlined in our analytical framework. The more decentralized the production and enforcement of law, the more contested a system tends to be, and the more likely that legal change will occur in the courts and in private lawmaking efforts (contractual innovations, lobbying-induced regulations, or legislation). Contestation is possible in more centralized, coordinative systems, too, but demand for new governance forms in such systems is likely to be filtered through and mitigated by a different set of agents, such as bureaucrats, legislatures, or business elites. The rate of legal change may be comparatively slower, and the locus of legal change less court-centered, than in decentralized systems.

We again acknowledge the affinities between our framework for understanding legal systems and the canonical taxonomy of common-law and civil-law systems, particularly as they relate to the role of the courts as agents of legal change. But we now see that the variation in the role of the courts in countries around the world is a function of deeper structural differences in the way demand for legal governance is transmitted through a given system. And our framework suggests that not all forms of legal change will have identical effects on a legal system. In particular, changes that alter the incentives of those who operate the system such as procedural changes lowering the cost of filing suit or providing attorneys with greater incentives to use the courts have the potential to gradually alter the underlying characteristics of a legal system by changing the avenues of contestation available to law's consumers.

Legal Transplants

Legal transplants are perhaps the most common form of legal development around the world (see Watson 1993).[7] Transplants are so common in part because, as Friedman (1969, 46) put it, leaders believe that "modern law must come from the advanced countries and that it is a kind of capital good or technology that cannot be locally supplied." The institutional autopsies also highlighted the borrowing of law from other countries as a prominent form of legal change. With the notable exception of the United States, recent legal development in each of the countries we have examined involves the transplantation[8] of foreign law to address a perceived problem or institutional weakness in the domestic system.[9] Moreover, as our discussion of the E.U. Takeover Directive in connection with the Mannesmann case suggests, another prominent form of legal change in the past decade is the effort at harmonization, explicitly designed to produce a common legal framework for a given economic activity across many countries.

As we have noted, a line of scholarship claims that the origin of a country's legal system—the legal family to which it belongs—is a significant determinant of the *effectiveness* of its legal institutions. Countries belonging to the English common-law family are found to have more effective investor protections than countries belonging to the French and German civil-law family, and members of the Scandinavian civil-law family fall somewhere in between. Membership in a legal family is also found to affect enforcement. La Porta et al. (1998) find that after controlling for GDP per capita (which is highly correlated with enforcement), French and German civil-law countries have poorer enforcement than English common-law countries, while enforcement in Scandinavian countries is similar to that in the latter.[10] These findings suggest that where a country's law comes from may affect economic growth by leading to relatively stronger or weaker legal institutions.

These empirical results are fascinating, but they contradict the real-world experience of law reformers. The two major "law and development" movements in the twentieth century, the first taking place after World War II and the second after the collapse of the Soviet Union and its satellite states in Eastern Europe, reached exactly the opposite conclusion. They left little doubt that changes in formal law have little impact on the effectiveness of legal institutions. Indeed, the experience so dispirited members of the first movement that they publicly declared it a failure (Trubek and Galanter 1974). The second movement seems to have fared little better, though perhaps it is too early to reach a final judgment. Far from suggesting that legal rules from the most effective legal systems can be imported to jump-start lagging economies, these experiences, like the studies by Hausman et al. (2005) and our own research discussed in chapter 1, suggest that over time there is no meaningful relation between economic growth and the purely formal attributes of a country's legal system, including the legal family to which it belongs.

Many commentators have suggested that legal transplants that do not comport with local culture will fail (for example, Frankel 1995; Smith 1993; Montesquieu 1977). But this observation is too broad to be of much predictive value, particularly because the open-ended concept of "culture" opens a Pandora's box of interpretive nightmares.

A demand-adaptation theory of legal change is a more promising way to approach the question of whether effective legal rules can be imported. Drawing on our prior work with others (Berkowitz, Pistor, and Richard 2003; Kanda and Milhaupt 2003), we sketch a theory of legal transplants that explains the conditions under which legal transplants will be effective as a mode of legal change, and, conversely, when transplants will fail to play a meaningful role in the host country's legal system—a phenomenon we have previously labeled the "transplant effect" (Berkowitz, Pistor, and Richard 2003; Milhaupt 2001). Consistent with the overall conceptual approach we employ in this book, our theory is that the nature of legal demand for the transplanted law and the process by which it is incorporated into the host country's institutional structure significantly affect whether and how the transplant will function. The findings of the economic studies clash with real-world experience of law reform because the studies make no attempt to differentiate between countries that developed their legal systems internally from those that received their law by way of legal transplantation. Consistent with the predisposition of economists to view law as exogenous to markets and to remain indifferent to the actual mechanics of lawmaking, these studies implicitly assume that the *process* of legal development is irrelevant to the effectiveness of a given legal system. Yet this is the key to understanding the transplant phenomenon.

We begin by asking why this is such a common form of legal change. The motivation for transplants is important because it affects demand. First and most obvious, a legal transplant is a cheap, quick, and potentially fruitful source of new law. Learning effects associated with the rule in the home country can potentially be utilized in the host country, providing a "market-tested" product to local consumers of law. Developing countries or developed countries that are experiencing a given economic phenomenon of first impression (such as hostile acquisitions) would be remiss if they did *not* piggyback on other countries' experience in devising legal responses to similar phenomena. This use of foreign law is the closest analogue to technology transfer, and we refer to this as the "practical utility" motivation for transplantation.

Second, legal transplantation has often followed colonization or military conquest as the new regime seeks to transform the governance structure of the colony or occupied territory. We will call this the "political" motivation for legal transplants, and it is commonly associated with sweeping, system-wide legal transplants of the kind experienced by Korea under Japanese occupation, Latin America under Spanish rule, or the French colonies in Africa.[11] Note that the political motivation accounts for most of the groupings of countries into legal families in the canonical taxonomy used by the law and finance scholarship. We return to this point below, because it helps explain the mismatch between the economists' findings and the real-world results of legal reform.

Third, as we suggested in the introduction, law has an expressive function. Conscious of the signaling power of law and legal reform, political actors and members of the legal community may use foreign as opposed to home-grown law to signal some desired quality of their governance. Two examples from Japan at different historical moments illustrate the point. At the turn of the twentieth century, Meiji leaders enacted virtually verbatim translations of European legal codes. Whatever the practical utility of this strategy,[12] it was also motivated to a significant degree by a desire to escape the threat of Western domination—which had become manifest in the Unequal Treaties imposed on Japan—by showing that Japan was a modern, advanced nation on a par with the West. More than a century later, Japan borrowed Delaware judicial standards for takeovers in part to signal adherence to "global standards."[13] Signaling has always been and remains a powerful motivation for legal transplants.

The final reason for the prevalence of transplants is not motivation but shortcomings in human cognition and decision making: legal rules are sometimes borrowed in haste and without adequate preparation or familiarity ("blind copying"). For example, in the middle of the nineteenth century, Colombia enacted virtually all eleven hundred articles of the Spanish Commercial Code of 1829 without change (Means 1980). More recently, observers of the Eastern European countries, which joined the European Union in 2004, have likened the legal reforms undertaken prior to their accession to a "legislative tornado." European directives in principle permit lawmakers substantial discretion in formulating domestic implementing legislation. Given the sheer magnitude of the legal change that was required, however, and the lack of capacity on the ground, many countries simply copied law "by the meter" from other member states (Pistor 2004).

The motivation or reason for a legal transplant is important because it affects the conduct of the legal community that subsequently interprets and enforces the law. The second step of our theory is that the performance of a legal transplant depends on the extent to which the changes are aligned with the conduct of lawyers, judges, and bureaucrats in applying and enforcing the law.[14] And just as with a home-grown law, enforcement conduct is deeply affected by demand for the legal transplant among the relevant constituencies that support the current system of governance. Our theory is that a legal transplant fits the host jurisdiction if it is sufficiently responsive to demand that the legal community integrates the transplanted law into the surrounding legal system. We call this type of integration "micro-fit."[15] For example, for the transplantation of a protective legal rule from a decentralized legal system to a more coordinative system, the relevant issues include whether there are mechanisms in place to enforce the new rule. Do plaintiffs and lawyers have incentives to bring suits that make use of the new rule? Are judges familiar with the concept or doctrine underlying it? Are they inclined to side with the normative implications of the legal change? Demand sufficient to motivate this integrative activity by the local legal community is more likely to exist if the transplanted rule complements the political economy of the host country. We call complementarity between the transplant and the political economy "macro-fit."[16] Here the important issues are whether the foreign legal rule responds to an actual governance gap in the host country's institutional structure that is not filled by nonlegal mechanisms and whether the rule is likely to be used, given the local interest group structure.

This theory generates two main predictions: First, all else being equal, internally developed legal systems will function more effectively in support of markets than will legal systems developed via transplantation. The reason is that internal development typically occurs via the rolling relation between legal and market development we described in chapter 2. By definition, law developed in this manner is at least broadly responsive to demand and consistent with the political economy in which it was enacted. Moreover, the legal community will not only be familiar with the rule from its inception but may have played a large role in its production. As such, complementarities between the new rule and the surrounding infrastructure are typically built into the enactment and enforcement processes. This does not mean, of course, that all internally developed law is optimal for the circumstances or that every internally developed law is superior to each possible foreign alternative. It simply means that legal systems developed internally enjoy important advantages over transplanted legal systems.

Second, legal systems developed via transplantation—those of most of the world—will vary in their effectiveness depending in significant part on how well the local community adapts the law to local circumstances. Among the important variables are the motivation for the transplant (with practical necessity being the most conductive to adaptation), whether demand by relevant constituencies for the law exists (or conversely, whether nonlegal substitutes exist that would diminish demand), whether the legal community is familiar with the transplanted law, and whether the law is broadly consistent with the political economy of the host country, such that it is compatible with other governance mechanisms at work in society.

In separate research projects, we have found evidence consistent with these predictions. Berkowitz et al. (2003) find that the way in which a law is transplanted is a more important determinant of a legal system's effectiveness than whether the legal system was supplied by a particular family. Note again that the categorizations used by the economists are based entirely on the first wave of legal transplantation that took place at the end of the nineteenth century, which was principally motivated by politics and symbolism. It is thus natural to expect less familiarity and adaptation by local communities with respect to these transplants.

Using qualitative analysis of a single rule, Kanda and Milhaupt (2003) reach conclusions highly consistent with the cross-country empirical analysis of Berkowitz et al. (2003). They analyze the transplantation of the duty of loyalty principle into Japanese corporate law as part of the amendments to the Commercial Code under the American-led occupation in 1950. The transplanted duty of loyalty played virtually no role in the governance of directors' conduct during the period of high economic growth, because it had poor micro- and macro-fit with Japan's legal system and political economy at that time. Enforcement mechanisms were not well developed to encourage the use of litigation to enforce the rule. And a high-growth economy with little labor mobility greatly reduced managerial incentives to engage in transactions that posed conflicts of interest in violation of the rule. But as lawyers and judges gained familiarity with the duty of loyalty standard, as procedural obstacles to its enforcement in the legal system were removed, and as the economic institutions of Japan began to break down in the late 1980s, opening new opportunities and incentives for ex-propriation of firm assets by insiders, the duty of loyalty came to play a role in the governance of Japanese firms.

The larger lessons from both studies are remarkably similar: local de-mand and adaptation appear to be the keys to effective use of legal trans-plants. Put differently, transplants play a meaningful role in a legal system when, but only when, they become part of the rolling relation between law and markets, with local constituencies playing a critical role in mediating between the two.

Convergence

What insights might a demand-adaptation approach to legal change offer for the question of whether legal systems and corporate governance struc-tures are converging on an Anglo-American shareholder-oriented model? The convergence question has preoccupied scholars of comparative corpo-rate governance for some time,[17] yet the debate has devolved to essentially two positions. On one side is the strong-form convergence theory rooted in evolutionary concepts advanced by Hansmann and Kraakmann (2001), discussed above. On the other, Bebchuk and Roe (1999) argue that path dependencies based on efficiencies and rent-seeking will slow corporate change and block convergence.

Certainly the forces for convergence of legal rules have never been more powerful: foreign institutional investors seek a common set of rules to gov-ern their capital investments. Information technology has made knowledge of foreign law accessible instantly and at low cost. International organiza-tions such as the World Bank and the IMF have pursued policy programs that require or encourage the adoption of a standard package of legal reforms. Delaware state officials travel the globe promoting the benefits and low cost of incorporation in Delaware, putting pressure on other jurisdictions to mimic features of Delaware corporate law. Scholarship has contributed to these homogenizing influences as the investor protection index of La Porta et al. has become something of a benchmark in the evaluation of corporate law quality around the world.[18] Now arcana that are of debatable real-world significance, such as cumulative voting for directors,[19] are dutifully emulated by law reformers around the world. The cumulative effect of these developments is the increasing commodification of law, and there is little question that laws governing economic organizations and activities in major countries are taking on similar outward characteristics, a phenomenon that has come to be known as formal convergence (see Gilson 2001).

Nothing in our analysis, however, suggests that formal convergence per se is meaningful to the governance of markets beyond potential signaling and credibility enhancement functions. We suspect, for example, that portions of the Sarbanes-Oxley Act have proved to be attractive transplants in some other countries—despite the fact that it was enacted in response to a set of governance challenges distinctly rooted in late twentieth-century U.S. capitalism—for the same reason the law was enacted in the United States: because it signals governmental seriousness about corporate governance and white-collar crime. Even the signaling and credibility enhancement effects of formal convergence will vary, depending on the extent to which a given country has in the past actually used and enforced transplanted law as opposed to simply enacting it. The protective and coordinating functions of law may be very difficult to perform through legal transplants because they are deeply connected to home-country power relations and institutions. Assuming that the transplanted law is integrated and enforced, the introduction of laws from a protective, decentralized system such as that of the U.S. into legal systems traditionally characterized by their centralized and coordinative features, such as those of Korea, Japan, and Germany— the trend in the world today—may fundamentally alter the character of the latter systems. This may explain, for example, the staunch resistance around the world to U.S.-style mechanisms for bringing class-action suits as a device for shareholder protection.

The dichotomous convergence debate, which depicts systems as either converging on a U.S.-style shareholder-oriented model or being blocked from that trajectory owing to path-dependence, masks important features of the actual process of legal and market reform revealed in our institutional autopsies. A more informative analytical construct for thinking about how foreign legal knowledge is incorporated into local regimes is *institution telescoping and stacking.* In practice, the home country's experience with the formation, interpretation, and enforcement of the rule—that is, massive amounts of implicit knowledge—is "telescoped" when the host country transplants a law. In the process, a portion (perhaps most) of this implicit knowledge is left behind. The law is presented as a convenient or politically palatable package and stacked atop existing institutions in the host country. Only through repeated strategic and adaptive responses by local actors can the transplanted rule and the preexisting institutions eventually be welded together into something new and functional. Telescoping and stacking may be mechanisms of institutional convergence, but that is not the inevitable outcome of the process. Legal transplants contain a Jurassic Park quality:[20] mutations are commonplace. Recall that a legal intervention, from whatever source, is likely to elicit strategic and adaptive responses by those affected by the new rule. Thus, the set of possible responses to a legal transplant is not binary rejection or acceptance but an unpredictable range of actions based on strategic maneuvering whose precise contours are difficult to anticipate.

This analysis suggests that a potentially important force for the convergence of legal systems lies somewhere no one has noticed: change in the education and structure of the legal profession around the world. A demand-adaptation analysis suggests that familiarity of local legal communities with transplanted rules is a key determinant of whether the rules will be used in the host system as governance mechanisms. The increasing influence of the United States in the market for graduate legal education has significant implications for the transplantation phenomenon. Each year, thousands of foreign graduate students (virtually all of whom are already lawyers, judges, prosecutors, government officials, in-house providers of corporate legal services, or legal academics) study law in the United States. In 2004–5, for example, almost one thousand foreign students were enrolled in graduate LLM degree programs at the top ten American law schools alone.[21] This represents a major expansion in such training over the course of the past two decades. Equally important, the U.S. model of legal education has become highly influential in other parts of the world. Japan recently introduced major changes to its system of legal education explicitly patterned after the U.S. system. Along with these reforms, the size of the legal profession is being expanded in a direct response to greater demand for legal services in a society that now relies more heavily on legal governance than during Japan's postwar period of high growth. Korea has just embarked on similar reforms for precisely the same reasons.

An ever-growing number of legal professionals around the world who are intensely familiar with U.S. legal doctrines, practices, and theories implies an increasingly powerful U.S. influence on legal systems around the world. Network effects similar to those that have helped make English a global language or Delaware the predominant corporate law jurisdiction in the United States could take hold: regardless of the intrinsic merits of the U.S. legal system vis-à-vis any other, the greater the number of legal professionals who are expert in U.S. law, the greater the benefits of learning and adopting U.S. law in one's home country. These "network externalities" accrue from many sources. To name only two, the spread of U.S. law enhances the ability of far-flung legal professionals to speak a common legal language in transactions as well as adversarial settings. And this expanding base increases the incentives of parties all over the world to select U.S. law as the governing law, conferring a benefit on those equipped to provide expert advice on that law. As these network effects proliferate, local legal communities trained in U.S. law schools will constitute a mechanism of demand for and adaptation of U.S. legal transplants.[22]

This influence of U.S. law may be felt most acutely in transactional work on behalf of global market players. As such, it may be relatively limited in its impact on the structure of foreign legal systems, although there is evidence that thorough exposure to the U.S. legal system changes the way foreign legal professionals view their own legal systems and law-making processes.[23] Legislative law-making processes, by contrast, may be particularly resistant to change. Indeed, as our analysis of countries from Germany to China suggests, lawmakers appear to be acutely aware that the decentralization of legal governance by way of encouraging decentralized law enforcement may alter the legal systems and affect the ability of other agents to coordinate socially or politically desirable outcomes. Moreover, the diffusion of legal mechanisms borrowed from one system may not necessarily produce the same outcome everywhere. Although it is but a single example, adoption of the poison pill defense in Japan is powerfully suggestive of this phenomenon. In form it looks familiar to a lawyer trained in the U.S. system, but the ramifications of the transplantation are by no means certain or predictable. In other words, as others have suggested before, "looks can be deceiving,"[24] not only with regard to the contents of substantive legal rules, but also as to the meaning and usage of procedural enforcement devices.

The larger point is that if the modes of legal governance should converge over time (a proposition for which we have at best mixed evidence at present), this does not predict convergence in outcomes. Indeed, the creeping decentralization of legal governance we appear to be witnessing in many countries may make legal governance more responsive to local circumstances and thus promote further diversification.

Legal Standardization

We suggested above that the evolutionary approach to legal change spurs harmonization efforts and the standardization of best practices as mechanisms of legal and economic development. The expectation is that standardization will accelerate the process of legal convergence, with the dual benefit of reducing transaction costs and improving the quality of legal institutions in countries whose institutions are less well developed. Given the realities of law and law production that we have emphasized, however, legal harmonization has a weak theoretical basis as good policy. Instead of improving domestic legal institutions, standardization may undermine the development of effective legal systems. The reason for this can be found in two essential features of legal systems. The first is the interdependence of legal rules, concepts, and doctrines. Few rules can be understood without reference to other legal doctrines or concepts. The second is the fact that legal systems (as distinct from legal rules) include the people who interpret, apply, and enforce the rules. The understanding of a rule by the legal profession is integral to its operation and enforcement. In order for a rule to be standardized, there must be multinational agreement about the basic concepts behind the rule, and those concepts must be shared by diverse populations of legal professionals.

In order to accomplish this formidable task, those involved in legal harmonization efforts typically resort to one of two strategies: the lowest-common-denominator approach or a synthetic approach (Pistor 2002). In the lowest-common-denominator approach, the minimum standard in force among the relevant countries is applied to all of them. The synthetic approach is to create a new legal concept that is based on comparative research but is not actually in force anywhere, and to incorporate it into a standardized rule. Both approaches represent a compromise between the desire to reduce transaction costs and improve governance institutions across a range of countries and the reality of distinct preexisting legal systems in those countries.

But these approaches to standardization may actually undermine the goal of improving governance in countries with less well-developed institutions. In order to be effective, laws need local constituencies with an interest in and understanding of the laws. This is a prerequisite for new law—whether home-grown or transplanted from abroad—to become part of the continuous process of legal and market change, without which the law will remain largely irrelevant as a governance device. Yet the standardization of best practices or "higher-quality" law as actually implemented may replace a Schumpeterian rolling relation between markets and law with an idealized conception of law unfamiliar to local constituencies. Thus, standardization and legal harmonization, far from being means for building effective legal systems around the world, are to be approached with considerable caution.

Conclusion

Our analysis suggests that law mediates changes in governance. Law stipulates the normative goals of governance by emphasizing the rights and interests of different constituencies. By means of procedural devices, law allocates or denies these constituencies the right to enforce their interests against others and determines the extent and form of their participation in lawmaking and enforcement. Law not only responds to demand but also shapes demand by serving as a focal point for strategic and adaptive responses among those who enforce and are subject to it. The signaling function of law is important in this regard. Some legal reforms, whether by altering substantive or procedural rights or simply by sending certain signals may trigger a dynamic process of change that helps alter the character of a legal system in important ways. This quality of law, coupled with the contestability of a legal system, opens the possibility that legal reform can at times escape the twin traps of public choice–based capture and path-dependence. Our institutional autopsies suggest that countries do not remain in legal stasis. Both the degree to which economic systems rely on legal governance and the nature of legal governance in a given system can change significantly over time.

ELEVEN

Conclusion

We began the book by noting that the quest to link economic success with particular features of a legal system has attracted the attention of prominent scholars for more than a century. We hope that our book has made several contributions to this long line of debate. We have taken seriously George Fletcher's admonition (Fletcher 1998, 690) that comparative law should be a "subversive" discipline in its attempt to "understand[ ] the way in which law develops and functions in legal cultures other than our own." Our "subversive" goal has been to challenge many aspects of the prevailing view of the way in which law supports markets—not only in faraway legal systems but in the United States, the implicit paradigm of "good law" against which many legal systems are compared today.

Most fundamentally, we have argued that it is time for new thinking about legal systems and their relation to markets. The first step is the realization that law should not be viewed as fixed but as fluid; a rolling relation, not an endowment. To this end, we have urged a new approach for analyzing legal systems focusing on their organization, the functions they perform, and their relation to the political economy. We have emphasized the need to delve deeply into a given country's *process* of lawmaking and law enforcement, as well as the *demand* for law by market actors and the mechanisms by which law changes. One of the book's major arguments is that commentators should pay less attention to the origins and formal characteristics of legal systems and focus instead on how legal systems change. We have developed a demand-adaptation theory of legal change, which has allowed us to identify pressure points within legal systems with the potential to trigger deeper legal change than legal-origin theories might predict.

We do not dispute the fact that there are affinities between the organization and function of legal systems as analyzed here and the legal-origin approach as explicated in the law and finance literature. The most decentralized and protective system in our matrix is the United States, which also happens to be a common-law country. With the exception of Singapore, the coordinative legal systems in our study are all of civil origin. But there is less overlap between the two analytical constructs than meets the eye. Whereas legal origin analysis places countries into inert historical categories and emphasizes seemingly fixed characteristics of legal systems, our focus on organization, function, and demand opens a more dynamic window onto analysis of legal systems.

Several key conclusions emerge from our study. First, as a historical matter, no single type of legal system is uniquely associated with economic success. Indeed, the countries examined in our book—all of which, with the exception of Russia,[1] qualify as economic success stories—display a wide array of legal characteristics. Pushing the conclusion further, we have seen that in several of the countries economic development preceded a "rule of law" as that term is widely understood and discussed in the literature today. Among countries at roughly equivalent stages of advanced economic development such as the United States, Germany, and Japan, legal systems vary substantially in the process of lawmaking and law enforcement. The structure of the legal professions and their respective roles in the legal system vary significantly among the three countries as well.

Our analysis has shown that even in the U.S. legal system, which some may view as the one that most closely approaches the rule-of-law ideal, vast proliferation of protections and enforcement agents creates complexities and uncertainties that are in considerable tension with the ideal of a predictable, efficient legal system as a foundation for economic activity. Ironically, Weber himself would probably not have been surprised by this conclusion. In his day he struggled to explain England's leadership among the industrializing countries of the West despite having a legal system that in many ways defied his criteria for rationality—what is often referred to as the "England problem" in Weber's work. The lesson we draw from the tension between the Weberian rule-of-law ideal and the actual operation of law in the most successful capitalist countries both in Weber's time and today is that the rule-of-law concept is too general to provide much guidance on the construction or analysis of real-world legal systems. This becomes clear if we return to the issue of property rights protections, which looms so large in collective thinking about law and development. Although universally recognized as the key role for law in support of markets, protection of property rights is not self-defining or self-enforcing. Which rights receive protections, by whom are they enforceable, and how? Who benefits from a given assignment of property rights, and who is disadvantaged? How are new forms of property allocated and protected? Different countries have provided very different answers to these questions. In reality, to say that property rights protection is the foundation of economic development is to say very little about the characteristics of a legal system that is conducive to investment and growth.

The diversity of viable legal supports for markets and the existence of an array of nonlegal supports for market activity is not cause for discouragement but rather grounds for optimism. As a historical matter, we have seen that centralized, coordinative legal systems as well as decentralized, protective legal systems are capable of supporting sustained economic growth. Law can support markets in a variety of crucial ways—not only by providing property rights protections but also by coordinating market actors, sending signals to the consumers and enforcers of law, and enhancing the credibility of government policy. We have seen that the functions law plays in support of markets differs across countries, markets, and stages of development. The process by which markets interact with law, examined carefully across diverse societies as we have done, suggests that each country reaches its own balance between legal governance and its other market and political institutions. Our analysis suggests that many high-growth economies in the postwar period have gotten by with less (or at least different) law than the United States.

An important point follows from this line of analysis: the *benchmarking* problem merits much more attention than it has received in the literature. By this we mean the use of a specific legal rule or procedure from one system as a benchmark against which to measure the quality of other legal systems. The system typically held up as a benchmark in the past decade has been that of the United States. It is now quite common for corporate law and governance scholars from other countries, for example, to frame their entire analysis of their home country's institutional environment as if U.S. law provided a standard against which the quality of their own laws and enforcement institutions should be measured. Often, this exercise is conducted with minimal acknowledgment that the governance problems in the system for which legal solutions are sought differ significantly from those in the United States, even if a common label such as "agency problem" is applied in both settings. We have shown that on a variety of dimensions the United States is an outlier in its use of law. The U.S. legal system is highly decentralized, extremely demand-driven, and highly adaptable but also highly complex, unpredictable, and not particularly well suited to achieving swift, coordinated solutions to governance problems. It is thus not obvious that legal solutions developed in the United States should figure so centrally in reforms designed to address governance problems faced elsewhere. However well intentioned, the intense focus on U.S. legal approaches may lead to a poverty of imagination in seeking solutions to other countries' governance problems.

The World Bank appears to be coming around to this conclusion as well. A recent publication surveying lessons that it drew from the reforms of the 1990s concludes: "[I]f solutions must be found in specific-country contexts, rather than applied from blueprints, those who advise or finance developing countries will need more humility in their approaches, implying more openness on the range of solutions possible, more empathy with the country's perspective, and more inquisitiveness in assessing the costs and benefits of different possible solutions" (World Bank 2006, 26).

To say that no single legal system is best suited for economic success, however, is not to throw up our hands in despair. Although present in varying degrees, there are certain features common to all of the legal systems we have studied in this book, with the exception of modern-day Russia. Successful legal systems for market economies must perform market-supporting functions while being flexible enough to respond to market shifts. This tension between stasis and change is achieved, in our terms, when a legal system is contestable rather than monopolized for the protection of incumbents. All legal systems struggle with the rivalry for protection between incumbents and newcomers, but successful legal systems manage this balance over time, either by giving newcomers extensive rights to challenge existing rules and doctrines, as in the United States, or by mediating competing interests at the state level and leaving the door open a crack to legal challenge by outsiders, as is done in most European and Asian legal systems associated with market economies.

Successful legal systems distinguish themselves by their institutional capacity to adapt to new market realities and to shifts in demand for legal governance resulting from new social or economic phenomena. This does not mean that effective legal solutions to new problems will always be generated or that the laws produced will always be optimal from an efficiency standpoint. It simply means that the legal system rolls with the market and provides at least a backdrop for adaptation to emerging governance problems. Effective legal governance is an ongoing institutional inclination or state of being, not a static point or fixed endowment that depends on a checklist of formal legal rules or enforcement institutions. From this perspective, the notion of an effective legal system for economic growth as a neutral third-party agent of contract enforcement and property rights protection (North 1990) misses the mark.

We began sketching our analytical framework with the simple insight that law and markets respond to each other in highly iterative fashion. We ended chapter 10 with some conjectures about the process of legal change, particularly in an increasingly globalizing world. A major topic for future research is the way the processes of lawmaking and law enforcement are being affected by globalization. Viewed at close range and across several systems simultaneously, globalization appears to be forcing legal systems built on the centralized, coordinative model to become more decentralized and protective in their orientation. The mechanism of change in this direction has often been a transaction or series of encounters pitting a market newcomer (sometimes foreign, sometimes domestic) against an incumbent. The newcomer is less respectful of existing rules for market activity (whether legal or nonlegal), forcing both private- and public-sector actors to reevaluate the rule system or to adapt their conduct to the new state of play. The rise of private equity may be the latest example of this process of creative legal destruction. But we lack detailed studies of how various actors in the law-making and enforcement processes are responding to this phenomenon and how it is affecting the production and enforcement of law.

As we have noted at various points in the book, the process of globalization as it affects legal systems means that not only newcomers but also incumbents have access to the newly built legal machinery. This means that law reform contains a great irony that is not fully appreciated: newfound forms of legality can be used to block as well as facilitate institutional and market change.

Moreover, and equally important, key legal actors such as the courts have not necessarily themselves undergone globalization to the same extent as have other parts of the legal system, such as practicing lawyers or the formal law on the books. So several of the countries we have studied—and, we suspect, many others beyond the scope of the book—are currently caught in a twilight zone of legal governance. Statutory law has been modernized, new actors have appeared in the markets and in the courts, and the legal machinery is being put to use like never before, but the outcomes are rather contradictory and unpredictable, sometimes suggesting openness to new forms of legality in the governance of market relations and sometimes displaying rather xenophobic tendencies.[2] The recent experiences of Japan and Korea that we have examined epitomize in many ways the ambiguity and contradictions in the globalization of legal governance to which we have just adverted. But much more work needs to be done if we are to understand the effects of global flows of capital, information, technology, managerial talent, and other factors of production on domestic legal systems.

In methodological terms, we argued that focusing on a moment of stress is highly revealing of the underlying dynamics of a complex system, permitting unique insights into its vulnerabilities and its propensity for change. We have applied this methodology only with respect to corporate governance crises, but we believe that it could prove useful in understanding other features of a country's governance system as well. For example, the institutional autopsy might prove revealing in the context of financial crises, labor unrest, or even environmental catastrophes. We hope the book might inspire further studies of breakdowns of governance in other realms as a means of understanding complex institutional relationships, stasis, and transition in the political economy.

As we noted at the outset, our instinct was to see a complex world where many have seen straight lines of causation. The complexity of the subject matter places great demands on the reader as well as the investigator. We hope that this book has shown that complex systems can be examined on their own terms—as messy and to some extent unpredictable—without dispensing with an analytical framework that exposes dead ends in the prevailing wisdom and brings a new order to our collective thinking about a fascinating and important topic. Of course, no single work can provide definitive answers to the big questions about the relation between legal systems and economic development that have occupied generations of scholars. But we hope that this book has altered, if modestly, the way these questions are approached.

NOTES

INTRODUCTION

1. Europe and Central Asia Judicial Reform, General Overview, available at the World Bank Web site: http://www.worldbank.org.
2. Assif Shameen, "Dream and Controversy," Asiaweek.com. http://www.pathfinder .com/asiaweek/99/0625/biz4.html; "Financial Crisis in Korea" (19 January 1998), Korean-U.S. Business Council. http://www.dwnam.pe.kr/021%20imf-980119.html.
3. For Weber, rationality of law stemmed from its autonomous, universal, and consciously constructed character.
4. We discuss this literature extensively in chapter 1.
5. See chapter 10. There is, however, an extensive literature about the existence of transnational networks among national regulators, courts, and lawmakers and its effect on the making and enforcement of law globally. For a recent review of this literature, see Slaughter (2004).
6. In some cases it can be difficult to disentangle corporate governance problems from macroeconomic problems. For example, observers disagree about the precise origins of the financial crisis that afflicted South Korea and other countries in 1997 and 1998. Some emphasize weak corporate governance and legal institutions, and others fault exchange rate and interest rate policies and related macroeconomic trends.
7. See chapter 1.
8. Weber did not see a firm link between English common law and economic development.
9. We do not wish to delve deeply into the voluminous literature concerning the definition of the rule of law and the various ends to which scholars have used the term. In the policy world and the academic literature most closely related to our topic, the rule of law signifies an infrastructure of generally applicable legal rules that lend predictability to economic behavior and constrain discretionary governmental intervention in the economy. Ohnesorge (2003) discusses at length the definition of the rule of law in the literature of law and development.
10. Hong (1999), 147.
11. For a critical perspective on this Weberian legacy, see Sabel (2005).
12. Dorf and Sabel (1998). As discussed in chapter 2, we use the term in a somewhat broader sense than do prior scholars.

13. As discussed in chapter 1, the notion that mechanisms of governance may be more or less centralized is not new, but the implications of the relative centralization of legal systems have not been consistently explored.

14. Note that we do not claim that the legal system is actually capable of a complete and clear allocation of rights. Instead, we are referring to the aspirations of legal systems as reflected in substantive law and in the legal mechanisms available for enforcement of rights.

15. See Banner (1998).

16. Characteristically, Weber defined "law" not by reference to some commonly accepted usage of the term but according to his own conceptual framework. Weber believed that social conduct has validity to the extent that it complies with legitimate order. He calls that order "law" when violation is likely to be met with coercion of some kind exercised by a group of people who stand ready to perform that role. This conceptual framework studiously avoids exclusive reference to state-created law enforced by agents of the sovereign. Rheinstein (1954), lxiii.

CHAPTER ONE

1. Chen (2003) includes this nuance after reciting the prevailing view.

2. These authors' article, "Law and Finance" (1998), provided the name by which this line of research would come to be known.

3. Because the focus of these studies was financial market development, they excluded countries that had not developed a meaningful stock market. Subsequent studies, however, include a larger set of countries.

4. For a full list of publications by this group (with various others), see Rafael La Porta's home page at http://mba.tuck.dartmouth.edu/pages/faculty/rafael.laporta/publications.html.

5. Note that in some regressions the negative impact of the French legal system disappears, but the overwhelming evidence produced by this line of scholarship places common law above (French) civil law systems in relation to financial market development.

6. In fact, the notion that legal institutions can be separated from a country's sociopolitical governance structure distinguishes modern-day endowment theorists from Max Weber, who was deeply concerned with the interaction between legal and sociopolitical structures and the institutions they produced (Weber 1968). To be fair, La Porta and colleagues have not openly endorsed the exportation of the legal indicators that, their studies suggest, are conducive to development—but neither have they objected to others (Levine 1999), including the World Bank, using their work to this end.

7. In particular, Djankov et al. (2003) criticize North and others for excluding politics from their analysis.

8. For an exception see La Porta et al. (1999).

9. Legislatures still have a role to play in a system dominated by courts that hear cases brought by individuals. Their role, however, is confined to correcting case law gone astray. Clearly, this argument assumes a benevolent legislature, the existence of which is denied in Hayek's critique of centralized law-making patterns.

10. See, e.g., World Bank (1996), in particular chap. 5, p. 87 concerning legal institutions. See also chapter 3 (esp. p. 48) regarding property rights and enterprise reform. The World Bank has funded much of the group's subsequent research.

11. http://www.doingbusiness.org/.

12. In the original law and finance paper, the authors avoid this shortcut by pointing out that "France and Belgium, after all, are both very rich countries." See La Porta et al. (1998), 1152.

13. For an attempt to conceptualize the endogenous evolution of institutions, see Aoki (2001) and Greif (2006).

14. See, e.g., Eiras (2003, 3): "The rule of law is the only mechanism that a society has to punish crime, protect private property, enforce contracts, and maintain reforms."

15. See also Aoki (2001) and Greif (2006).

16. As discussed in chapter 10, demand has entered the existing analysis only in very general evolutionary theories of legal change.

17. Russia's 1997 bankruptcy law was modeled on the new German version, which in turn had been inspired by the U.S. bankruptcy law of 1978. See Black and Tarassova (2003).

18. The literature about economics provides no explanation for in-country variations in the use of law to govern markets. Variations of this sort are very problematic for the canonical view.

CHAPTER TWO

1. The extent to which they are addressed by the legal system in a given country requires a further level of analysis, which we provide below.

2. Some scholars have coined the terms "rolling rules" and "rolling regulation" to describe a recent trend toward using ongoing benchmarking and information exchange as a regulatory approach, in contrast to the command-and-control style of regulation (Dorf and Sabel 1998). We borrow the term "rolling" but use it to describe the larger phenomenon of ongoing, mutual influence that has always characterized the development of law and markets. A more technical approach is to describe institutions as endogenously created. See Greif (2006).

3. This relation does not mean that we exclude the possibility that legal change might be triggered by factors other than markets. In fact, legal change frequently occurs to correct problems encountered with existing law (that is, endogenously) because of poor drafting, because the legislature originally failed to anticipate the ways a law might be applied to real-world cases, or because the law proved ineffective.

4. Winter et al. (2002).

5. Lamfalussy (2001).

6. In the United Kingdom, the Department of Trade and Industry typically assembles committees comprising legal practitioners and business people for the purpose of reforming the country's company law. In Delaware, changes in corporate law are proposed by a legislative committee, which includes members of the bar with great expertise in matters of corporate law.

7. A prime example is the Takeover Directive. The High Level Group of Company Law Experts' proposals were substantially watered down in the directive as finally enacted.

8. Yet Delaware does not enjoy a monopoly on the regulation of corporate affairs. Its dominant role in corporate law has been checked to some degree by the massive growth of securities regulation at the federal level, from the enactment of the securities laws in 1933 and 1934 through the passage of the Sarbanes-Oxley Act in 2002 (Roe 2002). These major federal interventions were triggered by a severe market downturn and a major corporate governance scandal, respectively, which empowered interest groups that have little or no influence in the lawmaking process in Delaware (Roe 2005).

9. According to art. 4 of the French Civil Code, judges have the obligation to interpret the law; art. 5 prohibits them explicitly from making law. Article 5 states : "Il est défendu aux juges de prononcer par voie de disposition générale et réglementaire sur les causes qui leur sont soumises." (The code is available in English and French at http://www.legifrance.gouv.fr/html/index.html.) For a discussion of judicial interpretation of the code in France, see Germain (2003).

10. The most famous examples are typically drawn from the area of torts, in which courts have reinterpreted the provisions of the code—arguably *contra legem*—in order to respond to the needs of an industrializing country with growing numbers of car accidents and increased product liability. The famous case that introduced essentially strict liability into French tort law is *Jand'heur v. Les Galeries Belfortaise*, Cass. ch. réun. (February 13, 1930), 1930 D.P. I. 57 (Cours de Cassation).

11. When we say "protective," we do not mean that such a legal system necessarily provides greater substantive protections than does a coordinative legal system. We use the term to characterize legal systems that specify desired substantive rights or outcomes and allocate residual enforcement rights to private parties.

12. Although monitoring of property rights and enforcement of contract rights are sometimes analyzed separately in the literature, we view the two as subspecies of the protection function of law.

13. The varieties-of-capitalism literature has come under substantial critique lately, mostly because the explanatory variables used to characterize the system have lost much of their power. See, e.g., Siaroff (1999). For a more comprehensive reassessment see Streeck and Thelen (2005).

14. For a comparative analysis of the U.K. and U.S. takeover regimes, see Armour and Skeel (2006).

15. For a review of the range of pre-bid defenses available in legal systems across the European Union, compare Winter et al. (2002).

16. Note that the legal dispute in the Mannesmann case, which we discuss in greater detail below, was not so much about absolute pay levels but the ability of a board or committee to grant extra compensation ex post. The public debate, however, focused on the amounts that changed hands.

17. As discussed in chapters 8 and 9, Russia's legal practice at times resembles hierarchy more than coordination. But among the countries we analyze this is the exception, not the rule.

18. See Kenworthy (2000) for the corporatism debate and La Porta, Lopez-de-Silanes, and Shleifer (2006) for the legal origins debate, wherein the proponents of the legal origin classification system concede that the "French effect" disappears in some of the specifications when one tests the quality of securities regulations.

19. A useful definition is provided by Posner (1997, 365): a norm is simply a rule that is not promulgated by an official source nor enforced through legal sanction, yet is regularly complied with.

20. Note that the tendency to define governance devices that are not legally enforceable principally in contradistinction to their legally enforceable counterparts—as "nonlaw," "soft law," and so on—implicitly suggests their inferiority. Posner (1996) uses game theory to argue that norms are often inferior to formal law as a means of dealing with social dilemmas of coordination and cooperation. We note only that every society, from the most to the least economically successful, uses a wide array of governance devices. Like a discussion of whether a hammer is a better tool than

a screwdriver, there does not seem to be much point in debating whether law is superior to nonlaw as a means of governing the economy.

21. One of the great internal contradictions of the literature that follows from the work of La Porta et al. is that while it recognizes the political origins of legal systems as in Djankov et al. (2003), it fails to incorporate this insight into the analysis of the operation of legal systems.

22. This point is not novel (Upham 2002), and the impact of politics (in the sense of left or right political preferences) on law has been used to explain differences in economic outcomes, specifically corporate governance structures, around the world (Roe 2000). Gourevitch and Shinn (2005) argue that political preferences determine law, which in turn drives corporate governance.

23. We want to emphasize that we are not claiming, as was fashionable in the 1980s, that "industrial policy" set by smart bureaucrats created Japan's economic success. Quite to the contrary, we are arguing that the ground rules for economic activity emerged from intense interactions between the public and the private sectors in which bureaucrats played an important coordinating role that is sometimes played by legal institutions in other systems. Nor do we claim that the informal ground rules developed in Japan were always optimal for economic activity. As with law, sometimes the informal ground rules lacked predictability or provided poor incentives for market actors.

24. Note that the reach of informal mechanisms of governance is, to considerable extent, a function of information costs. Advances in information technology have dramatically reduced information costs, suggesting that the demand for legal governance should have declined, at least in some markets. Arguably, the development of the relatively "law-free" environment of the Internet is consistent with this prediction.

25. By contrast, incumbents may be slow to realize the growing discrepancy between the prevailing institutional setup and what is feasible or even necessary. See Greif (2006, 338). Our institutional autopsies of the Mannesmann case and the SK case illustrate this point.

26. Black and Kraakman reject a purely enabling model for Russia's corporate law. Instead they opt for what they term a "self-enforcing model"—somewhere between the extremes of an enabling model and mandatory law. See Black and Kraakman (1996).

27. In the European Union in particular, a growing chorus is advocating a change in mandatory capital maintenance rules that were the hallmarks of the early directives that harmonized law. See Wymeersch (1999). This, however, has not yet been translated into actual changes to these directives.

CHAPTER THREE

1. Readers who desire detailed accounts of the scandal itself can turn to a host of other sources (e.g., Rapoport and Dharan 2004).

2. Several years later, the Supreme Court overturned Arthur Andersen's criminal conviction—far too late to save the firm.

3. For example, a single book of collected works about Enron (Rapoport and Dharan 2004) contains a number of conflicting hypotheses advanced by various commentators: (1) "Enron is more a tale of greed and ego run amok than it is a tale of why certain business models fail" (89); (2) "The Enron meltdown is a result of massive failure of corporate control and governance" (122); (3) the "problem with viewing

Enron as an indication of any systematic governance failure is that its core facts are maddeningly unique" (125). Other commentators have suggested that Enron and other scandals notwithstanding, "the evidence is not consistent with a failed U.S. system. If anything, it suggests a system that is well above average" (Holmstrom and Kaplan 2003, 1).

4. For critical differences between the United States and the United Kingdom in terms of the ownership structure of firms and the role of institutional investors see Black and Coffee (1994).

5. The actual impact of the PSLRA on securities fraud class actions is still being debated. Although the number of such suits declined in the immediate wake of the statute's enactment, by the middle of the first decade of the twenty-first century, the number of suits filed annually reached and sometimes exceeded pre-PSLRA levels. For a variety of perspectives on the PSLRA's impact on securities fraud litigation, see Peng and Roell (2004); Perino (2003); Choi (2005).

6. In order to maintain partisan balance, no more than three commissioners may belong to the same political party.

7. This is available at http://www.sec.gov/news/speech/spch516.htm.

8. "Harvey Pitt's Credibility," *Wall Street Journal*, 8 May 2002, at A18.

9. The law even seeks to regulate the ethics of securities lawyers. See section 307.

10. Even this requirement, however, is partly a repackaging of existing law. Since the 1970s, the Foreign Corrupt Practices Act has required internal controls for large corporations. Section 404 added the requirement that these controls be audited by outside auditors and publicly evaluated by management.

11. Vice Chancellor Leo E. Strine of the Delaware Chancery Court described SOX as a "strange stew" of sensible ideas and "narrow provisions of dubious value" (Taub 2005, n.p.).

12. The following description of SOX is typical: "The Act represents the most dramatic change to the securities laws and their administration since the Great Depression. Wide ranging in scope, the Act . . . is intended to be a comprehensive and permanent solution to management malfeasance" (Huber 2004, 1).

13. The act did add $776 million to the SEC's budget. Most of the money was used to hire additional enforcement staff.

14. Indeed, the Enron defendants were prosecuted under pre-SOX law (because the law had not been enacted at the time of their alleged misconduct). Even a former federal prosecutor and director of the government's Enron task force conceded that the heightened criminal penalties provided by SOX are not necessary to deter this type of corporate wrongdoing. Remarks of Leslie Caldwell, University of California, Berkeley, 17 March 2006.

15. Reflecting this change in emphasis, the FBI increased the number of agents involved in corporate and securities fraud investigations and referred more of such cases to U.S. Attorneys' offices in fiscal year 2004 than in fiscal year 2000 (U.S. Department of Justice 2005, 52–53).

16. See "Rivals for Spitzer's Job Play Down Wall Street Role," Bloomberg.com, 27 July 2006. http://www.bloomberg.com/apps/news?pid=20601070&refer=home &sid=am0.JV2Lvzok.

17. The Martin Act of 1921 is a "Blue Sky law," a state law designed to combat securities fraud enacted prior to the enactment of the federal securities laws. The law was used occasionally in the 1970s against abusive sales tactics by brokerage firms, but it was

less frequently used once the SEC and the NASD became more actively involved in the regulation of brokers.

18. See, e.g., "The Martin Act: Spitzer's Blank Check." http://www.overlawyered .com/archives/001124.html; "The Martin Act: A Weapon of Mass Destruction," Corporate Law Blog, 4 May 2004. http://www.corplawblog.com/archives/000329.html.

19. Senator Arlen Specter introduced the Attorney-Client Privilege Protection Act of 2007, S. 286, 110th Cong., 1st sess. (2007).

20. United States v. Stein, 435 F. Supp. 2d. 330, 336 (S.D.N.Y. 2006).

21. "Principles of Federal Prosecution of Business Organizations: Memorandum to Heads of Department Components and United States Attorneys from Paul J. McNulty, Deputy Attorney General" (the McNulty memo) can be found at http://www.usdoj.gov/dag/pubdoc.html.

22. Lately, the regulatory competition story has been challenged. Kahan and Kumar (2002) find no evidence for continued regulatory competition among U.S. states. And Mark Roe has suggested that Delaware's real competition is with the federal government, not with other states. See Roe (2002). Nonetheless, there is little dispute about the fact that regulatory competition—in particular, with New York and New Jersey—was critical for the early stages of the development of Delaware's corporate law. See Arsht (1976).

23. In re The Walt Disney Company Derivative Litigation, No. Civ. A. 15452. 2005 WL 2056651 (Del. Ch.), decided 9 August 2005. Quotations in text are from this decision.

24. Note that the plaintiff's principal and most promising claim was focused on an indirect issue—the adequacy of the board's decision-making process with respect to Ovitz's contract—and *not* on the amount of Ovitz's compensation. The claim that Ovitz was simply paid too much was subjected to the "waste" test, a plaintiff-unfriendly standard, and summarily rejected by the court.

25. The ruling was affirmed by the Delaware Supreme Court in 2006. In re The Walt Disney Company Derivative Litigation, 906 A.2d 27 (Del. Supr. 2006).

26. Interim Report of the Committee on Capital Markets Regulation, November 30, 2006. http://www.capmktsreg.org/pdfs/11.30committee—interim—reportRev2. pdf.

27. "New Independent Nonpartisan Committee to Study Capital Markets Regulation," press release, 12 September 2006. http://www.capmktsreg.org/pastpress_releases .html#9_12.

28. "Committee on Capital Markets Regulation Recommends Enhancing Shareholder Rights," press release, 30 November 2006. http://www.capmktsreg.org/pastpress _releases.html#11_30.

CHAPTER FOUR

1. See the World Bank's World Development Indicators for 2006. http://devdata .worldbank.org/wdi2006/contents/4f.htm.

2. German corporate law stipulates a two-tiered management structure. The management board is the executive body, and its members are appointed by the supervisory board. Half of the members of the supervisory board are elected by shareholders and half by the company's employees.

3. HutchisonWhampoa had acquired 10 percent of Mannesmann shares in exchange for a 45 percent stake in the British telecommunications firm Orange in October 1999 for US$36 billion. Top managers of Orange had been paid an award of £10

million (paid equally by Mannesmann and Hutchison) when they were forced out as a result of the transaction.

4. The resolution is quoted in the ruling of the Landgericht in Düsseldorf of 22 July 2004. http://www.justiz.nrw.de/nrwe/lgs/duesseldorf/lg_duesseldorf/j2004/ XIV_5_03urtei120040722.html, (AktZ XIV/05/03) at recital 93.

5. The exact wording in German is as follows: "Nach Auffassung der Herren Zwickel und Ladberg ist die Höhe des genannten Betrages den Arbeitnehmern schwer vermittelbar. Sie nehmen daher die Entscheidung zur Kenntnis." See the decision of the court of First Instance (Landgericht), ibid. at 28 (translation by Katharina Pistor).

6. Details about the postacquisition restructuring of Mannesmann, including the sale of some of its operations, are available at Vodafone's investor relations Web site: http://www.vodafone.com/article/0,3029,CATEGORY_ID%253D406%2526LAN-GUAGE_ID%253D0%2526CONTENT_ID%253D232102,00.html. According to this information, Atecs was sold to Siemens AG and Robert Bosch GmbH in 2000–1. Orange was disposed of subject to requirements imposed by the European competition authorities. The Arcor Rail Business was sold to Deutsche Bahn.

7. See Joachim Jahn, "Staatsanwaltschaft erklärt Sinneswandel" (Prosecutor Explains Change of Mind), *Frankfurter Allgemeine Zeitung*, 17 November 2006. http://www .faz.net.

8. The relevant provision (sec. 266 of the Straßgesetzbuch, or StGB, Germany's criminal code) reads: "Any person who by law, administrative delegation or contract has dispositional power over the assets of others or power to commit these assets to a third party [and] abuses and breaches the duty laid on him by law, administrative delegation or trust relationship to protect the property interests of another, and in this way causes damage to the property interests that he should protect, shall be punished with arrest of up to five years or with a monetary fine."

9. For a citation to the full text of the decision (in German), see note 4.

10. Sec. 296, StPO states that both the defense and the prosecutor may invoke appeal procedures. Moreover, the prosecutor, as the general agent for lawfulness, may invoke such procedures in the interests of the accused. By implication, even an acquittal can be appealed by the prosecutor for violation of substantive or procedural law, including the failure of the court to assess the evidence based on relevant legal standards. The relevant appeal procedure invoked in the present case is the revision; see sec. 333 StPO.

11. The decision of the BGH, with the filing number (Aktenzeichen) 3 StR 470/04, is available in German at http://www.bundesgerichtshof.de/. All quotations are from this full-text version. A summary of the core findings in English can be found at http://www.germanlawjournal.com/article.php?id=735.

12. See the story "Aberwitzige Vereinbarung" by West German public radio. http://www .wdr.de/themen/wirtschaft/wirtschaftsbranche/mannesmann_abfindungen/interview _experten.jhtml?rubrikenstyle=wirtschaft.

13. Ibid.

14. See *Süddeutsche Zeitung*, 20 January 2004, http://www.sueddeutsche.de/wirtschaft/ artikel/198/25173/.

15. "111 Millionen und ein bisschen mehr" (DM 111 million and a little more), *Handelsblatt*, 15 January, 2004. Note that even this pro-business paper stated the total amount of the appreciation award in deutschmarks, the currency that had meanwhile been replaced by the euro. The effect is that the amount seems about twice as high.

16. See Uwe Hüffer, "Die Kritik der Staatsanwaltschaft bleibt im Allgemeinen stecken und trifft auch nicht zu" (The Prosecutor's Critique Remains Overly General and Is Incorrect), *Frankfurter Allgemeine Zeitung*, 21 January 2004.

17. Marcus Lutter and Wolfgang Zöllner, "Die Mannesmann-Prämien durften nicht gezahlt werden" (The Mannesmann Awards Should Not Have Been Paid), *Frankfurter Allgemeine Zeitung*, 10 February 2004.

18. Janet Guyon, "In Germany High Pay Is a Crime," *Fortune*, 13 October 2003. http://money.cnn.com/magazines/fortune/fortune_archive/2003/10/13/350890/index.htm.

19. According to the *Süddeutsche Zeitung*, Merkel opined that the criminal investigation amounted to an attack against Germany as an international marketplace (*Wirtschaftsstandort Deutschland*). See "Just Like in a Bazaar." http://www.sueddeutsche.de/wirtschaft/artikel/198/25173.

20. "Mannesmann-Prozess: Kein Scherbengericht für die deutsche Wirtschaft" (Mannesmann Trial: Not an Ostracism Procedure for German Business), *Frankfurter Allgemeine Zeitung*, 18 November 2004. http://www.faz.net.

21. "Freisprüche im Mannesmann-Prozess: Gericht sieht keine Beweise für Käuflichkeit, rügt aber Manager-Gier" (Acquittals in the Mannesmann Trial: Court Does Not See Evidence for Bribes, but Reprimands Management Greed), *Frankfurter Neue Presse*, 23 July 2004. See also Henning Peitsmeier "Sieg ohne Victory-Zeichen" (Victory without Victory Sign), *Frankfurter Allgemeine Zeitung*, 23 July 2004. http://www.faz.net/s/RubEC1ACFE1EE274C81BCD3621EF555C83C/Doc~E229492015E404FEB99E589BBD5098948~ATpl~Ecommon~Scontent.html. "Victory Sign" refers to the gesture Josef Ackermann gave before entering the court on the first day of the proceedings.

22. Note that the requirement of a "severe breach" to elicit punishment under sec. 266, StGB (see n.8) was developed in case law and is therefore not immediately apparent from reading the provision.

23. The opinion of the prosecutor's office is contained in a lengthy brief filed on 15 October 2004 (29 Js 159/00). The brief, which is not publicly available, is on file with the authors.

24. 3 StR 470/04, available in German at http://www.bundesgerichtshof.de/.

25. Ibid at 11.

26. Ibid at 16.

27. See press announcement no. 09/2006 of the Landgericht Düsseldorf, 29 November 2006, http://www.lg-duesseldorf.nrw.de/presse/dokument/09-06.pdf.

28. See the public radio report "Das Gericht hat gesprochen" (The court has ruled), 29 November 2006, www.wdr.de.

29. Note that in Germany the discourse about corporate law employs language referring to the traditional factors of production, capital and labor first identified by David Ricardo (1772–1832) and more fully developed by Karl Marx in *Das Kapital* (1859). "Capital" in contemporary parlance includes shareholders, creditors, and management.

30. Gesetz über die Mitbestimmung der Arbeitnehmer, or MitBestG (Law on codetermination by employees) of 4 May 1976 (BGBl I, p. 1153), http://bundesrecht.juris.de/mitbestg/BJNR011530976.html.

31. Gesetz über die Mitbestimmung der Arbeitnehmer in den Aufsichtsräten und Vorständen der Unternehmen des Bergbaus und der Eisen und Stahl erzeugenden Industrie (Montanmitbestimmungsgesetz) (Law on codetermination of employees

234 / Notes to Pages 76–79

in the supervisory boards and management boards of companies in mining, iron, and steel production sectors) of 21 May 1951, BGBl I, p. 347, last amended 25 November 2003, BGBl I, p. 2304. A clean version of the law as amended is available in BGBl III, no. 801–2.

32. The relevant sections of art. 14 of the Basic Law read in full: "(1) Property and the right of inheritance shall be guaranteed. Their content and limits shall be defined by the laws. (2) Property entails obligations. Its use shall also serve the public good." English translation available at http://www.bundestag.de/htdocs_e/info/030gg.pdf. For an insightful analysis of Germany's concept of private property and how it differs from the concept in the United States, compare Alexander (2003).

33. See note 31.

34. The major difference between full-parity codetermination under the 1951 law governing the coal and steel sectors and the quasi-parity codetermination law of 1976 is that in the latter the balance is tilted in favor of shareholders by allowing shareholders to elect the chairman of the supervisory board and by giving him or her the decisive vote in case no consensus can be reached in the first round of voting. See sec. 27 II MitbestG, supra note 30.

35. For a critical review of codetermination, however, see Adams (2006).

36. The median is 51 percent. See La Porta et al. (1998), table 7, p. 1147.

37. Voting power may deviate from ownership concentration when companies issue more than one class of stock with different voting powers, when shareholders enter into voting agreements, or when custodians of stock commonly vote the shares they hold on behalf of small investors.

38. La Porta et al. (1998) table 1, p. 1052. The role of banks in German capitalism remains a matter of dispute. In the comparative corporate governance literature, Germany has been characterized as a bank-centered system in which banks not only provide finance, mostly in the form of debt, but also own substantial equity stakes in corporations (Cable 1985; Baums 1992; Roe 1993). Comparative data about debt finance and ownership structures give a slightly different picture, however. Whereas Germany's share of debt finance, 33 percent, is 10 percent higher than the comparable figure in the United States, the prototypical market-based system, it is 10 percent *lower* than in the United Kingdom, which is also typically classified as a market-based system in which equity dominates over debt finance (Rajan and Zingales 1995). Moreover, according to Edwards and Fischer, nonbank corporate blockholders are more characteristic of the German governance system than are bank blockholders (Edwards and Fischer 1994).

39. See Martin Höpner, "Ende der Deutschland AG?" (The end of Germany, Inc.?), *Magazin Mitbestimmung*, November 2000, www.boeckler.de.

40. Detailed data about Mannesmann's ownership structure are available in Höpner and Jackson (2001).

41. See http://www.bankgeschichte.de.

42. This was most notable in the pharmaceutical sector, as evidenced by the triangular takeover war between Merck (Germany), Schering, and Bayer. See "Merck Sells Schering Shares, Paves Way for Bayer Buy," 14 June 2006, www.bloomberg.com.

43. Gesetz zur Kontrolle und Transparenz im Unternehmensbereich (KonTraG), BGBl I, 30 April 1998, p. 786.

44. "Ackermann: Es war kein Bereicherung" (Ackermann: This was not an enrichment), *Frankfurter Allgemeine Zeitung*, 23 January 2003; "Deutsche Bank Executive to Have His Day in Court," *New York Times*, 18 October, 2003; "Es geht um sehr viel Geld,

doch das ist kein Problem" (A lot of money is at stake, but this is not a problem), *Frankfurter Allgemeine Zeitung*, 21 January 2004.

45. "Telefonterror bis hin zu regelrechten Drohungen" (Telephone terror all the way to real threats), *Börsenzeitung*, 23 July 2004, quoting the introductory statement of the judge. Toward the end she remarked, in apparent reference to Ackermann's statement, that only in Germany were corporate managers prosecuted for creating value: "[In a criminal court] we do not evaluate corporate governance culture, even though the evidence presented has perplexed some. Nevertheless—and this should be stated clearly—a corporation and its representatives do not operate in Germany in a lawless environment, irrespective of whether they create value or not." Ibid.

46. On the genesis of the E.U. Takeover Directive, see Winter et al. (2002).

47. For a comparison of the legal framework for takeovers in the United Kingdom and the United States (mainly Delaware) see Armour (2006).

48. This context challenges the argument put forward by Gordon, namely, that Germany vetoed the takeover directive in order to accelerate the European integration project Gordon (2000a).

49. Wertpapier- und Übernahmegesetz (German Takeover Law), 20 December 2001, BGBl I, p. 3822. Prior to the adoption of this law, Germany had only a voluntary takeover code. Few companies subjected themselves to this code, however. See Hopt (1976).

50. Directive 2004/25/EC of the European Parliament and of the Council of 21 April 2004 on takeover bids. www.europa.eu.int.

51. See ibid., art. 9.

52. See ibid., art 12.

53. The decision must specify the kind of defensive measure that may be employed and requires a three-quarter supermajority vote of shareholders as well as approval by the supervisory board. Sec. 33, German Takeover Law, BGBl I, p. 3822.

54. Gesetz über die Offenlegung der Vorstandsvergütungen (Law on the disclosure of executive compensation), 3 August 2005, BGBl I, p. 2267.

55. The law known as UMAG was adopted 22 September 2005, BGBl 2005 I, p. 2860.

56. If the supervisory board declines to take action, the court appoints a special shareholder representative to pursue the litigation.

57. Gesetz zur Einführung von Kapitalanleger-Musterverfahren, or KapMuG (Act on the initiation of model case proceedings with respect to investors in the capital market), 16 August 2005, BGBl I, p. 2437; an English version of the law is available at http://www.bmj.bund.de/media/archive/1110.pdf.

58. KapMuG, sec. 7.

59. See sec. 16 of the act: "The model case ruling shall be binding on the courts trying the matter, whose decisions depend on the establishment made on the model case or the legal question to be resolved in the model case proceedings."

60. Note that in Germany, as in most other member states of the European Union, contingency fees are considered unethical.

61. See the discussion of the coordination function of law in chapter 1.

62. This is a critical element of Germany's collective bargaining system as set forth in the Tarifvertragsgesetz (Act on wage scale contracts), enacted on 9 April 1949 (WiGBl 1949, 55, 68), last amended 25 November 2003, BGBl I, p. 2304. See sec. 5 of the act.

63. See note 34.

64. Peter Hartz, the mastermind of Germany's recent labor and unemployment reform during the tenure of Chancellor Gerhard Schroeder, received a two-year suspended sentence plus a fine of €560,000 in March 2007 for forty-four counts of breach of trust for having paid expensive airfares to union representatives and members of Vokswagen's Workers' Council in order to assure their support. See "Hartz Sentenced in VW Bribe Case," *BBC News*, 25 January 2007.

65. See "Ackermann, Raffke & Co" (Ackermann, Grabber & Co.), *Berliner Zeitung*, 23 July 2004; "Mannesmann-Prozess: Im Spannungsfeld zwischen Recht und Moral" (Mannesmann trial: Tension between law and morals), *Financial Times Deutschland*, 23 July 2004.

66. According to the seat theory, all firms that locate their operations or headquarters in Germany must incorporate under German law and thus adopt the mandatory German governance structures. German courts interpreted this rule as requiring companies that had been incorporated elsewhere but had moved their headquarters to Germany to reincorporate in Germany. Otherwise German law would not recognize them as duly incorporated legal entities. See BGH of 1 July 2002, II ZR 380/00. The critical case that finally led to the demise of the seat theory in Germany is the Überseering decision. The European Court of Justice found the seat theory to be in violation of the European Treaty's principle of the free movement of persons, which includes legal persons. Judgment of the European Court of Justice, 5 November 2002 (2002/C 323/13).

67. Council Regulation no. 2157/2001 on the Statute for a European Company (Societas Europaea, or S.E.). The regulation entered into force after member states had enacted a complementary directive on workers' rights in the context of establishing an S.E.

68. See Council Directive 2001/86/EC.

69. See http://www.allianz.com/en/allianz_group/press_center/news/company_news/corporate_governance/news1.html for details. As a result of this merger, the size of the supervisory board has been reduced from twenty members to twelve (Germany's Codetermination Law requires a company with more than twenty thousand employees to create a supervisory board with twenty seats, ten of which must be reserved for employees). See MitBestG, sec. 7. In addition, a new works council has been crated with thirty-seven members from twenty-four different countries, including ten representatives from Germany and three each from Italy, France, and the United Kingdom (ibid.).

70. See Merrill Lynch, "Deutsche Bank: Clearer Strategy and Improved Diversification Prompt Upgrade to Buy," in Merrill Lynch, In-Depth Report on Multi-National Banks, 6 September 2005.

CHAPTER FIVE

1. This chapter is based on research and interviews conducted by Milhaupt in the first six months of 2005 and published as (Milhaupt 2005). Readers are directed to that publication for more extensive citations and support for the factual and analytical assertions made in this chapter.

2. Securities and Exchange Act, Law no. 25 of 1948, art. 27–2(1). In the wake of the Livedoor controversy, this provision was amended to subject even off-exchange trades to the mandatory tender offer rule.

3. Commercial Code, Law no. 488 of 1899, art. 280–21(1).

4. "Nippon Broadcasting: Increased Likelihood That President Kamebuchi Will Resign for Failing to Prevent Takeover," *Mainichi Shimbun*, 9 April 2005, http://www

.mainichi.msn.co.jp/shakai/wadai/news/20050409k0000e04002400c.html (in Japanese).
5. See chapter 4, p. 80–81.
6. The dynamics behind the E.U. Takeover Directive were somewhat different from those at work in Japan, however. In Europe, the directive was intended to create a level playing field for takeovers among the members of the E.U. In Japan, momentum to create guidelines for takeover defenses was provided by the emergence, for the first time, of hostile takeovers in the Japanese economy.
7. "70% Perceive Threat of Hostile Takeover," *Asahi Shimbun*, 30 April 2005, at 1 (in Japanese).
8. See, e.g., Lucier (2002, 13), showing that Japanese CEOs have "the lowest proportions of merger-driven and performance-related departures; the smallest impact of CEO performance upon tenure; the oldest CEOs at ascension; and the least orientation toward shareholder returns" of CEOs in the United States, Europe, and the Asia-Pacific region.
9. The business judgment rule, a judge-made doctrine, essentially provides that judges will not second-guess a good-faith decision of corporate directors or officers that turns out poorly, unless the decision-making process or the substance of the decision was obviously improper.
10. Nippon Hoso K.K. v. Livedoor K.K., Appeal from Injunction Against Issuance of Warrants, 1173 Hanrei Taimuzu 125, Tokyo High Court, March 23, 2005. Translation by Curtis Milhaupt.
11. Both Horie and Livedoor received far more severe legal treatment than is typical for this type of wrongdoing in Japan. Executives convicted of white-collar crime usually receive suspended sentences, and a company embroiled in a high-profile investigation for accounting fraud at around the same time as the Livedoor case received a monetary fine but was not delisted from the Tokyo Stock Exchange. See Norimitsu Onishi, "Livedoor Founder Is Sentenced to Prison," *International Herald Tribune*, 17–18 March 2007, at 13.
12. The German Takeover Code was adopted after Germany voted down the Thirteenth Directive on Takeovers in 2000. When a greatly modified Thirteenth Directive was finally adopted years later, Germany changed the Takeover Code but largely retained a flexible response system based on supervisory board approval. See chapter 4 for details.
13. See chapter 10.
14. The Takeover Code was adopted by the Takeover Panel in 1968. For details see www.thetakeoverpanel.org.uk.
15. It could be argued, however, that the self-governing model contemplated by the City Code is quite different from the regulatory approach of postwar Japan, in which industry players operated under the ostensible tutelage of economic ministries. Viewed in this light, the U.K. approach may have represented a rather radical departure from past regulatory practices.
16. Japan's tender offer regulation in place at the time of the Livedoor bid (see note 2 and accompanying text above) was a mandatory tender offer rule for purchases of more than 33.3 percent but not a City Code–style mandatory bid rule because a bidder in Japan need not bid for all outstanding shares.
17. Exactly what constitutes independence in the Japanese context is now the subject of substantial debate. The corporate law does not require the presence of *independent* directors on corporate boards, and there is no formal definition of independence

in any regulation or judicial ruling. Rather, the corporate law refers to "outside" (*shagai*) directors, the definition of which is broad enough to include directors from a parent company or sibling subsidiary. Commercial Code sec. 188.

18. As the Delaware Chancery Court put it, "Since the 1980s, [corporate takeover law], largely judge made, has been racing to keep abreast of the ever-evolving and novel tactical and strategic developments so characteristic of this important area of economic endeavor." Carmody v. Toll Brothers, 723 A.2d 1180 (Del. Ch. 1998).

19. See Milhaupt (2001) for some evidence of low demand for corporate law in the postwar period.

20. Data concerning share ownership are from the Tokyo Stock Exchange, http://www.tse.or.jp/english/market/data/shareownership/index.html.

21. See, e.g., Justice System Reform Council 2001.

CHAPTER SIX

1. For example: "'I will root away the noisome weeds which, without profit, suck the soil's fertility from wholesome flowers.' Shakespeare, *Richard II*" (Sovereign Asset Management 2005).

2. Sovereign's share ownership in SK was effectively capped at 14.9 percent by a variety of considerations. For example, crossing the 15 percent threshold would have triggered antitrust review, including unwelcome financial disclosures by Sovereign.

3. Don Kirk, "Stakeholder Speaks out to Koreans," *New York Times*, 29 April 2003, W1.

4. Chey and the banks had good reason to cooperate, particularly if the cost of that cooperation could be borne by SK's shareholders: the banks held Chey's personal guarantee and could have bankrupted him because of the SK Global insolvency. At the same time, however, the continued viability of SK was crucial to the banks, which had sustained major impairments to their capital during a recent wave of credit card defaults.

5. "South Korean Court Rejects Sovereign's Petition against SK Corp.," Agence France Presse, 23 December 2003.

6. One candidate jointly nominated by Sovereign and SK was elected to the board.

7. Seoul Central District Court, 2004 Bi Hap 347, 15 December 2004.

8. In support of its ruling, the court's opinion contains the rather remarkable observation that although Sovereign's stated objective in barring a convicted criminal from serving on the board is to improve corporate governance, SK's business does not require a particularly high level of morality.

9. Sovereign Asset Management, press release, 12 June 2005, http://www.prnewswire.co/uk/cgi/news/release?id=147902.

10. Salving Sovereign's wounds, however, was the $800 million profit it made on its two-year investment in SK, whose share value increased 500 percent after the saga began. A portion of the share price increase was attributable to rising oil prices during the period in question.

11. Korean Fair Trade Commission (2005). "Article 9" is a reference to the Fair Trade Act provision according to which they are regulated.

12. A more nuanced, and complementary, explanation for why the controlling shareholder problem persists is that the incremental wealth gain to be realized from selling a controlling block would not compensate for the loss of nonpecuniary benefits (power, prestige, and so on) attendant on relinquishing control. (Gilson 2006).

13. Moreover, the lack of a broad investor base reduced demand for investor protections.

14. More than a decade later, under very different political and legal circumstances, Korea's Constitutional Court ruled the dissolution unconstitutional.

15. Today, the Korean FTC is promoting the use of holding companies as a means of mitigating problematic *chaebol* ownership structures. In 2007 the SK Group announced that it would adopt a holding company structure.

16. In our view, what Ginsburg calls a "systematic under-capacity in the [Korean] legal system" (Ginsburg 2004, 3) is actually a reflection of low demand for formal law. In other words, given low demand, the legal system was operating at full capacity although it had few lawyers, prosecutors and judges.

17. To see how legal thresholds can affect the exercise of minority shareholder rights, consider that given the average market capitalization of Korea's listed firms in 1997, shareholders would have needed $3.5 million worth of shares to meet the 5 percent threshold for filing a derivative suit (Kim and Kim 2003, 386).

18. See chapter 1, discussing the assumptions underlying this standard reform package.

19. Class-action suits are permitted for misleading disclosure, accounting fraud, and insider trading and manipulation.

20. The media appeared to play a major role in the SK saga, which is to say that Sovereign clearly lost the public relations aspect of its undertaking. There are several possible (nonexclusive) reasons for this defeat, full analysis of which is beyond the ambition or expertise of the authors. One possibility is that the Korean media are heavily influenced by the *chaebol*, so that alternative perspectives are not aired fully or objectively. Another possibility is that Sovereign would have received better press if it had somehow managed to form a partnership with one of the domestic corporate governance advocacy groups such as PSPD (discussed in the text above). Precisely because of the public relations factor, however, it is unlikely that PSPD would view a partnership with a foreign investor as an attractive strategy. Of course, it is also possible that Sovereign simply made tactical errors in its public relations campaign.

21. Securities and Exchange Act, arts. 200–1, 200–3.

22. Securities Exchange Act Implementation Decree, art. 86–7.

23. Securities Exchange Act, amendment of January 17, 2005.

24. Marcus Noland, "Foreign Investor or a Progressive Force?" *Korea Times*, 22 September 2005.

CHAPTER SEVEN

1. "China Aviation Oil's US$550 million Derivatives Disaster," 1 December 2004, SIAS newsletter, http://www.sias.org.sg.

2. Quoted in John Burton, "CAO's 'Risky Gambles' Made Losses Worse," *Financial Times*, 30 March 2005, at 27.

3. Energy Intelligence Group, "Trading Turbulence Downs China Aviation," *International Petroleum Finance* vol. 27, sec. 12 (1 December 2004). For an overview of historic oil prices, see http://www.oilnergy.com/10post.htm#since78.

4. At this time Temasek apparently did not own any shares in CAO. But the company acquired some of the shares that CAOHC placed on the market in the ill-fated transaction of October 2004. For details, see note 30 below and accompanying text.

5. A *New York Times* article suggested that block trades "exist in a legal twilight in Singapore." Wayne Arnold and Keith Bradsher, "Bank Says Chinese Assured It Filing Company Was Healthy," *New York Times*, 6 December 2004, at A5. Nevertheless, under existing rules the company was obliged to disclose any "material" information to its investors.

6. See "China Aviation Oil's Suspended Chief Executive Freed on Bail: Reports," *Agence France Presse,* 11 June 2005, www.singapore-window.org/sw05/050611af.htm.

7. Section 218(2)(a) of the SFA prohibits a person who is in possession of material price-sensitive information concerning a corporation (to which he is connected), which he knows is not generally available, from subscribing for, purchasing, selling, or entering into an agreement to subscribe for, purchase, or sell the securities of that corporation.

8. The role of CAOHC as one of CAO's creditors came about when it lent the proceeds of its October 2004 offering of CAO shares to CAO. At the time CAO filed for bankruptcy, the company's main creditors included MERM (Mitsui & Co.), Fortis Bank, Barclays Capital, J. Aron & Co. (Singapore), Standard Bank London, Sumitomo Mitsui Banking, and Macquarie Bank. See "Trading Turbulence Downs China Aviation," International Petroleum Finance, 1 December 2004.

9. See Monetary Authority of Singapore, press release, "MAS Takes Civil Penalty Enforcement Action Against China Aviation Oil Holding Company for Insider Trading," 19 August 2005, http://www.mas.gov.sg/masmcm/bin/pt1MAS_Takes_Civil _Penalty_Enforcement_Action_Against.htm (last visited 7 April 2006).

10. For example, "CAO's Shine All Due to One Man," *Business Times* (Singapore), 19 August 2004.

11. The extent to which Jia's conduct was still informed by China's state-controlled system is suggested by allegations made by Chen concerning Jia's handling of the CAO crisis. According to Chen, Jia was incommunicado during a critical request for assistance because he had turned off his cell phone during a Communist Party training session. When CAO sent an emergency request a few days later, it took a week for managers at CAOHC and Communist Party leaders to look into the case. Mure Dickie, "Ex-CAO Chief Attacks CAOHC," *Financial Times,* 19 February 2005, at 6.

12. "Trading Turbulence Downs China Aviation." See also Singapore Exchange Limited Annual Report FY 2004–2005, at 64, http://sgx.com (hereinafter SGX 2005 Annual Report).

13. Elliot Wilson, "Scandal Cools Taste for China Plays," *Standard* (Hong Kong), 7 March 2005, http://www.thestandard.com.hk. See also SGX 2005 Annual Report.

14. SGX 2005 Annual Report, at 59.

15. The report by PricewaterhouseCoopers is not publicly available. Press reports, however, have detailed its findings. See, e.g., "CAO's 'Risky Gambles' Made Losses Worse," Financial Times, 10 April 2005.

16. "China Aviation's Chen Gets 4 Years, 3 Months in Jail," *Bloomberg News,* 21 March 2006.

17. "Oil Firm Officials Ordered to Pay Fines," *China Daily,* 3 March 2006 (reporting that jail time would be served only if the convicted were unable to pay the fines).

18. "Three Chinese Indicted in New York for BoC Fraud," *China Daily,* 15 February 2005.

19. Mure Dickie, "CAO Arrests Fade from Official View: Emphasis Is on Good News Not Bad on Industry Website," *Financial Times,* 10 June 2005, at 27.

20. "The High Court Approved the Debt Structuring Plan of Chinese Jet Fuel Importer China Aviation Oil (Singapore)," *Petroleum Intelligence Weekly,* vol. 44, issue 25 (20 June 2005).

21. Tom Grimer, "China's Taking Notes on Corporate Justice, Singapore-Style," *Globe and Mail* (Toronto), June 15, 2005, at 2.

22. Burke v. China Aviation Oil (Singapore) Corp. Ltd., 421 F. Supp.2d 649 (S.D.N.Y. 2005).

23. The SIAS defines itself as an investor lobby group and a financial market watchdog committed to ensuring transparent and fair treatment of investors in Singapore and throughout Asia. The organization currently has sixty-one thousand members. It was quick to respond vocally to the CAO scandal but did not take any legal action. See http://www.sias.org.sg/about/ for details.

24. Douglas Wong, "China Second-Largest Stock Issuer after U.S.," *Bloomberg News*, 7 June 2005.

25. David Barboza, "Horse Trading for a Venture in China," *New York Times*, 5 March 2005, at C1.

26. The company, though not publicly traded, has adopted governance practices that are on a par with best practices in publicly listed companies and proclaims a firm commitment to enhance shareholder value rather than the interests of the Singapore government. Yet as a nonpublic company the firm has considerable discretion in the content and timing of disclosure. In fact, Temasek only began issuing annual reports in 2004. See "In Issuing First Annual Report, Investment Vehicle Aims to Move Further onto World Stage," *Asian Wall Street Journal*, 12 October 2004, http://www.singapore-window.org/sw04/041012aw.htm.

27. "China Construction Bank and Temasek Holdings Established Strategic Partnership in Beijing," 4 July 2005, http://www.temasekholdings.com.sg/news_room/press_speeches/05_07_2005.htm.

28. The chairman of the board, S. Dhanabalan, is also chairman of DBS Group Holdings, a financial institution in which Temasek holds a 28 percent stake. Also serving on the board is the chairman of Singapore Airlines, which is controlled by Temasek.

29. See http://www.temasekholdings.com.sg/about_temasek/board_of_directors.htm.

30. Temasek acquired 0.5 percent directly; the remaining 1.5 percent was acquired by other companies belonging to the group. See Jake Lloyd-Smith, "Temasek Keen to Finish Talks with CAO Parent: Agreement with Scandal-Hit Chinese Jet Fuel Importer May Be in Sight," *Financial Times*, 24 August 2005, at 24.

31. "Trading Turbulence Downs China Aviation," supra note 8.

32. "Temasek Keen to Finish Talks with CAO Parent Financial Times, 23 August 2005."

33. John Burton et al., "Creditors to Recover 40% under Bail-Out China Aviation Oil," *Financial Times*, 24 January 2005, at 23.

34. Jake Lloyd-Smith and Andrew Yeh, "CAO Head Was Kept 'in the Dark,'" *Financial Times*, 2 February 2005, at 17.

35. In 2006 China implemented a scheme aimed at reducing state holdings in listed companies. Many of the previously nontradable shares were converted into tradable ones, and outside shareholders received a proportion of the newly traded shares. For a detailed account of this scheme, see Kister (2006).

36. To be sure, Russian privatization posed its own acute problems, the consequences of which are still being felt in the political economy. We explore these consequences in our institutional autopsy of the Yukos case in chapter 8.

37. Before 1985, industrial enterprises required not only permission but active sponsorship and supervision from the government and its agents, the bureaucrats. A century earlier, new firms established in the 1870s and 1880s were known as *guandu shangban* (government supervision and merchant management enterprises). In a close parallel to today's listed firms, merchants put up the capital and managed the firms under the supervision of government officials. The merchants bore the financial risks of the enterprise and were forced to operate under the supervision of

officials who followed their own agendas, frequently leading to corruption and poor corporate management. Goetzmann and Koll (2003).

38. Pistor and Xu (2005) present descriptive data and some correlation coefficients suggesting that regions whose companies perform better on the stock market obtain higher IPO quotas from the central government in future years.

39. For an English-language version of the law, see http://www.novexcn.com.

40. According to the 1987 bankruptcy law, the debtor had the primary right to file for bankruptcy and required approval by the relevant ministry, which typically functioned as its controlling shareholder. See art. 7, Law of the People's Republic of China on Enterprise Bankruptcy, adopted 2 December 1986. According to arts. 17 and 20 of the same law, the "superior departments in charge of the enterprise" have the power to initiate and supervise reorganizations. An English-language translation of the 1987 bankruptcy law is available at www.novexcn.com/enterprise _bankruptcy.html. A new bankruptcy law was adopted in August 2006.

41. See "China's Top Legislature Adopts Corporate Bankruptcy Law," *Xinhua* (*China View*) (Beijing), 27 August 2006, www.chinaview.cn. The law entered into force on 1 June 2007.

42. In English translation, the relevant parts of the court's guidelines read as follows: People's Supreme Court Notice on the Temporary Suspension on the Hearing of Securities Related Civil Compensation Cases . . . : Our country's capital markets are in a period of continuous standardization and development and a number of problems have arisen including insider trading, cheating, market manipulation and other behaviors. These behaviors harm the fairness of the securities market, infringe upon investor's legal rights, and have influenced the safe and healthy development of capital markets and should be progressively normalized. Currently, in the court's administration of justice, this new situation and these new problems that require attention and research have already emerged. However, under current legislative and judicial limits, courts still don't have the conditions to accept and hear this type of case. As the result of research, civilian compensation cases arising from the aforementioned behavior temporarily should not be heard. (Translation provided by Daniel Magida.) See also Magida (2003).

43. This is not to say that civil courts in China are beyond the reach of the party or state bureaucrats. In the long term, however, decentralized litigation brought by nonstate agents may be more difficult to monitor and control than actions brought or enforced by state agents such as prosecutors or regulators.

44. The Trojan horse effect was, however, anticipated or hoped for by many foreigners who advised China about legal reforms. See Stephenson (2000). Note that throughout the book we use the term "lawmaker" generically without referring to a particular institution such as a parliament or legislature.

45. In the original investor protection ranking by La Porta et al. (1998), for example, Singapore scores 4 out of 6. Singapore ranks fifth in the world on Transparency International's Corruption Perception Index and second in the Economic Freedom Index.

46. See Cris Prystay, "Executives on Trial: Three CAO Singapore Officials Are Fined in Derivatives Case," *Wall Street Journal*, 3 March 2006, at C4.

47. Ibid.

48. This is reflected in Singapore's location in the upper left-hand corner of the matrix reproduced in chapter 9. See figure 9.1, p. 183.

49. In this context "rule of law" is understood as law establishing the rules of the game. It does not include the use of law to constrain government actors.

50. A similar point has been made for Sweden, where the Wallenberg family has been a dominant shareholder without displaying strong tendencies to expropriate minority shareholders. See Högfeldt (2003).

51. We are grateful to Donald Langevoort for suggesting this analogy to us.

52. For a discussion of the willingness of foreign banks to pay substantial premiums for minority stakes in state-owned banks, see World Bank, "Financial Sector Policies and Development," *China Quarterly Update*, November 2005, at 13. http://www.worldbank.org under "Countries and Regions."

CHAPTER EIGHT

1. See, however, Shleifer and Treisman (2005).

2. Decree of the President of the Russian Federation no. 1403 of 11 November 1992, "On Specific Features of Privatization and Reorganization into Joint-Stock Companies of State-Sector Enterprises, Production and Scientific and Industrial Amalgamations in the Oil and Oil-Refining Industry and Oil Supplies." SAPP RF, vol. 22, no. 1878, p. 1997.

3. Decree of the President of the Russian Federation no. 354 of 15 April, 1993, SAPP RF, vol. 17, no. 1547, p. 1755.

4. See Hellman, Jones, and Kaufmann (2003).

5. C. J. Chivers and Erin Arvedlund, "Khodorkovsky Gets 9-year Sentence," *International Herald Tribune*, 1 June 1995.

6. "Rosneft Wins First Yukos Auction," *BBC News*, 27 March 2007. See also "Italian Firm Wins Yukos Auction" (referring to the second auction in the liquidation proceedings), *BBC News*, 10 April 2007.

7. The abbreviation AO stands for "aktionernoye obshchestvo," the Russian term for a joint stock company.

8. Chrystia Freeland, "A Falling Tsar," *Financial Times* 1 November 2003.

9. See also Peter Foster, "The Crime of Destroying Yukos," *National Post* (Canada), 10 December 2004 (WLNR 13806562); "Liberal Members of the Russian Cabinet Angered by the Tax Service's Activities," *Russian Business Monitor*, 15 December 2004 (WLNR 14042322).

10. "Creditors Vote to Bankrupt Yukos," *BBC News*, 25 July 2006.

11. The following account of Khodorkovsky's rise and fall during Russia's transition period relies heavily on Freeland (2000), 120.

12. The scheme was devised to ensure a rapid transfer of ownership. Each citizen received one voucher, which she could invest in a company, transfer into a voucher investment fund, or trade on the next street corner (Boycko, Shleifer, and Vishny 1994). On average, 29 percent of the shares of state-owned enterprises were transferred in this way—typically after 51 percent of shares had first been secured by management, employees, and other company insiders (Pistor 1995). The remaining 20 percent was retained by the state and frequently sold in investment tenders.

13. Three Russian banks (Rossisky Kredit, Inkombank, and Alfa) that were not part of the original consortium that had conceived of the loans-for-shares program nevertheless dared to bid for Yukos. Their bid was excluded for technical reasons: the guarantee it gave to a front company through which it was placing the bid exceeded the bank's total capital (Freeland 2000).

14. Presidential Decree on the Procedure for Transferring Shares in Public Ownership into Security Interests, SZ RF, vol. 26, no. 3527, p. 6600, signed 31 August 1995.
15. Note that the world market price for a barrel of oil at the time was US$12 (unadjusted for inflation). See http://www.wtrg.com/prices.htm.
16. Corporate Governance in Russia, Sponsored by the Investor Protection Association, http://www.corp-gov.org/bd/db.php3?db_id=342&base_id=3.
17. As is now well known, Yeltsin chose his successor before stepping down three months prior to the official end of his term in office and handed over the reins of power to Prime Minister Vladimir Putin on New Year's Eve 1999.
18. http://www.jbholston.com/mtype/week_2003_11_02.html.
19. See, e.g., Valeria Korchagina, "Yukos Murder Probe Opened," *Moscow Times*, 21 July 2003 (NEXIS no. 2723).
20. "Russian Duma Confirms Putin as Prime Minister," CNN, 16 August 1999. http://www.cnn.com/WORLD/europe/9908/16/russia.putin.03/.
21. This follows from Russia's constitution. Article 92(2) provides, first, that the powers of the president are terminated on his resignation, and, second, that "in all cases when the President of the Russian Federation is unable to perform his duties such duties are temporarily performed by the chairman of the Government of the Russian Federation." The Constitution of the Russian Federation is available (in Russian) at http://www.duma.gov.ru/.
22. According to Gazprom's annual report for 2005, 50.0002 percent of shares (an increase of 10 percent from the previous year) are controlled by the Russian Federation. Another 29.482 percent of the shares are owned by "Russian legal entities," which may include private as well as state-owned legal persons. Russian individuals own a total of 13.068 percent of the company, and nonresidents 7.448 percent. The report is available in English at http://www.gazprom.ru/documents/Annual_Report_Eng_2005.pdf. See p. 68.
23. Article 90 of the Constitution of the Russian Federation vests the president with the power to issue "decrees" (*ukazi*) on all matters within the jurisdiction of the Russian Federation unless they are preempted by federal laws or in conflict with the constitution. http://www.duma.gov.ru/.
24. "The Motherland sells out," *Kommersant Online*, 13 October 2004. http://www.kommersant.com/p514492/The_Motherland_Sells_Out/.
25. See Committee to Free Mikhail Khodorkovsky, http://www.supportmbk.com/timeline/index.cfm (8 December entry).
26. Ibid. (16 December entry).
27. "The Yugansk Coverup Operation," *Moscow Times*, 30 December 2004 (WLNR 15347357).
28. Yukos Oil Co. v. Russian Fed'n (in re Yukos Oil Co.), 320 B.R. 130 (Bankr. S.D. Tex. 2004).
29. In re Yukos Oil Co., 321 B.R. 396 (Bankr. S.D. Tex. 2005).
30. "Deutsche Bank Has Challenged the U.S. Department of State in the Yukos Affair," *Russian Finance Report*, WOS Media Monitoring Agency, 17 December 2004, WLNR 14248429.
31. Erin E. Arvedlund and Steven Lee Myers, "An All-but-Unknown Company Wins a Rich Russian Oil Stake," *New York Times*, December 20, 2004, WLNR 14366018.
32. Ibid.
33. "Russian Banks Secretly Financed Rosneft's Purchase of Yuganskneftegaz," *Moscow News*, 5 February 2005.

34. Templeton Thorp, "Yukos Asks London to Halt Rosneft IPO," 26 June 2006. http://templetonthorp.com/en/news1283.
35. Catherine Belton, "BP Pulls out of Yukos Auction," *Financial Times*, 27 March 2007.
36. Article 125, Constitution of the Russian Federation. http://www.duma.gov.ru/.
37. Federal Law on Joint Stock Companies, 26 December 1995, SZ RF, 1996, no. 1, p. 1. The law was inspired by a draft written by two American law professors. See Black, Kraakman, and Hay (1996).
38. This was accomplished by a constitutional change that eliminated direct election of the governors and instead allows the president to appoint them.
39. Brian Withmore, "Russia: The End of Loans-For-Shares," Radio Free Europe/Radio Liberty, 29 September 2005.
40. "Deals between Rosneftegaz and Gazprom's Subsidiaries Clinched," *Capital Link Russia*, 24 June 2005.
41. See Gazprom's annual report for 2005, at 68, http://www.gazprom.ru/documents/ Annual_Report_Eng_2005.pdf.
42. See text accompanying note 32.
43. The chairman of Gazprom, Dmitri Medvedev, for example, is Russia's first deputy prime minister. And the chairman of Rosneft's board of directors, Igor Sechin, is Putin's deputy chief of staff. Rosneft's CEO is Sergei Bogdanchikov (Twining 2006).
44. See Goriaev and Sonin (2005), table 1, p. 26, for statistics relating to these companies. They include six companies in the oil or gas sector, seven utility companies, five telecom companies, and one bank; the remaining companies are in metallurgy, food and beverages, and airlines.
45. See our critique of the literature in chapter 1.
46. In 2005 natural resources contributed 80 percent of Russia's exports and a large share of the government's revenue. See http://www.buyusa.gov/russia/en/ccg.html.
47. Arguably, political change brought about by the elections indicates a change in the demand side. Note, however, that Putin was Yeltsin's hand-picked successor. Although he was confirmed by parliament in 2000 and reelected in 2004, the strong state control over the media casts doubt on the ability of his opponents to voice their preferences.

CHAPTER NINE

1. See the review of the literature in chapter 1 for details.
2. Using the canonical classification scheme as a basis for predicting economic outcomes also conflicts with evidence showing that many of the relevant indicators used in the empirical law and finance studies emerged only over the course of the past century (Pistor et al. 2002).
3. Note, however, that it is closely related to the M-form and the U-form organization of political systems discussed in Qian et al. (2006).
4. Although courts of first and second instance are technically "state courts" in Germany, an appeal goes to the federal supreme court, the Bundesgerichtshof.
5. The argument is similar to Mancur Olson's suggestion that the most powerful forces for change are wars, revolutions, and competition. See Olson (1982).
6. The notion that contracts are incomplete is, of course, well established in the economics literature. See Hart and Moore (1999). This literature defines property rights as the inherently indefinable residual rights. It has not been fully recognized, however, that the delineation of residual rights of control held by different owners is

also affected by the incompleteness problem, which results from the fact that law is incomplete. See Pistor and Xu (2003).

7. In 1996, 244,467 private cases were filed, but only 44,272 suits against the state (for wrongful fines, taxation, and the like) (Pistor 1996). By 2003, there were 502,000 cases brought against the state, but only 449,778 against private parties. In 2005, 418,071 new private lawsuits were filed and 1,169,836 suits against the state. See statistics on the Web page of the court at http://www.arbitr.ru.

8. In the chapter "The King and the Dean: Melvin Belli, Roscoe Pound, and the Common Law Nation," Witt describes how Melvin Belli mobilized attorneys in order to prevent a coordinated legislative effort to impose worker safety standards, a measure that would have greatly reduced the lucrative market for tort litigation for lawyers.

9. On Germany, see Pistor (2005).

10. Empirical evidence suggests that many medium-sized companies delisted in the years immediately following the enactment of SOX (Karaca-Mandic, Kamar, and Talley 2006). The authors of this study attribute this trend to SOX, but the causal relation is not undisputed.

11. Floyd Norris, "Panel of Executives and Academics to Consider Regulation and Competitiveness," *New York Times*, 13 September 2006. The panel brings together academics as well as business insiders but deliberately excludes regulators.

12. The Second Circuit adopted the strictest pleading test, requiring plaintiffs to plead "facts that give rise to a strong inference of fraudulent intent." See Shields v. Cititrust Bankcorp, 25 F.3d 1124 (2nd Cir. 1994). By contrast, the Ninth Circuit adopted the most permissive pleading standard, requiring plaintiffs only to plead that the defendant had acted with scienter. See Decker v. Glenfed, 42 F.3d 1541 (9th Cir. 1994).

13. Securities class actions did not abate after the PSLRA was enacted. There is, however, some evidence that the incidence of strike suits has declined. See Peng and Röell (2004).

14. See Haley (1978) for a discussion of Japan.

15. No one we interviewed in connection with the SK case suggested that any untoward influence was exerted on the court by any interested party.

16. As noted above, there had been some shareholder litigation in Korea prior to the SK case. But most cases had been brought by organizations that represented investor interests, not by individual shareholders. See Milhaupt (2004).

17. This, at least, is our sense from discussions with academics and practitioners in Korea.

18. The notion of embeddedness was first developed by Michael Granovetter. See Granovetter (1985).

19. The Livedoor case in Japan is less clear, because both parties scored a victory at one point in time—Livedoor in the case against Nippon Broadcasting, and incumbents because of the criminal proceeding against Horie.

CHAPTER TEN

1. This is not to say that each system has changed at the same pace. Pistor et al. (2003) present evidence that some countries do not change their legal systems for long periods of time.

2. The legal historian Lawrence Friedman noted this long ago. See Friedman (1969).

3. See, e.g., Hadfield (2000), discussing how U.S. lawyers benefit from complex legal rules.

4. A subsequent study finds that legal change can influence the behavior of banks (Haselmann et al. 2006). The behavioral change is much more pronounced for foreign lenders than for domestic lenders, suggesting that strong signaling effects may be at work.

5. See also Greif (2006, 55), who uses the term "institution" to describe a system consisting of rules, organizations, beliefs, and norms that creates regularity of behavior.

6. Note that contestability, though a desirable and perhaps essential trait in any legal system, is not an unalloyed good. Contestability often increases the complexity and cost of legal governance while reducing predictability.

7. Schauer (2000, 253) claims that "[l]aw has traditionally been among the least global of social phenomena" because of its close association with national sovereignty. Thus, he argues, we tend to witness "a desire to engage in indigenous law-making even when the product . . . may be otherwise sub-optimal" (255). This conclusion does not appear to be supported by historical experience or by the institutional autopsies presented in this book.

8. Scholars debate whether "legal transplant" is the best metaphor to describe the phenomenon of enacting foreign law into domestic legal systems. For better or for worse, the transplant metaphor has stuck, and there seems little point in engaging in a debate about whether this is the analytically optimal term. The important point is not to allow analysis to become captive to metaphor, regardless of which one is used.

9. To recap: Germany introduced laws (loosely modeled on the U.S. system) that expanded the ability of shareholders to sue directors and managers in derivative actions. Japan transplanted key features of Delaware judicial doctrine to address the rise of hostile takeovers in its economy. China has transplanted rules governing independent directors and other features of U.S. corporate law such as the mechanism by which a shareholder may file a derivative suit. Korea transplanted shareholders' rights and disclosure rules from U.S. corporate and securities laws. Russia transplanted major features of U.S. corporate law as part of its privatization process.

10. See, however, Berkowitz et al. (2003), who show that legal origin is a poor predictor of the effectiveness of law.

11. We are using the term "political" differently than at least one other commentator uses the term. Kahn-Freund (1974) suggests that political factors are more important than cultural factors in explaining why successful legal transplants are rare. But he uses the term "political" to refer to constitutional structure and interest group coalitions.

12. To be sure, translating and enacting the European civil code structure was quicker and outwardly more predictable than building up a common-law system from scratch. A case can be made, however, that the Tokugawa legal system, which preceded the Meiji Restoration, had a closer affinity to the common-law than the civil-law tradition.

13. China's compliance with World Trade Organization rules is another contemporary example of the importance of signaling.

14. Pistor developed and tested this theory in Berkowitz et al. (2003), as we discuss below.

15. The term comes from Kanda and Milhaupt (2004).

16. The term comes from Kanda and Milhaupt (2003).

17. For a sampling of views concerning this question, see Gordon and Roe (2004).

18. We were amused by a scholar from Beijing who began a presentation about China's new Company Law by highlighting the fact that it scores significantly higher on the investor protection index of La Porta et al. than the law it replaced. But he noted a bit wistfully that the index had been recently updated and that the new law would no longer score as high.

19. Cumulative voting is a form of proportionate representation that allows minority shareholder representation on the board of directors. Its real-world significance is debatable because even where it is permitted, it is rarely used. For example, cumulative voting is nonexistent in large, publicly traded U.S. corporations, though it is universally allowed under state corporate statutes.

20. This wonderful description of legal transplants was coined by Walter Hutchins (2005).

21. Data were collected by the Graduate Legal Studies Office of Columbia Law School.

22. Of course, this assumes that the United States will retain its competitive position in the education of legal professionals and the worldwide provision of legal services. The United Kingdom certainly presents a challenge in this regard.

23. For example, in our experience, U.S.-trained lawyers and legal academics from a diverse range of countries are often quite vocal in their criticism of the law-making processes and judiciaries in their home countries (see, e.g., Liu 2003).

24. This is the title of an article that compares U.S. and Japanese securities regulations. See Beller, Terai, and Levine (1992).

CHAPTER ELEVEN

1. The most ardent supporter of the Russian reform strategy argues that Russia is a "normal country," not that it has been a major success. See Shleifer (2005).

2. See e.g., Kim (2008), analyzing recent Korean lawsuits involving foreign investors and *chaebol* managers. He finds that the judgments display considerable "schizophrenia." Sometimes, judges adhere closely and formalistically to the statutes. At other times, they take considerable liberties and reach conclusions not supported by the statutes. Looking at the outcomes of the cases, Kim concludes that one possible interpretation is that the courts are simply finding justifications to rule in favor of Korean firms.

REFERENCES

Adams, Michael. 2006. Das Ende der Mitbestimmung. *Zeitschrift für Wirtschaftsrecht (ZIP)* 34:1561–1568.

Alexander, Gregory S. 2003. Property as a fundamental constitutional right? The German example. *Cornell Law Review* 88:733–778.

Allen, Franklin, Jun Qian, and Meijun Qian. 2005. Law, finance, and economic growth in China. *Journal of Financial Economics* 77:57–116.

Allen, Robert C. 2001. Community and market in England: Open fields and enclosures revisited. In *Communities and markets in economic development*, ed. M. Aoki and Y. Hayami, 42–69. Oxford: Oxford University Press.

Amsden, Alice H. 1989. *Asia's next giant: South Korea and late industrialization.* New York: Oxford University Press.

Amsden, Alice H., and Yoon-Dae Euh. 1993. South Korea's 1980s financial reforms: Good-bye financial repression (maybe), hello new institutional restraints. *World Development* 21 (3):379–390.

Amsterdam, Dean, and Robert Peroff. 2007. Abuse of state power in the Russian Federation. http://www.robertamsterdam.com/.

Aoki, Masahiko. 2001. *Toward a comparative institutional analysis.* Cambridge: Cambridge University Press.

Armour, John, and David A. Skeel Jr. 2007. Who writes the rules for hostile takeovers, and why? The peculiar divergence of US and UK takeover regulation. *Georgetown Law Journal* 95-1727–1794.

Arsht, Samuel S. 1976. A history of Delaware corporation law. *Delaware Journal of Corporate Law* 1 (1):1–22.

Auyang, Sunny Y. 1999. *Foundations of complex-system theories in economics, evolutionary biology, and statistical physics.* Cambridge: Cambridge University Press.

Axelrod, Robert. 1984. *The evolution of cooperation.* New York: Basic.

Balzer, Harley. 2005. Vladimir Putin on Russian energy policy. *National Interest,* 11 November.

Banner, Stuart. 1998. *Anglo-American securities regulation: Cultural and political roots, 1690–1860.* Cambridge: Cambridge University Press.

Barber, John. 1994. Russia: A crisis of post-imperial viability. *Political Studies* 42 (special issue 1):34–51.

Baums, Theodor. 1992. Corporate governance in Germany: The role of the banks. *American Journal of Comparative Law* 40:503–526.

———. 1996. Vollmachstimmrecht der Banken—Ja oder Nein? *Die Aktiengesellschaft* 1996 (1):11–26.

———. 1997. Shareholder representation and proxy voting in the European Union: A comparative study. In *Comparative corporate governance: The state of the art and emerging research*, ed. K. J. Hopt, H. Kanda, M. J. Roe, and S. Prigge, 545–564. Oxford: Oxford University Press.

Bebchuk, Lucian Ayre. 1999. A rent-protection theory of corporate ownership and control. *National Bureau of Economic Research Working Paper ser.* 7203. Cambridge, MA.

Bebchuk, Lucian, and Mark Roe. 1999. A theory of path dependence in corporate governance and ownership. *Stanford Law Review* 52:127–170.

Becht, Marco, and A. Roell. 1999. Blockholdings in Europe: An international comparison. *European Economic Review* 43 (4–6):1049–1056.

Beller, Alan L., Tsunemasa Terai, and Richard M. Levine. 1992. Looks can be deceiving: A comparison of initial public offering procedures under Japanese and U.S. securities laws. *Law and Contemporary Problems* 55:77–118.

Berglöf, Erik, and Patrick Bolton. 2002. The great divide and beyond: Financial market architecture in transition. *Journal of Economic Perspectives* 16 (1):77–100.

Berglöf, Erik, and Anete Pajuste. 2003. Emerging owners, eclipsing markets? In *Corporate governance and capital flows in a global economy*, ed. P. Cornelius and B. Kogut, 267–303. Oxford: Oxford University Press.

Berkowitz, Daniel, Katharina Pistor, and Jean-François Richard. 2003a. Economic development, legality, and the transplant effect. *European Economic Review* 47:165–195.

———. 2003b. The Transplant Effect. *American Journal of Comparative Law* 51 (2):163–203.

Berle, Adolf Augustus, and Gardiner Means. 1932. *The modern corporation and private property.* New York: Council for Research in the Social Sciences, Columbia University.

Bernstein, Lisa. 1996. Merchant law in a merchant court: Rethinking the Code's search for immanent business norms. *University of Pennsylvania Law Review* 144:1765–1821.

Bhagat, Sanjai, and Bernard Black. 2002. The non-correlation between board independence and long-term firm performance. *Journal of Corporation Law* (27):231–273.

Black, Bernard. 2000. The legal and institutional preconditions for strong securities markets. *UCLA Law Review* 48 (4):781–856.

Black, Bernard, and John C. Coffee, Jr. 1994. Hail Britannia? Institutional investor behavior under limited regulation. *Michigan Law Review* 92 (2087):1997–2087.

Black, Bernard, Hasung Jang, and Woochan Kim. 2006. Does corporate governance predict firms' market value? Evidence from Korea. *Journal of Law, Economics, and Organizations* 22 (2):366–413.

Black, Bernard, and Reinier Kraakman. 1996. A self-enforcing model of corporate law. *Harvard Law Review* 109:1911–1982.

Black, Bernard, Reinier Kraakman, and Jonathan Hay. 1996. Corporate law from scratch. In *Corporate governance in Eastern Europe and Russia*, ed. R. Frydman, C. W. Gray, and A. Rapaczynski, 245–302. Budapest: Central European University Press.

Black, Bernard, Reinier Kraakman, and Anna Tarassova. 2000. Russian privatization and corporate governance: What went wrong? *Stanford Law Review* 52:1731–1803.

Black, Bernard, and Anna S. Tarassova. 2003. Institutional reform in transition: A case study of Russia. *Supreme Court Economic Review* 10:211–278.

Blum, Vanessa. 2005. Justice deferred: DOJ gets companies to turn snitch. *Legal Times*, 25 March 2005.

Boycko, Maxim, Andrei Shleifer, and Robert W. Vishny. 1994. Voucher privatization. *Journal of Financial Economics* 35:249–266.

Butler, William E. 1988. *Soviet law*. 2d ed. London: Butterworths.

Cable, J. 1985. Capital market information and industrial performance: The role of West German banks. *Economic Journal* 95 (377):118–132.

Calabresi, Guido, and Douglas Melamed. 1972. Property rules, liability rules, and inalienability: One view of the cathedral. *Harvard Law Review* 85:1089–1128.

Carney, William J. 1997. The political economy of competition for corporate charters. *Journal of Legal Studies* 26:303–330.

Chandler, Andrea. 2001. Presidential veto power in post-Communist Russia, 1994–1998. *Canadian Journal of Political Science* 34 (3):487–516.

Chandler, William B., III, and Leo E. Strine Jr. 2003. The new federalism of the American corporate governance system: Preliminary reflections of two residents of one small state. *University of Pennsylvania Law Review* 152 (2):953–1006.

Chen, Zhiwu. 2003. Capital markets and legal development: The China case. *China Economic Review* 14:451–472.

Clark, Robert C. 1981. The four stages of capitalism: Reflections on investment management treatises. *Harvard Law Review* 94:561–582.

Clarke, Donald. 2003. Coporate governance in China: An overview. *China Economic Review* 14:494–507.

———. 2006. Independent directors in Chinese corporate governance. *Delaware Journal of Corporate Law* 31:125–213.

Clarke, Donald C., Peter Murrell, and Susan H. Whiting. 2006. The role of law in China's economic development. Public Law Research Papers, George Washington University Law School. http://papers.ssrn.com/sol3/papers.cfm?abstract_id=878672.

Coase, Ronald H. 1960. The problem of social cost. *Journal of Law and Economics* 3:1–44.

Coffee, John C., Jr. 2002. Racing towards the top? The impact of cross-listings and stock market competition on international corporate governance. *Columbia Law Review* 102 (7):1757–1831.

———. 2004. What caused Enron? A capsule social and economic history of the 1990s. *Cornell Law Review* 89 (2):269–309.

———. 2006. Gatekeepers: The Professions and Corporate Governance, Oxford: Oxford University Press.

———. 2007. Law and the market: The impact of enforcement. Unpublished manuscript.

Conk, George W. 2005. People's Republic of China Civil Code: Tort liability law. *Private Law Revew* 5 (2):77–111.

Corporate Fraud Task Force. 2004. Second year report to the president. July 20. United States Department of Justice. http://www.usdoj.gov/dag/cftf/2nd_yr_fraud_report.pdf.

Corporate Value Study Group. 2005. Corpate value report. http://www.meti.go.jp/press/20050527005/3-honkokisho-honntain-set.pdf.

Cunningham, Lawrence A. 2003. The Sarbanes-Oxley yawn: Heavy rhetoric, light reform (and it just might work). *Connecticut Law Review* 35:915–988.

Dam, Kenneth. 2006. China as a test case: Is the rule of law essential for economic growth? *Law and Economics Olin Working Paper*, University of Chicago.

Damaška, Mirjan. 1975. Structures of authority and comparative criminal procedure. *Yale Law Review* 84:480–544.

———. 1986. *The faces of justice and state authority*. New Haven: Yale University Press.

DeFond, Mark L., Jere R. Francis, and Joseph V. Carcello. 2005. Audit research after Sarbanes-Oxley. *Auditing* 24:5–30.

Desai, Padma. 2005. Russian retrospectives on reforms from Yeltsin to Putin. *Journal of Economic Perspectives* 19 (1):87–106.

Djankov, Simeon, Edward Glaeser, Rafael La Porta, Florencio Lopez-de-Silanes, and Andrei Shleifer. 2003. The new comparative economics. *Journal of Comparative Economics* 31 (4):595–619.

Djankov, Simeon, Caralee McLiesh, and Andrei Shleifer. 2007. Private credit in 129 countries. *Journal of Financial Economics* 84 (2):299–329.

Dorf, Michael, and Charles Sabel. 1998. A constitution of democractic experimentalism. *Columbia Law Review* 98 (2):267–473.

Edwards, Courtney, Mark H. Lang, Edward L. Maydew, and Douglas A. Shackelford. 2004. Germany's repeal of the corporate capital gains tax: The equity market response. *Journal of the American Taxation Association* 26:73–97.

Edwards, J. S. S., and K. Fischer. 1994. *Banks, finance and investment in Germany*. Cambridge: Cambridge University Press.

Eiras, Ana I. 2003. Make the rule of law a necessary condition for the Millenium Challenge Account. *Heritage Foundation Backgrounder* no. 1634, March 7.

Ellickson, Robert C. 2001. The market for social norms. *American Law and Economics Review* 3:1–49.

Enriques, Luca. 2004. Silence is golden: The European Company Statute as a catalyst for company law arbitrage. *Journal of Corporate Law Studies* 4:77–95.

Fang, Liufang. 1995. China's corporatization experiment. *Duke Journal of Comparative and International Law* 5:149–269.

Fields, Karl. 1997. Strong states and business organization in Korea and Taiwan. In *Business and the State in Developing Countries*, ed. Sylvia Maxfield and Ben Ross Schneider, 122–151. Ithaca: Cornell University Press.

Fletcher, George P. 1998. Comparative law as a subversive discipline. *American Journal of Comparative Law* 46:683–700.

Frankel, Tamar. 1995. A recipe for effecting institutional changes to achieve privatization. *Boston University International Law Journal* 13:295–312.

Freeland, Chrystia. 2000. *Sale of the century: Russia's wild ride from communism to capitalism*. New York: Random House.

Friedman, Lawrence M. 1969. Legal culture and social development. *Law and Society Review* 4:29–44.

Gao, Xi-Qing. 1996. Developments in securities and investment law in China. *Australian Journal of Corporate Law* 6:228–243.

Germain, Claire M. 2003. Approaches to statutory interpretation and legislative history in France. *Duke Journal of Comparative and International Law* 13:195–206.

Gerschenkron, Alexander. 1962. *Economic backwardness in historical perspective*. Cambridge: Harvard University Press.

Gerum, Elmar, Horst Steinmann, and Werner Fees. 1988. *Der mibestimmte Aufsichtsrat, eine empirische Untersuchung*. Stuttgart: Poeschel Verlag.

Gilson, Ronald J. 2001. Globalizing corporate governance: Convergence of form or function. *American Journal of Comparative Law* (49):329–357.

———. 2004. The poison pill in Japan: The missing infrastructure. *Columbia Business Law Review* 2004 (1):21–44.

———. 2006a. Catalyzing corporate governance: The evolution of the U.S. system in the 1980s and 1990s. *Company and Securities Law Journal* 24 (143):143–160.

————. 2006b. Controlling shareholders and corporate governance: Complicating the comparative taxonomy. *Harvard Law Review* 119 (6):1641–1679.

Gilson, Ronald, and Curtis Milhaupt. 2005. Choice as regulatory reform: The case of Japanese corporate governance. *American Journal of Comparative Law* (553):343–377.

Gilson, Ronald, and Curtis Milhaupt. 2008. Economic growth, benevolent dictators, and the irrelevance of legal origin. Mimeo on file with the author.

Ginsburg, Tom. 2004. *Legal Reform in Korea*. London: RoutledgeCurzon.

Glaeser, Edward L., and Andrei Shleifer. 2002. Legal origins. *Quarterly Journal of Economics* 117 (4):1193–1229.

Goldman, Marshall. 2004. Putin and the oligarchs. *Foreign Affairs* 83 (6):33–44.

Gordon, Jeffrey. 2002a. An American prspective on the new German antitakeover law. ECGI Working Paper Series. http://www.ssrn.com/abstract=336420.

————. 2002b. What Enron means for the management and control of the modern business corporation. *University of Chicago Law Review* 69 (3):1233–1250.

————. 2006. The rise of independent directors in the United States, 1950–2005: Of shareholder value and stock market prices. *Stanford Law Review* 59:1465–1568.

Goriaev, Alexei, and Konstantin Sonin. 2005. Is political risk company-specific? The market side of the Yukos affair. http://ssrn.com/abstract_id=676875.

Gourevitch, Peter, and James J. Shinn. 2005. *Political power and corporate control: The new global politics of corporate governance*. Princeton: Princeton University Press.

Granovetter, Mark. 1985. Economic action and social structure: The problem of embeddedness. *America Journal of Sociology* 91 (3):481–510.

Green, Stephen, and He Ming. 2004. China's stock market: Out of the valley in 2004? *Royal Institute of International Affairs Briefing Paper* (U.K.), February 2004 (1):1–11.

Greif, Avner. 2006. *Institutions and the path to the modern economy: Lessons from medieval trade; Political economy of institutions and decisions*. Cambridge: Cambridge University Press.

Greif, Avner, Paul Milgrom, and Barry R. Weingast. 1994. Coordination, commitment, and enforcement: The case of the merchant guild. *Journal of Political Economy* 102 (4):745–776.

Grundfest, Joseph A., and A. C. Pritchard. 2002. Statutes with multiple personality disorders: The value of ambiguity in statutory design and interpretation. *Stanford Law Review* 54 (4):627–736.

Guriev, Sergei, and Andrei Rachinsky. 2004. Ownership concentration in Russian Industry. CEFIR Working paper No. 45. http://www.cefir.ru.

Hadfield, Gillian. 2006. The quality of law in civil code and common law regimes: Judicial incentives, legal human capital and the evolution of law. http://www.ssrn.com/abstract=967494.

Haley, John O. 1978. The myth of the reluctant litigant. *Journal of Japanese Studies* 4 (2):366–389.

Hall, Peter A., and David Soskice, eds. 2001. *Varieties of capitalism*. Oxford: Oxford University Press.

Hansmann, Henry, and Reinier Kraakman. 2001. The end of history for corporate law. *Georgetown Law Journal* 89:439–471.

Hart, Oliver, and John Moore. 1999. Foundations of incomplete contracts. *Review of Economic Studies* 66 (226):115–138.

Hashim, Mohsin S. 2005. Putin's *Etatization* project and limits to democractic reforms in Russia. *Communist and Post-Communist Studies* 38 (1):25–48.

Hausmann, Ricardo, Lant Pritchett, and Dani Rodrik. 2005. Growth accelerations. *Journal of Economic Growth* 10:303–329.

Hayek, Friedrich A. 1944. *The road to serfdom.* Chicago: Chicago University Press.

———. 1973. *Law, legislation and liberty—rules and order.* Vol. 1. Chicago: University of Chicago Press.

Hellman, Joel S., Geraint Jones, and Daniel Kaufmann. 2003. Seize the state, seize the day: An empirical analysis of state capture and corruption in transition. *Journal of Comparative Economics* 31 (4):774–794.

Hendrick, Max III. 2001. Opinion letter from Max Henrick III to James Derrick. 2001. WL17642

Hertig, Gerard, and Joseph A. McCahery. 2003. Company and takeover law reforms in Europe: Misguided harmonization efforts or regulatory competition? ECGI Law Working Paper. http://www.ssrn.com/abstract=438421.

Högfeldt, Peter. 2003. The history and politics of corporate ownership in Sweden. ECGI Working Paper. http://papers.ssrn/abstract=449460.

Holmstrom, Bengt, and Steven Kaplan. 2003. The state of U.S. corporate governance: What's right and what's wrong? ECGI Working Paper Series in Finance. http://papers.ssrn.com/abstract_id=394721.

Hong, Joon-Hyung. 1999. The rule of law and its acceptance in Asia: A view from Korea. *Asia Perspectives* 2 (2):11–18.

Höpner, Martin. 2001. Corporate governance in transition: Ten empirical findings on shareholder value and industrial relations in Germany, Discussion Paper 01/5, Max Planck Institute for the Study of Societies, Cologne, Germany.

Höpner, Martin, and Gregory Jackson. 2001. Entsteht ein Markt für Unternehmenskontrolle? Der Fall Mannesmann. *Leviathan* 29:544–563.

Hopt, Klaus J. 1976. Der Wandel vom Gesellschafts—zum Kapitalmarktrecht? *Zeitschrift für Handelsrecht* 140: 201–235 (pt. 1), 389–441 (pt. 2).

———. 1994. Labor representation on corporate boards: Impacts and problems for corporate governance and economic integration in Europe. *International Review of Law and Economics* 14:203–214.

Hoskins, Lee, and Ana I. Eiras. 2002. Property rights: Key to economic growth. In *Index of Economic Freedom*, ed. J. Gerald P. O'Driscoll, Kim Holmes, and Mary Anastasia O'Grady, 37–48. Washington, DC: Heritage Foundation.

Huang, Yasheng. 1996. *Inflation and investment controls in China.* Cambridge: Cambridge University Press.

Huber, John J. 2004. *The practitioner's guide to the Sarbanes-Oxley Act.* American Bar Association, Section of Business Law. http://www.loc.gov/catdir/toc/ecip0420/2004015928.html.

Hughes, James W., and Edward A. Snyder. 1999. Litigation and settlement under the English and American rules: Theory and evidence. *Journal of Law and Economics* 38 (1):225–250.

Huntington, Samuel P. 1965. Political development and political decay. *World Politics* 17:386–430.

Hutchens, Walter. 2005. Jurassic Park in China's legal system: An essay in honor of Stanley Lubman. Paper presented at Columbia Law School, 15 April, on file with the authors.

Ietswaart, Heleen F. P. 1990. The international comparison of court caseloads: The experience of the European Working Group. *Law and Society Review* 24 (2):571–594.

Johnson, Simon, Edward Glaeser, and Andrei Shleifer. 2001. Coase vs. Coasians. *Quarterly Journal of Economics* 116 (3):853–899.

Johnson, Simon, Rafael La Porta, Florencio Lopez-de-Silanes, and Andrei Shleifer. 2000. Tunneling. *American Economic Review* 90(2):22–27.

Joint Committee on Taxation. 2003. *Report of investigation of Enron Corporation and related entities regarding federal tax and compensation issues, and policy recommendations,* 108th Cong., 1st sess. S. Rep. JCS-3-03. Washington, DC: GPO. http://www.gpo.gov/congress/joint/jcs-3-03/vol1/index.html.

Justice System Reform Council. 2001. Recommendations of the Justice System Reform Council: For a justice system to support Japan in the twenty-first century. http://www.kantei.go.jp/foreign/judiciary/2001/0612report.html.

Kagan, Robert A. 2001. *Adversarial legalism: The American way of law.* Cambridge: Harvard University Press.

Kahan, Marcel, and Ehud Kamar. 2002. The myth of state competition in corporate law. *Stanford Law Review* 55:679–750.

Kahan, Marcel, and Edward B. Rock. 2002. How I learned to stop worrying and love the pill: Adaptive responses to takeover law. *University of Chicago Law Review* 69 (3):871–916.

Kahn-Freund, Otto. 1974. On uses and misuses of comparative law. *Modern Law Review* 37 (1):1–27.

Kali, Raja. 1999. Endogenous business groups. *Journal of Law, Economics and Organization* 15 (3):615–636.

Kamar, Ehud. 1998. A regulatory competition theory of indeterminacy in corporate law. *Columbia Law Review* 98:1908–1959.

Kanda, Hideki, and Curtis J. Milhaupt. 2003. Re-examining legal transplants: The director's fiduciary duty in Japanese corporate governance. *American Journal of Comparative Law* 51 (4):887–902.

Karaca-Mandic, Pinar, Ehud Kamar, and Eric Talley. 2006. Going private decisions and the Sarbanes-Oxley Act of 2002: A cross-country analysis. Unpublished manuscript.

Karube, Takuya. 2005. Livedoor ushers in era of hostile takeover. *Japan Today,* 24 February 2005.

Kenworthy, Lane. 2000. Quantitative indicators of corporatism: A survey and assessment, Discussion Paper 00/4, Max Planck Institute for the Study of Societies, Cologne, Germany.

Kim, Joongi. 2005. A forensic study of Daewoo's corporate governance: Does responsibility lie beyond the *chaebol* and Korea? Working paper, Hills Corporate Governance Center-Yonsei, Seoul.

Kim, Kon-Sik. 2008. The role of judges in Korean corporate governance. In *Transforming corporate governance in East Asia,* ed. Hideki Kanda, Kon-Sik Kim, and Curtis Milhaupt. London: Routledge.

Kim, Kon-Sik, and Joongi Kim. 2003. Revamping fiduciary duties in Korea: Does law matter in corporate governance? In *Global markets, domestic institutions: Corporate law and governance in a new era of cross-border deals,* ed. C. J. Milhaupt, 373–399. New York: Columbia University Press.

Kirk, Don. 2003. Stakeholder speaks out to Koreans. *New York Times,* 29 April, W1.

Kister, Sandra. 2006. China's share-structure reform: An opportunity to move beyond practical solutions to practical problems. *Columbia Journal of Transnational Law* 45 (1):312–363.

Korean Fair Trade Commission. 2005. Bo-do Ja-ryo, 2005 Nyun Dae-gyu-mo-gi-up-jip-dan So-yoo-ji-bae-goo-jo-ae Dae-han Joung-bo-gong-gae [Press Release, Disclosure of Large Enterprise Groups' Ownership Structure in 2005], July 13 (in Korean). http://

ftc.go.kr/data/hwp/giup/20050713_bodo.hwp. A downloadable viewer is available at http://www.haansoft.com/hnc5_0/haansoft_en/product_info/hangul/hangul2007 _info.php.

Kraakman, Reinier, Paul Davies, Henry Hansmann, Gerard Hertig, Klaus J. Hopt, Hideki Kanda, and Edward B. Rock. 2004. *The anatomy of corporate law.* Oxford: Oxford University Press.

Kydland, Finn, and Edward Prescott. 1977. Rules rather than discretion: The inconsistency of optimal plans. *Journal of Political Economy* 85 (3):473–492.

Lamfalussy, Alexandre. 2001. Final report of the Committee of Wise Men on the regulation of European securities markets. Brussels: European Union.

Landa, Janet T. 1981. A theory of the ethnically homogeneous middleman group: An institutional alternative to contract law. *Journal of Legal Studies* 10:349–362.

Landes, William M., and Richard A. Posner. 1975. The independent judiciary in an interest-group perspective. *Journal of Law and Economics* 18:875–901.

La Porta, Rafael, Florencio Lopez-de-Silanes, and Andrei Shleifer. 2006. What works in securities laws? *Journal of Finance* 61 (1):1–32.

La Porta, Rafael, Florencio Lopez-de-Silanes, Andrei Shleifer, and Robert W. Vishny. 1997. Legal determinants of external finance. *Journal of Finance* 52 (3):1131–1150.

———. 1998. Law and finance. *Journal of Political Economy* 106 (6):1113–1155.

———. 1999. The quality of government. *Journal of Law, Economics and Organization* 15 (1):222–283.

La Porta, Raphael, Florencio Lopez-de-Silanes, Cristian Pop-Eleches, and Andrei Shleifer. 2004. Judicial checks and balances. *Journal of Political Economy* 112 (2):445–470.

Lee, Eun-Jong. 2005. The social impact of Sovereign's purchase of SK shares. *Corporate Governance Structure Research* 16:48–58 (in Korean).

Lee, Yeon-ho. 1997. *The state, society, and big business in South Korea.* London: Routledge.

Levine, Ross. 1999. Napoleon, bourses, and growth: With a Focus on Latin America. Mimeo.

Li, Shuguang. 1999. Bankruptcy law in China: Lessons from the past twelve years. *Harvard Asia Quarterly Online,* http://www.asiaquarterly.com/content/view/95/40.

Lichtenstein, Natalie G. 1993. *Enterprise reform in China: The evolving legal framework,* Policy Research Working Papers #1198, World Bank.

Lieberman, Ira, Stilpon Nestor, and Raj Desai. 1997. *Between state and market—Mass privatization in transition economies.* Washington, DC: World Bank.

Lieberman, Robert Charles. 2005. *Shaping race policy: The United States in comparative perspective.* Princeton: Princeton University Press.

Liebman, Benjamin. 2005. Watchdog or demagogue? The media in the Chinese legal system. *Columbia Law Review* 105:1–157.

Liebman, Benjamin, and Curtis J. Milhaupt. 2008. Reputational sanctions in China's securities markets. *Columbia Law Review* (forthcoming).

Liu, Lawrence S. 2003. Global markets and parochial institutions: The transformation of Taiwan's corporate law system. In *Global markets, domestic institutions: Corporate law and governance in a new era of cross-border deals,* ed. Curtis Milhaupt, 400–434. New York: Columbia University Press.

Lubman, Stanley. 1995. Introduction: The future of Chinese law. *China Quarterly* 141 (March):1–21.

Lucier, Chuck, Rob Schuyt, and Eric Spiegel. 2002. Why CEOs fall: The causes and consequences of turnover at the top. McLean, VA: Booz Allen Hamilton.

Macey, Jonathan, and Geoffrey Miller. 1987. Toward an interest-group theory of Delaware corporate law. *Texas Law Review* 65:469–524.

Magida, Daniel. 2003. Establishing an effective regulatory regime: Corporate and securities case studies from Russia and China. Mimeo, Columbia Law School.

Mahoney, Paul. 2001a. The common law and economic growth: Hayek might be right. *Journal of Legal Studies* 30 (2):503–525.

———. 2001b. The political economy of the Securities Act of 1933. *Journal of Legal Studies* 31 (1):1–31.

Mathernova, Katarina. 1995. The World Bank and legal technical assistance: Initial lessons. Washington, DC: World Bank.

Mattei, Ugo. 1994. Efficiency in legal transplants: An essay in comparative law and economics. *International Review of Law and Economics* 14:3–19.

Maxfield, Sylvia, and Ben Ross Schneider. 1997. Business, the state, and economic performance in developing countries. In *Business and the State in Developing Countries*, ed. B. R. Schneider and S. Maxfield, 3–35. Ithaca: Cornell University Press.

Means, Robert Charles. 1980. *Underdevelopment and the development of law*. Chapel Hill: University of North Carolina Press.

Mendelson, A. 2002. A control-based approach to shareholder liability for corporate torts. *Columbia Law Review* 102:1203–1303.

Milhaupt, Curtis J. 1996. A relational theory of Japanese corporate governance: Contract, culture, and the rule of law. *Harvard International Law Journal* 37 (1):3–64.

———. 1998. Property rights in firms. *Virginia Law Review* 84:1145–1194.

———. 2001. Creative norm destruction: The evolution of nonlegal rules in Japanese corporate governance. *University of Pennsylvania Law Review* 149:2083–2129.

———. 2004. Nonprofit organizations as investor protection: Economic theory and evidence from East Asia. *Yale Journal of International Law* 29:169–208.

———. 2005. In the shadow of Delaware? The rise of hostile takeovers in Japan. *Columbia Law Review* 105:2171–2217.

Milhaupt, Curtis J., and Mark D. West. 2004. *Economic organizations and corporate governance in Japan: The impact of formal and informal rules*. Oxford: Oxford University Press.

Ministry of Economy, Trade, and Industry and Ministry of Justice. 2005. Takeover Defense Guidelines for Protecting and Enhancing Corporate Value and the Common Interests of Shareholders. http://www.meti.go.jp/press/20050527005/3-shishinn-honntai-set.pdf.

Montesquieu, Charles-Louis. 1977. *The spirit of laws*. Berkeley: Univeristy of California Press.

Nam, Rafael. 2003. Creditors seek to protect SK. *Korea Herald*, 19 December.

Naughton, Barry. 1996. *Growing out of the plan*. Cambridge: Cambridge University Press.

Nesvetailova, Anastasia. 2004. Coping in the global financial system: The political economy of nonpayment in Russia. *Review of International Political Economy* 11 (5):995–2021.

Noack, Ulrich, and Dirk A. Zetsche. 2005. Corporate governance reform in Germany: The second decade. *European Business Law Review* 15 (5):1033–1064.

North, Douglass C. 1990. *Institutions, institutional change, and economic performance*. Cambridge: Cambridge University Press.

North, Douglass C., and Barry R. Weingast. 1989. Constitutions and commitment: The evolution of institutions governing public choice in seventeenth-century England. *Journal of Economic History* 49 (4):803–832.

Ogus, A. 1999. Competition between national legal systems: A contribution of economic analysis to comparative law. *International and Comparative Law Quarterly* 48 (2):1–14.

Ohnesorge, John. 2003. The rule of law, economic development, and the developmental states of Northeast Asia. In *Law and development in East and Southeast Asia*, ed. Christoph Antons, 91–127. London: Routledge.

Olson, Mancur. 1971. *The logic of collective action: Public goods and the theory of groups.* Cambridge: Harvard Univeristy Press.

———. 1982. *The rise and decline of nations: Economic growth, stagflation, and social rigidities.* New Haven: Yale University Press.

Organization for Economic Cooperation and Development. 2004. *Economic reports: Korea.* Paris: OECD.

Ostrom, Elinor. 1990. *Governing the commons—The evolution of institutions for collective action.* Cambridge: Cambridge University Press.

Owen, Thomas C. 1991. *The corporation under Russian law, 1800–1917.* Cambridge: Cambridge University Press.

Patrick, Hugh T., and Yung Chul Park. 1994. *The financial development of Japan, Korea, and Taiwan: Growth, repression, and liberalization.* New York: Oxford University Press.

Peng, Lin, and Alisa Röell. 2004. Executive pay, earnings manipulation and shareholder litigation. Working paper. http://www.ssrn.com/abstract-488148.

Pils, Eva. 2005. Land disputes and social unrest in China: A case from Sichuan. N.Y.U. Law School, Global Law Working Paper, www.nyulawglobal.com/GLWP0705pils.rtf.

Pistor, Katharina. 1995. Privatization and corporate governance in Russia: An empirical study. In *Privatization, conversion and enterprise reform in Russia*, ed. M. McFaul and T. Pelmutter, 69–84. Boulder: Westview.

———. 1996. Supply and demand for contract enforcement in Russia: Courts, arbitration, and private enforcement. *Review of Central and East European Law* 22 (1):55–87.

———. 1997. Company law and corporate governance in Russia. In *The rule of law and economic reform in Russia*, ed. J. D. Sachs and K. Pistor, 165–187. Boulder: Westview.

———. 1999. Codetermination in Germany: A socio-political model with governance externalities. In *Employees and corporate governance*, ed. M. Blair and M. Roe, 163–193. Washington DC: Brookings Institute.

———. 2002. The standardization of law and its effect on developing economies. *American Journal of Comparative Law* 50:101–134.

———. 2004. Enhancing corporate governance in the new member states: Does EU law help? In *Law and governance in an enlarged European Union*, ed. G. Berman and K. Pistor, 339–368. Oxford: Hart.

———. 2005. Legal ground rules in coordinated and liberal market economies. In *Corporate governance in context: Corporations, states, and markets in Europe, Japan and the US*, ed. Klaus Hopt, Eddy Wymeersch, Hideki Kanda, and Harald Baum, 249–280. Oxford: Oxford University Press.

———. 2008. Who tolls the bells for firms? Tales from transition economies. *Columbia Journal of Transnational Law*. Forthcoming.

Pistor, Katharina, Yoram Keinan, Jan Kleinheisterkamp, and Mark West. 2002. The evolution of corporate law. *University of Pennsylvania Journal of International Economic Law* 23 (4):791–871.

Pistor, Katharina, Martin Raiser, and Stanislav Gelfer. 2000. Law and finance in transition economies. *Economics of Transition* 8 (2):325–368.

Pistor, Katharina, and Philip Wellons. 1999. *The role of law and legal institutions in Asian economic development.* Hong Kong: Oxford University Press.

Pistor, Katharina, and Chenggang Xu. 2003a. Fiduciary duties in (transitional) civil law jurisdictions—Lessons from the incompleteness of law theory. In *Global Markets, Domestic institutions: Corporate law and governance in a new era of cross-border deals*, ed. C. Milhaupt, 77–106. New York: Columbia University Press.

———. 2003b. Incomplete law. *Journal of International Law and Politics* 35 (4):931–1013.

———. 2005. Governing stock markets in transition economies: Lessons from China. *American Review of Law and Economics* 7 (1):184–210.

Posner, Eric. 1996a. Law, economics, and inefficient norms. *University of Pennsylvania Law Review* 144:1971–1986.

———. 1996b. The regulation of groups: The influence of legal and non-legal sanctions on collective action. *University of Chicago Law Review* 63:133–197.

Posner, Richard. 1995. *Overcoming law*. Cambridge: Harvard University Press.

———. 1997. Social norms and the law: An economic approach. *American Economic Review* 87 (2):365–369.

Potter, Pitman B. 1994. The administrative litigation law of the PRC: Judicial review and bureaucratic reform. In *Domestic law reforms in post-Mao china*, ed. P. B. Potter, 270–304. Armonk, NY: Sharpe.

Powers, William C., Raymond S. Troubh, and Herbert S. Winokur. 2002. *Report of investigation by the special investigative committee of the board of directors of Enron Corp*. 2002 WL 198018.

Qian, Yingyi. 2000. Government control in corporate governance as a transitional institution: Lessons from China. In *Rethinking the East Asian miracle*, ed. J. Stiglitz and S. Yusuf, 295–321. Oxford: Oxford University Press.

———. 2003. How reform worked in China. In *In search of prosperity: Analytical narratives on economic growth*, ed. D. Rodrik, 227–333. Princeton: Princeton University Press.

Qian, Yingyi, Gerard Roland, and Chenggang Xu. 2006. Coordination and experimentation in M-form and U-form organizations. *Journal of Political Economy* 114 (2):366–402.

Rajan, Raghuram G., and Luigi Zingales. 1995. What do we know about capital structure? Some evidence from international data. *Journal of Finance* 50 (5):1421–1460.

Ramseyer, J. Mark. 1994. The puzzling (in)dependence of courts: A comparative approach. *Journal of Legal Studies* 23:721–747.

Rapoport, Nancy B., and Bala G. Dharan. 2004. *Enron: Corporate fiascos and their implications*. New York: Foundation Press.

Rauch, James E. 1999. Networks versus markets in international trade. *Journal of International Economics* 48 (June):7–35.

Reese, William, and Michael Weisbach. 2001. Protection of minority shareholder interests, cross-listings in the United States, and subsequent equity offerings. Cambridge, MA: National Bureau of Economic Research.

Rheinstein, Max. 1954. Introduction. In *Max Weber on law in economy and society*, ed. M. Rheinstein. Cambridge: Harvard University Press.

Roe, Mark. 1990. Political and legal restraints on ownership and control of public companies. *Journal of Financial Economics* 27:7–41.

———. 1993. Some Differences in corporate structure in Germany, Japan, and the United States. *Yale Law Journal* 102:1927–2003.

———. 1996. Chaos and evolution in law and economics. *Harvard Law Review* 109:641–668.

———. 2000. Political foundations for separating ownership from corporate control. *Stanford Law Review* 53:539–606.

260 / References

————. 2003. Delaware's competition. *Harvard Law Review* 117:588–646.

————. 2005. Delaware's politics. *Harvard Law Review* 118 (8):2492–2543.

Romano, Roberta. 2005. The Sarbanes-Oxley Act and the making of quack corporate governance. *Yale Law Journal* 114:1521–1611.

Ross, Michael. 2004. What do we know about natural resources and civil war? *Journal of Peace Research* 41 (3):337–356.

Sabel, Charles. 2005. Bootstrapping development: Rethinking the role of public intervention in promoting growth. Paper read at Protestant Ethic and the Spirit of Capitalism, Cornell University, Ithaca, New York.

Sachs, Jeffrey D., and Katharina Pistor. 1997. Introduction: Progress, pitfalls, scenarios, and lost opportunities. In *The rule of law and economic reform in Russia*, ed. J. D. Sachs and K. Pistor, 1–21. Boulder: Westview.

Sachs, Jeffrey D., and Andrew Warner. 1995. Natural resource abundance and economic growth. Cambridge, MA: National Bureau of Economic Research.

Saxenian, Annalee. 1994. *Regional advantage: Culture and competition in Silicon Valley and Route 128*. Cambridge: Harvard University Press.

Schauer, Federick. 2000. The politics and incentives of legal transplantation. In *Governance in a globalizing world*, ed. Joseph S. Nye Jr. and John D. Donahue, 253–270. Washington, DC: Brookings.

Scott, Joanne, and David Trubek. 2002. Mind the gap: Law and new approaches to governance in the European Union. *European Law Journal* 8 (1):1–18.

Sheard, Paul. 1989. The Main Bank system and corporate monitoring and control in Japan. *Journal of Economic Behavior and Organization* 11:399–422.

Shleifer, Andrei, and Daniel Treisman. 2005. *A normal country: Russia after communism*. Cambridge: Harvard University Press.

Shleifer, Andrei, and Robert W. Vishny. 1997. A survey of corporate governance. *Journal of Finance* 52 (2):737–783.

Siaroff, Alan. 1999. Corporatism in 24 industrial democracies: Meaning and measurement. *European Journal of Policy Research* 36:175–205.

SK, woi 'gieop sanyanggam' dwoina? [Why has SK become a takeover target?]. 2003. *Maeil Business Newspaper*, 11 April.

Slaughter, Anne-Marie. 2004. *The new world order*. Princeton: Princeton University Press.

Smith, James. 1993. Confronting differences in the United States and Mexican legal systems in the era of NAFTA. *U.S.-Mexico Law Journal* (1):85–108.

Song, Kimberly. 2004. Moving the market—Tracking the numbers / Street sleuth: SK Corp. battle may spur overhaul in Korea inc., *Wall Street Journal*, 26 February, C3.

Sonoko, Nishitateno 1983. China's special economic zones: Experimental units for economic reform. *International and Comparative Law Quarterly* 32 (1):175–185.

Soskice, David. 1990. Reinterpreting corporatism and explaining unemployment: Co-ordinated and Non-coordinated market economies; The case for an extended perspective. In *Labour relations and economic performance*, ed. R. Brunetta and C. Dell'Ariga, 170–211. London: Macmillan.

Sovereign Asset Management. 2003. SK Corporation: A new beginning. Pamphlet.

————. 2005. SK Corporation: Broken trust in Asia's largest refiner. Pamphlet.

Spamann, Holger. 2006. On the significance and/or endogeneity of La Porta et al.'s "anti-director rights index" under consistent coding. In *Harvard John M. Olin Center for Law, Economics, and Business Fellow's Discussion Paper Series*. Cambridge: Harvard Law School.

Stephenson, Matthew. 2000. A Trojan horse behind Chinese walls? Problems and prospects of U.S.-sponsored "rule of law" reform projects in the People's Republic of China. *UCLA Pacific Basin Law Journal* 18:64–97.

———. 2003. When the devil turns . . . . The political foundations of independent judicial review. *Journal of Legal Studies* 32:59–89.

Streeck, Wolfgang, and Kathleen Thelen. 2005. *Beyond continuity: Institutional change in advanced political economies.* Oxford: Oxford University Press.

Sunstein, Cass. 1996. On the expressive function of law. *University of Pennsylvania Law Review* 144:2021–2053.

Taub, Stephen. 2005. *Influential Delaware judge slams Sarbox*, 6 July. http://proquest.umi .com/pqdweb?did=863500261&Fmt=7&clientId=15403&RQT=309&VName=PQD.

Thompson, Robert, and Hillary Sale. 2003. Securities fraud as corporate governance: Reflections on federalism. *Vanderbilt Law Review* 56:859–910.

Trebilcock, Michael, and Jing Leng. 2006. The role of formal contract law and enforcement in economic development. *Virginia Law Review* 92:1517–1580.

Trubek, David M. 1972. Max Weber on law and the rise of capitalism. *Wisconsin Law Review* (3):720–753.

Trubek, David M., and Marc Galanter. 1974. Scholars in self-estrangement: Some reflections on the crisis in law and development studies in the United States. *Wisconsin Law Review* (1974):1062–1102.

Twining, Daniel. 2006. Putin's power politics. *Weekly Standard*, 7 January.

Uemura, Tatsuo. 2005. Raibudoa tai Fuji Terebi: Shijo no Ruru wo Fumiarasu Mono wa Dare ka? [Livedoor v. Fuji TV: Who will trample the market rules?]. *Sekai*, May:58.

Upham, Frank K. 1987. *Law and social change in postwar Japan.* Cambridge: Harvard University Press.

———. 2002. Myth making in the rule of law orthodoxy. Carnegie Papers 30, http:// www.carnegieendowment.org/publications/index.cfm?fa=viewAuthorPublications &authorID=404&carAuth=0.

U.S. Department of Justice. 2005. The external effects of the Federal Bureau of Investigation's reprioritization efforts: U.S. Department of Justice, Office of the Inspector General Audit Division.

U.S. Senate. Permanent Subcommittee on Investigations. 2002. The role of the board of directors in Enron's collapse. 107th Cong., 2d sess., S. Rep. 107-70. Washington, DC: GPO.

Veasey, E. Norman, and Christine T. Di Guglielmo. 2005. What happened in Delaware corporate law and governance from 1992 to 2004? A retrospective on some key developments. *University of Pennsylvania Law Review* 153 (5):1399–1512.

Wade, Robert. 2003. *Governing the market: Economic theory and the role of government in East Asian industrialization.* Princeton: Princeton University Press.

Walder, Andrew, and Jean C. Oi. 1999. Property rights in the Chinese economy: Contours of the process of change. In *Property rights and economic reform in China*, ed. A. Walder and J. C. Oi, 1–26. Stanford: Stanford University Press.

Weber, Max. 1968. *Economy and society: An outline of interpretive sociology.* Berkeley: University of California Press.

———. 1981. *General economic history.* Social Science Classics Series. New Brunswick, NJ: Transaction.

West, Mark. 2001. Why shareholders sue: The evidence from Japan. *Journal of Legal Studies* 30:351–382.

Winter, Jaap, J. S. Christensen, Jose Maria Garrido Garcia, Klaus Hopt, Jonathan Rickford, Guido Rossi, and Joelle Simon. 2002. Report of the High-Level Group of Company Law Experts on issues related to takeover bids. Brussels: European Union. http://ec.europa.eu/internal_market/company/modern/index_en.htm#background.

Witt, John Fabian. 2007. *Patriots and cosmopolitans: Hidden histories of American law.* Cambridge: Harvard University Press.

Wójcik, Dariusz. 2002. Change in the German model of corporate governance: Evidence from blockholdings, 1997–2001. http://ssrn.com/abstract=294459.

World Bank. 1996. *World development report: From plan to market.* Washington, DC: Oxford University Press.

———. 2001. *World development report: Building institutions for markets.* Washington, DC: Oxford University Press.

Wymeersch, Eddy. 1999. Company law in the 21st century. Financial Law Institute Working Paper Series, no. 14, Brussels, Belgium.

Yousef-Martinek, Diana, Raphael Minder Knight-Bagehot, and Rahim Rabimoc. 2003. Yukos Oil: A corporate governance success story? *Chazen Web Journal of International Business* (Fall).